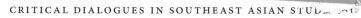

CRITICAL DIALOGUES IN SOUTHEAST ASIAN STUDIES

Charles Keyes, Vicente Rafael, and Laurie J. Sears

Series Editors

This series offers perspectives in Southeast Asian Studies that stem from reconsideration of the relationships among scholars, texts, archives, field sites, and subject matter. Volumes in the series feature inquiries into historiography, critical ethnography, colonialism and postcolonialism, nationalism and ethnicity, gender and sexuality, science and technology, politics and society, and literature, drama, and film. A common vision of the series is a belief that area studies scholarship sheds light on shifting contexts and contests over forms of knowing and modes of action that inform cultural politics and shape histories of modernity.

Imagined Ancestries of Vietnamese Communism: Ton Duc Thang and the Politics of History and Memory by Christoph Giebel

Beginning to Remember: The Past in the Indonesian Present edited by Mary S. Zurbuchen

Seditious Histories: Contesting Thai and Southeast Asian Pasts by Craig J. Reynolds

Knowing Southeast Asian Subjects edited by Laurie J. Sears

Making Fields of Merit: Buddhist Female Ascetics and Gendered Orders in Thailand by Monica Lindberg Falk

Love, Passion and Patriotism: Sexuality and the Philippine Propaganda Movement, 1882–1892 by Raquel A. G. Reyes

Gathering Leaves and Lifting Words: Intertextuality and Buddhist Monastic Education in Laos and Thailand by Justin Thomas McDaniel

The Ironies of Freedom: Sex, Culture, and Neoliberal Governance in Vietnam by Thu-hương Nguyễn-võ

Submitting to God: Women and Islam in Urban Malaysia by Sylva Frisk

No Concessions: The Life of Yap Thiam Hien, Indonesian Human Rights Lawyer by Daniel S. Lev

The Buddha on Mecca's Verandah: Encounters, Mobilities, and Histories along the Malaysian-Thai Border by Irving Chan Johnson

The
Buddha
— *on* —
Mecca's
Verandah

ENCOUNTERS, MOBILITIES, AND HISTORIES
ALONG THE MALAYSIAN-THAI BORDER

Irving Chan Johnson

UNIVERSITY OF WASHINGTON PRESS *Seattle & London*

This book is published with the assistance of a grant from the Charles and Jane Keyes Endowment for Books on Southeast Asia, established through the generosity of Charles and Jane Keyes.

Printed and bound in the United States of America

Designed by Ashley Saleeba

Composed in Minion by Robert Slimbach, Adobe Systems

Display type set in Linden Hill by Barry Schwartz, The League of Movable Type

16 15 14 13 12   5 4 3 2 1

UNIVERSITY OF WASHINGTON PRESS

PO Box 50096, Seattle, WA 98145, USA

www.washington.edu/uwpress

LIBRARY OF CONGRESS CATALOGING-IN-PUBLICATION DATA

Johnson, Irving Chan.

The Buddha on Mecca's verandah : encounters, mobilities, and histories along the Malaysian-Thai border / Irving Chan Johnson.

p. cm. — (Critical dialogues in Southeast Asian studies)

Includes bibliographical references and index.

ISBN 978-0-295-99203-7 (cloth : alk. paper)

ISBN 978-0-295-99204-4 (pbk : alk. paper)

1. Thais—Malaysia—Kelantan—Social life and customs. 2. Buddhists—Malaysia—Kelantan—Social life and customs. 3. Ethnology—Malaysia—Kelantan. 4. Borderlands—Malaysia—Kelantan. 5. Borderlands—Thailand—Narathiwat (Province) I. Title. II. Series: Critical dialogues in Southeast Asian studies.

GN635.M4J64 2012   306.09595—dc23   2012009925

The paper used in this publication is acid-free and meets the minimum requirements of American National Standard for Information Sciences—Permanence of Paper for Printed Library Materials, ANSI Z39.48–1984.∞

For my grandfathers and grandmothers,

wherever they may be

CONTENTS

PREFACE

THE BUDDHA ON MECCA'S VERANDAH IS ABOUT ENCOUNTERS. IT IS AS much an ethnographic account of a marginal community as it is a story about powerful cultural institutions, cartographies, histories, and global connections. The narrative is set somewhere between 2001 and 2002 in a small Thai Buddhist village in Malaysia's northeasternmost state of Kelantan, but it both carries forth into the present and entangles itself with an ancient and sometimes troublesome history. Delving into this terrain of ephemeral moments, I explore how comings and goings across locales near and far, past and present, real and surreal, banal and extraordinary can help us think about the way subjecthood and marginality are recognized, realized, and interpreted in the hinterlands of nation states.

The encounters I write about occurred in and around the village of Ban Bor On. My Thai mother grew up in the nearby market town of Bandar Tumpat and I have been visiting Ban Bor On since 1979. Doing anthropological fieldwork among friends, relations, and strangers was thus an exercise in reflexivity for me.[1] Many of the encounters that I write about and that are so crucial in framing identity politics in the village and the state are hidden from the prying eyes of non-intimates. These are often of a more personal and sometimes secretive nature, appearing only in the less perceivable realms of intimate moments — "the shadow side of fieldwork" as Annette Leibing and Athena McLean (2007) call it. The movements that form the ethnographic text in this book comprise not only physical travels along the settlement's potholed roads and sandy bicycle tracks but also dreams, events, narratives, fears, and other emotions. As with the vignettes of common American experiences that Kathleen Stewart (2007) mulls over, the experience of being Thai and Buddhist in Malay Muslim-majority Kelantan is located in a series of disjointed and messy moments. One's identity — one's Thainess — is never static. It revels in its ambiguity. The more one tries to rigidly define the boundaries of Thainess in Kelantan, the more one exposes oneself to the gaps inherent in its meaning.

Encounters forge and destroy the boundaries that seem to enclose their mobile subjects. Boundaries and the movements that flow across them have been central themes in many social scientific treatises since the nineteenth century. In his 1864 historical work, *The Ancient City*, de Coulanges suggested that the practices of everyday life and the memories they contained were instrumental in demarcating the parameters and sacred geographies of early Roman urbanism. Subsequent works by Durkheim and Mauss (1903), Evans-Pritchard (1940), Edmund Leach (1954), and Fredrik Barth (1969) have variously discussed the ways boundaries as space are produced through a culture's engagements with flows of people, economics, ecologies, and power. More recent discussions on mobility and spatial practices have focused on the trickier issues of displacement, circulation, memory, transnationalism, hybridity, and uncertainty (e.g., Appadurai 1996; Auge 1995; Feld and Basso 1996; Clifford 1997; Ho 2006; Tsing 1993; Ong 1999; Matory 2005; Green 2005; Tagliacozzo 2001, 2005). It was within this interstitial and shifting zone of traveling people, ideas, symbols, meanings, images, objects, and landscapes that people negotiated their social and historical identities. In the afterword to Feld and Basso's edited volume (1996), Clifford Geertz reminded the reader of the need to continue gazing at boundaries in order to reflect on the movements that cross and contest them (262). Boundaries, whatever their form, always matter. They have been—and will continue to be—"part of the classical conceptual tool-kit of social scientists" (Lamont and Molnár 2002: 167).

This book is about the politics of social and collective identification along a Southeast Asian frontier. Renato Rosaldo, in *Cultural Citizenship in Island Southeast Asia* (2003), observed that social, cultural, and political marginalizations have, at their core, the tense binary divide between the boundaries of the metropolitan state and its hinterlands. Minorities and other so-called marginal communities inhabit the gaps of national sovereignty and struggle to define themselves in light of the state's obsession with a "coercive conformity" (7). In their quest to define the parameters of subjecthood, individuals reflect on political citizenship in colorful "cultural" ways, ranging from acceptance to nonchalance and outright resistance. Kelantanese Thai visions of cultural agency result from their experiences of locatedness between diverse boundaries. These are lively sites of encounter and engagement from which definitions of self, other, nation, culture, core, and periphery emerge (Gupta and Ferguson 1992a; Herzfeld 2001).

As with Peter Sahlins's observations on the political boundary between

France and Spain in the Pyrenees (Sahlins 1989), the Kelantanese Thai villagers of Ban Bor On, like their European counterparts, ascribe their Thainess to the presence of politically constructed boundaries. Ban Bor On is saddled between two nation-states, each with varied political backgrounds and national motivations. Their proximity to Thailand means that Ban Bor On's residents are subject to the Buddhist nation-state's official discourse of citizenship, but they are also active recipients of Malaysian governmental discourses. The borderland world these villagers inhabit is a "living space" (Takamura 2004). Like the international border separating Malaysia from Thailand, the boundaries that define Ban Bor On's spatial and cultural parameters are not entirely imprisoning. Most are fascinating sites of movement, contradiction, and uncertainty where personal and collective identifications thrive and flourish (Rosaldo 1989; Gupta and Ferguson 1992b: 18). The "normal" locale of the subject, Gupta and Ferguson stated, is one that shifts and moves. It traverses a variety of landscapes and time frames. Just as they move between places, people also think about the past and the present, traveling ideologically between temporal worlds in their conversations, hopes, dreams, and fears. The past is not bounded from the present but instead permeates it in the way Ban Bor On's Thai residents (re)produce their Thainess. And it is through this Thainess that Kelantanese Thais make sense of their experiences of marginality. The forms in which Thainess materializes itself—stories, gossip, complaints, ritual performance, and humor—comprise the "cultural stuff" of the Kelantanese Thai community (Barth 1969). "Cultural stuff" emerged from the multiple and divergent perspectives on identity that people use to lay claims to the boundaries that define their group. But these are problematic boundaries that are at times lucid and at times ambiguous. Kelantanese Thais think about and reflect on Thainess differently. The spaces they crisscross and the encounters they have allow for a dizzying array of perspectives on self-definition.

Noting modernity's play with deterritorialization, displacement, migration, globalization, and transnationalization, anthropologists, historians, and other social scientists interested in borderland societies have tended to shift the academic gaze away from traditional essentialized identities prescribed in national rhetoric to a fluctuating definition of cultural personhood. Thus, as Lamont and Molnár observed for the Mexican-American border, "multiplex and transnational identities such as 'Chicano,' 'Latino,' and 'Hispanic'" have come to replace the classical "monolithic categories of 'Mexicans' and 'Americans'" (Lamont and Molnár 2002: 184). Yet, the salience of nationally defined identities has not simply disappeared. The interstitiality of borderland communities has resulted in a desire for clearer definitions of who they are. For many of these men, women, and children the cultural repertoire from which they produced their self-identifications continues to be firmly grounded in national categories. Because they inhabit the interface between two nation-states, Kelantanese Thais obsess over defining a unique identity for themselves that is unquestionably Malaysian but culturally neither one nor the other. The international border is instrumental in catalyzing this process of self-assertion. For many Mexican citizens living in the United States, for example, their cultural identity continues to remain undeniably Mexican even though they cross the international border regularly (Heyman 1994). Similarly, social encounters in Israel between Palestinian Muslims and Israeli Jews produce greater self-other awareness for both communities based on a common acknowledgment of the cultural differences between the two groups (Rabinowitz 1994). In her ethnography of Kella, a village that straddled the divide between what was once East and West Germany, Daphne Berdahl (1999) noted how the newfound fluidity of movement inherent in post–Cold War Germany across what was once an impenetrable political barrier resulted in Kella's inhabitants having clearer imaginings of their own communal identity. Historical and contemporary movements in and across Kelantan's Thai landscape have likewise shaped an intimate perception of selfhood that is highly mobile but at the same time concrete in its uncertainty.

Moving Subjects

How can the study of encounters in a Malaysian village add to current debates on the culture of movement? Academic musings on mobility have traditionally associated it with global capitalism, Western modernity, urbanization, and migration (Urry 2004; Brenner 1998; Berdahl 2001; Auge 1995; Featherstone 2004; Thrift 2004; Truitt 2008). When non-Western mobilities were studied, they were often discussed in relation to movements spurred on by Western-pioneered developments and globalization, thereby re-anchoring movement in imaginary Occidental roots rather than in indigenously crafted systems of circulation and connection (Ho 2006). The question that titillates anthropological thinking thus becomes one not of the origins of circulations, whether in the West or East, but of the effects these movements have on the articulations and negotiations of agency. Briefly put, how do local communities creatively respond to the mobilities that envelop their lives? The answer to this question lies in the interstices of social scientific and humanistic theorizing—blurred zones of interdisciplinary experimentation and cross-fertilization (Tagliacozzo and Willford 2009: 21). *The Buddha on Mecca's Verandah* dwells in this liminal zone. It narrates a traditional story of powerful state regimes, government structures, and global processes while foregrounding indigenous responses to feelings of marginality. By reflecting on the way people talk, laugh, sigh, and rage over the mobilities they forge and experience, *The Buddha on Mecca's Verandah* problematizes the very notion of an essentialized reading of history, selfhood, and community.

Ban Bor On's residents inhabit expansive but interconnected cultural universes that stretch a long way away from Kelantan. These are worlds that are part of the *longue duree* of Kelantanese Thai history with its lack of marked chronological dates. In this scenario, indigenous agency is not a simple set of deCerteuan "tactics" framed against powerful statist "strategies" but rather the product of a conversation between the two. In the case of marginal communities inhabiting national frontiers, these multi-voiced exchanges draw their interlocutors into both reified cultural worlds and unbounded universes (Carsten 1998; Steedly 1993; Green 2005; Tsing 1993, 2003; Asad 2004). But at the same time, the conversations that emerge from these fleeting moments of encountering also constrain, limit, and cement identities within older, established boundaries of identification. In sum, boundaries are zones where uncertainty and certainty mix and mingle. They are sites rich in the textures of global modernity and the ballast of the past, memories from which people fashion their cultural understandings (Verdery 1994; Oommen 1995; Ong 1996; Carsten 1998; Lamont and Molnár 2002).

Throughout this book's text, the voices of Kelantan's Thai villagers ring out loud and clear. Their stories bring the reader on journeys that move through the Thai village in Malaysia, accompanying the various protagonists on their fantastic travels as they wander near and far, building up and tearing down versions of personhood in the process. In brief, what concerns me here are not merely the topographical and cultural symbols of boundedness that Fredrik Barth (1969) popularized in studies of ethnic group association, but the social life of and at these boundaries. Alexander Horstmann and Reed Wadley (2006) rightly call for a subjective understanding of borders as living places and as "matrixes of social and cultural change" (1). In his critique of Benedict Anderson's famed *Imagined Communities* (1983), Shigeharu Tanabe added that looking at borders as reified political entities was only "half the story" (Tanabe 2008: 5). A fuller picture of the culture of the border and of the states it straddles emerges when we gaze at what happens at the margins, with their "disjunctive, ambivalent boundaries and identities" (ibid.). The hinterlands are therefore active sites for cultural imaginings and provide a window into the way power played itself out within and beyond nation-states. In a similar vein, the chapters in Michael Montesano and Patrick Jory's 2008 edited volume show how Malaysia's northern states and southern Thailand are part of a shared "plural peninsula"—a zone of interaction and connections that question artificial borders put in place by varying cultural and historical moments. Taking up from where Horstmann and Wadley, Tanabe, and Montesano and Jory left us, *The Buddha on Mecca's Verandah* is a narrative testimony that privileges local agency as it bridges territorial, historical, and subjective universes in a series of confusing encounters.

The border is not merely a political-jural divide between two nation-states, but an ideological partition that despite its appearance of boundedness encourages the movement of people and their diverse aspirations, dreams, and grievances. And it is through these physical and symbolic movements that people give meaning to their lives and create identities for themselves and their communities.

Thainess

The process of ethnic and cultural consolidation in Ban Bor On and other Thai villages in Kelantan may be seen as an exercise in locating Thainess—a use of the word that differs from the term's sociopolitical definitions as rooted in Thailand's national discourse of citizenry, which historian Thongchai Winichakul calls "a common Thai nature or identity" (Thongchai 1994: 5). To Thongchai, Thainess—like the state that grooms it—is circumscribed by the sovereign and cartographically mapped spaces of the nation-state. My use of the word Thainess takes on a more fluid definition that foregrounds its imagining not simply as a political idea but as an indigenous way of thinking about one's marginality outside the Thai state. Read this way, Thainess represents what Das and Poole (2004: 19) described as the "creativity of the margins." Thainess in the Kelantanese Thai context has little to do with Thailand per se (or Malaysia for that matter) but is more concerned with making meaning out of the interactive experiences that encounters across both boundaries bring about. The intersection of people, things, and ideologies slice across historical and contemporary landscapes and produce multiple articulations of Thainess by Thais living in Kelantan.

Everyone interprets Thainess in his and her own way—there is no consensus as to what it comprises or how it should be performed. The lack of a uniform definition of constituted Thainess is what reifies it. To some in Kelantan, it is about a *gut feeling of being Thai* as if one was part of a larger pan-Thai cultural community. Yet to others, it is about narratives of Malaysian difference and rupture as cultural and personal identities become entangled and turned topsy-turvy in opposition to Thailand's quintessential rhetoric of a common national essence. Thainess permeates everyday life in Kelantan's Thai villages. It is embodied, visualized, and performed in myriad ways. It is affective, sacred, tactile, and banal all at the same time. It is about the past but projects itself into an uncertain future. The fact that it is inseparable from one's person means that Kelantanese Thais do not have a word or phrase to describe Thainess. Thainess in Kelantan is a theoretical concept developed by the anthropologist to understand something that is both intimate and abstract and cannot be simply pinned down.

In Thailand's national rhetoric, Thainess is translated as *khwam pen thai* (the feeling of being Thai). It is a grand political-cultural metanarrative that overrides ethnic particularities in favor of sacrosanct citizenship status moored with a shared sense of belonging to the nation-state. In Kelantan, however, Thainess is what circumscribes the ethnic community. It is the sole monopoly of the Thai community, denied to non-Thais regardless of how close their inter-ethnic affiliations. Thainess in Kelantan refers to anything—food preferences, concepts of personal hygiene, aesthetic preferences, political inclinations, bodily deportment, and ritual life—as well as ways of speaking and remembering that specifically define one as being culturally and ethnically *Thai* but always politically Malaysian. Unlike in Thailand, Thainess in Kelantan is clearly dependent on the borderland location of the community. Although Thainess seems to override political sentiments, it remains constrained by them.

During my stay in Ban Bor On, villagers never referred to their behavior as an indicator of Thainess or *khwam pen thai*. When I asked my friends what they understood by the term, I was often greeted with the same puzzled looks and shrugged shoulders they gave me when I asked about origin stories or issues they found generally unimportant. Like Pierre Bourdieu's "habitus" (1990), Thainess is inscribed onto the body itself and is expressed in the taken-for-granted actions, words, and gestures that defined Kelantan's Thai villagers as members of an ethnic and cultural group.

Thainess is marked by ambiguity. It is emphasized during certain moments and downplayed during others, generating for interlocutors an identity that is real and lucid on the surface but problematic and shifting at the same time. This puzzle of Thainess that is clearly defined on the one hand and uncertain, contextual, and transformative on the other is the hallmark of Kelantanese Thai marginality. Seemingly simple and clear renditions of subjecthood mask larger issues of history, politics, economics, nationalism, religion, and ethnicity. The practical and taken-for-granted performances of cultural distinction inherent in indigenous understandings of Thainess draw an invisible boundary that both separates Ban Bor On's residents from everyone else and joins them together in a common community. Sometimes these boundaries are wide and encompass all Thais in Kelantan or all Thais globally, but at other times, Thainess remains a highly private and personal affair.

Ban Bor On's residents were (and continue to be) obsessed with their marginality, their Thainess. During my fieldwork, I heard them complain bitterly of being double marginals—of being treated unfairly by national policies of affirmative action by the Malaysian government and of suffering from cultural colonization emanating from Thailand's bureaucratic auxiliaries. Thoughts over what Thainess meant emerged in the thick of their grumbles. Yet despite their complaints, they were quick to point out the achievements their community had made and the positive qualities of living in Malaysia. They spoke of peace and tranquility in their nation-state, opposing it against the political turmoil that has rocked Thailand's many governments since the end of the Second World War. They told me of how the international border marked the furthest extremities of terrorism in South Thailand, but they were uncertain if and when Kelantan would succumb to similar acts of brutality. They proudly rattled off the names of their university students in Kuala Lumpur, Malaysia's federal capital city, and of their monks who had secured educational opportunities and promotions in faraway places like Bangkok, Singapore, and Colombo. They reminded me of their commercial successes in vegetable agriculture and construction and how they never spent entire mornings making small talk at coffeeshops—as did some *other* Kelantanese. And they pointed to large mansions with air-conditioned interiors and record-setting Buddhist statues as examples of their successful encounters with modernity, of capital, and of a positive rendition of Thainess. Yes, they were marginal, but they had also achieved remarkable feats.

During the seventeen months I spent in Ban Bor On, I observed that villagers constantly talked about Thainess. Younger Thais used the English word "identity" to refer to a sense of Thainess that did not exist in the local lexicon. Thainess was about identification. It revolved around the question of what it means to be Thai living in an Islamic state in today's Malaysia. This constant attempt to essentialize what was blurry and indeterminate drew me into the ethnographic project. Identity hinted at essentialisms and the search for some form of primordial cultural essence that could be pointed to as a symbol of a unique Kelantanese Thainess. But this is problematic due to the constant movements Kelantanese Thais are a part of. Movements draw and contest real and symbolic boundaries. The encounters that emerge from these mobile practices result in a slew of "creative possibilities" as to the definitions of what constitutes Thainess (Tsing 1993: 8). Thainess accompanies people on their journeys and animates conversations, thoughts, and stories. Thainess is full of contradictions but rife with promise, and it is through this elusive yet palpable process that Kelantanese Thai subjectivity is made and remade.

ACKNOWLEDGMENTS

THIS BOOK WOULD NOT HAVE BEEN POSSIBLE WITHOUT THE KIND assistance of many people. Of these, foremost are the Thai villagers of Kelantan and Terengganu who permitted me to enter into their lives. They patiently listened to my many questions and were always obliging and hospitable. In particular, I am most indebted to Than Chao Khun Iak, head of Kelantan's Thai monastic community. He was always encouraging and smiling, never failing to ensure the success of my fieldwork. To him and to Than Khru Di of Wat Chaengphutthawat and Than Khru Bun of Wat Uttamaram, I clasp my palms and bow my head.

My days in Kelantan were spent in enjoyable conversations with the monks, many of whom have since left the Order. It was largely through them that I was introduced to the lives of the villagers I write about. The late Mae Chi Ek was like a grandmother to me. Despite her own abstinence, she would always cook a fresh pot of rice for me in the evenings, scoffing at my suggestion that I eat leftovers.

Mae Thong and her husband, Pho Baen, treated me as their son. "Your parents are far away," Mae Thong reminded me time and again, "for now, we will be your parents. There is always rice for you here." In the evenings, Pho Baen would take me on journeys through the Kelantan of old, narrating episodes of cattle thieves, invisible gangsters, strange spirits, bullfights, and so on. The kindness Mae Thong and Pho Baen showed me cannot be expressed in words.

My undergraduate years at the National University of Singapore whetted my appetite for anthropology. Professors Maribeth Erb, the late Ananda Rajah, Geoffrey Benjamin, and Nancy Cooper have always been an inspiration. At Harvard, Michael Herzfeld, Engseng Ho, Mary Steedley, Nur Yalman, Lorand Matory, and Stanley Tambiah provided me with the tools needed to conceptualize the book and make theoretical sense of the ethnography. My fieldwork in Kelantan was made possible by the Overseas Research Scholarship I received from the National University of Singapore. I am also indebted to my colleagues at the university's Southeast Asian Studies Programme who have assisted me in thinking through the manuscript and its framework. Alexander Horstmann, Paritta Chalermpow-Koanantakool, Niti Pawakapan, Pattana Kitiarsa, Goh Beng Lan, Charles Keyes, Craig Reynolds, Tej Bunnag, Rusaslina Idrus, Patrick Jory, Mohamed Yusoff Ismail, Ajan Kamnuan, Mohamed Arafat, and Louis Golomb have shared my interest in Kelantan and deserve special mention. To them, I say "*khob chai mak mak.*" Finally, to my family in Singapore, Kelantan, and the United States, I extend my deepest gratitude. Pitra Narendra has helped me with the technical aspects of the manuscript's completion. I am also grateful to Lorri Hagman, Amanda Gibson, Marilyn Trueblood, and Tim Zimmermann of the University of Washington Press for their insights into editing the book. Last but not least, to my dear friend Foo Chen Loong for taking time to read through the manuscript and providing me with much needed companionship during the long nights I spent writing.

ORTHOGRAPHY AND TERMINOLOGY

UNLESS OTHERWISE STATED, ALL THAI WORDS IN THIS BOOK ARE in the Tumpat Tak Bai dialect of southern Thai as spoken by most Kelantanese Thais in the state. I have tried to replicate as closely as possible the phonology of Tumpat Tak Bai through spelling but with the elimination of tone marks. Since Kelantanese Thais also use a large number of Kelantanese Malay loanwords in their vocabulary, I have reproduced them in this context where necessary. These are often words that end with an aspirated "h" sound or contain the letters "z" and "g." Unlike standard (central) Thai, the Tumpat Tak Bai dialect includes a number of words that stress the sounds "j," "g," "ny," and "z," for example "jao" (long), "gerang" (a land grant), "nyai" (large), and "rizab" (reserved spaces). Standard Thai words are spelled according to the Royal Thai General System of Transcription (RTGST) established by the Royal Institute. Standard Malay words and place names are spelled according to Malaysia's national spelling system.

I have used pseudonyms in place of my interlocutors' given names and the names of villages. Historical figures such as Buddhist monks, Malay rulers, Thai kings, colonial officers, politicians, and local cultural heroes retain their real names. As with traditional Kelantanese Thai modes of address, all personal names are prefixed by a polite kinship term that denotes the person's relationship to the speaker as well as his/her social position within the community. Men who have not been ordained as monks are addressed by the prefix Ta. Men in one's parent's generation who have spent some time in the monkhood, as traditionally expected of them, are referred to by the honorific Chao or Na Chao. Older men, regardless of their ordination history, are often simply called Pho (Father) or the gender-neutral Na (Young Uncle/Auntie). Women can be Koe, Na, or Mae (Mother), the latter usually in reference to older women. Men in one's grandparent's generation are often respectfully addressed as Lung (Uncle) and women as Pa (Auntie). Those closer in age to the speaker are called Phi (elder sibling). Monks who have yet to become abbots are addressed as Khun. Abbots are addressed by the honorific title of Than or Pho Than. A number of minor honorifics are also used to designate kin and social status in the community. Some elderly women are referred to as Mae Kae (Grandmother) and men of their generation as Pho Kae (Grandfather). Sometimes the Malay word for grandparent, Tok, is used, but often only among close kin, usually women on one's mother's side of the family. Buddhist lay renunciate women are Mae Chi or Kae Chi—the latter used only for elderly women renunciates. Magical practitioners are referred to by their occupational designation as Tok Mo (Grandfather Magical Practitioner). Village headmen are called Tok Nai (Grandfather Headman) and school teachers as Khru or the standard Malay Cikgu.

The issue of how to refer to their community has been a contentious one in Kelantan's Thai villages. Although officially defined as Siamese (*orang Siam*) in Malaysian Malay and English language state records to distinguish them from their ethnic brethren in Thailand, the community never refers to itself as Siamese when speaking in Thai. During these face-to-face encounters, they refer to their ethnicity and community as simply *thai* (Thai). Thais from Thailand are *khon thai mueang thai* (Thais of Thailand) as opposed to *khon thai lantan* (Thais of Kelantan) or *khon thai rao* (our Thais). Throughout this book, I refer to the Thais of Kelantan as "Thai" according to local parlance. When I do use the term "Siamese," it is in historical reference to the Thai Buddhist people who inhabited what was then Siam until June 23, 1939, when the Siamese government changed the name of the polity to Thailand.

The
Buddha
— *on* —
Mecca's
Verandah

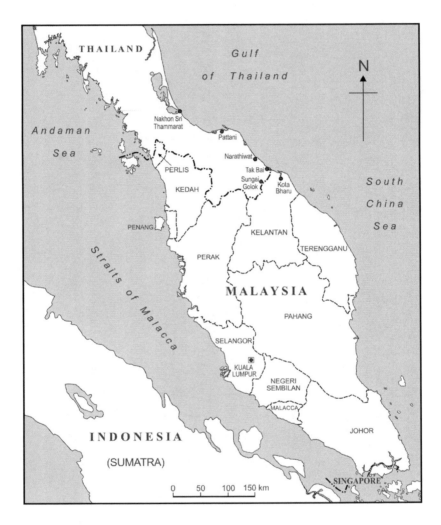

MAP 1. Kelantan and Southern Thailand

The Kelantanese World

KELANTAN IS A MARGINAL PLACE. GEOGRAPHICALLY, THE STATE is located at the peripheries of the Malay Peninsula. Flanked by the South China Sea along its eastern seaboard, Kelantan is framed by Thailand's southern province of Narathiwat to the north, and the Malaysian states of Terengganu and Pahang to the south and Perak to the west. Covering a surface area of 5,761 square miles, Kelantan is Malaysia's sixth-largest state, although a substantial part of its mountainous southern interior, known locally by its traditional Malay designation, Ulu, remains heavily forested. Here, the vast flat plains of rice fields and lush vegetable plots of the north give way to steep limestone cliffs and dense tropical rainforests. The state's sixty-mile stretch of sandy white beaches has attracted but a few travelers seeking out idyllic tropical paradises far from the crowded beach resorts of Thailand and Indonesia.

Historically, Kelantanese have prided themselves on their cultural and historical difference from the inhabitants of the rest of the Malay states. Today much of this sense of uniqueness is fueled by the state government's Islamic opposition. An Islamic front (Partai Islam SeMalaysia or PAS for short) that came into office in 1990, Kelantan's Muslim opposition party sees itself as morally superior to Malaysia's supposedly non-religious federal government based in Kuala Lumpur (Kershaw 1977; Stark 2004). Tok Kenali (1870–1933), one of Kelantan's foremost Islamic thinkers, once described his state as Mecca's Verandah (*serambi mekah*), a proud designation of uncertain provenance that Kelantan shares with Aceh in West Sumatra (Abdullah Al-Qari 1988). To many Kelantanese, Tok Kenali's observations on the Islamic nature of the state are spot on, a fact that they and the party that governs them are very proud of. Through a variety of religious and political acts and edicts in line with PAS's mandate of "Developing with Islam" (*Membangun Bersama Islam*), Kelantan's Islamic bureaucrats have attempted to forge Kelantan into a model Islamic political unit that would live up to its popular designation of Mecca's Verandah. By October 2005, the PAS-led state government had declared the capital Kota Bharu an "Islamic City" (*bandaraya Islam*) in the hopes of implementing an Islamic system of city administration that would eventually spread to surrounding districts. PAS's politicians regularly harp upon the state's Islamic governance and moral superiority, including the need to ban all forms of so-called "un-Islamic" entertainments such as popular Malay shadow plays (*wayang kulit*) and the traditional Mak Yong dance drama. The party has also called for the outlawing of Ferris wheels at fairs, which were believed to encourage sexual promiscuity, and the gendered segregation in supermarket checkout lanes, public benches, and hair salons, as well as the wearing of headscarves for all Malay Muslim women. On September 20, 2006, the Kelantan state government introduced "Islamic" currency in the state. The Kelantanese gold dinar was minted in strict accordance to classical sharia financial legislations of the original dinar of Caliph Umar. Although the Islamic state government had hoped that the quarter-, half-, and one-dinar coins would be legal tender, this was rejected by Malaysia's federal government and the coins today remain largely collectors' items. Islamization practices such as these were rhetorical devices for Kelantanese bureaucrats bent on conjuring up an idealized image of Islamic rule, thus showcasing the success of their party's political mission. In practice, however, policies were less rigidly enforced—shadow plays continued to be performed in villages, attracting large audiences, and men and women casually ignored the plastic signs calling for gendered segregation in supermarkets and public spaces.

To many non-Kelantanese Malaysians, Kelantan is a peculiar place. It is commonly imagined as an Islamic backwater ruled by conservative and radical Malay Islamicists. Malaysians, particularly those who have never traveled to the northern state, often think of Kelantan as a space of religious fervor and a museum of traditional Malay culture. William Roff, in the preface to his collection of articles on Kelantanese society and politics (1974), observes the state's marginality in terms not too different from those one hears today in popular descriptions of Kelantan. "Kelantan," writes Roff, "has come for many Malaysians and others to symbolize remoteness and beauty (of women, arts and crafts, and casuarina fringed beaches) in about equal proportion, allied with what is regarded as economic backwardness and religious Puritanism" (v).[1]

Islamic reformism is nothing new in the history of Kelantan. In an address to the members of the Royal Geographical Society in 1897, Sir Hugh Clifford, then British resident of the Malayan state of Pahang, who was himself an eminent explorer of the peninsula, noted how the former Kelantanese prime minister, the Datuk Maha Mentri (Saad bin Ngah), was a staunch Islamist. He had attempted to "prove his doctrine orthodox by apostolic blows" through ridding the Kelantanese state of syncretic practices, including the suppression of traditional "traveling theaters" (Clifford 1897: 37). Since 1990, the PAS government has also been attempting to transform Kelantan's legal constitution to include the implementation of Islamic Law Codes. The laws, known locally as *hukum hudud*, would include the amputation of thieves' hands and the stoning of adulterers. The punishments have yet to be approved by Malaysia's national judiciary and many Kelantanese view them with suspicion. They see in it another political strategy used by the state's hard-line Islamicists to create an image of Kelantan that is morally superior to that of Malaysia's federal government. It was, in other words, an attempt at foregrounding Kelantanese marginality as being distinct from the rest of Malaysia. And it was with this cultural distinction, albeit capped in political terms, that the party won votes across ethnic and religious divides in the state.

Kelantan was indeed Mecca's verandah. For a long time it had been a powerful center of Islamic learning in Southeast Asia. By the late nineteenth century, Kelantan's religious court was recruiting judges from Mecca (Talib 1995: 33). Tok Kenali himself had spent some twenty years in the Holy City before returning to Kelantan in 1909. The state's Malay rulers were also closely associated with the Malay Muslim sultanate of Patani in southern Thailand, which until Siamese annexation in 1902 had formed a powerful Islamic alliance across the peninsula.[2]

Kelantan's population has traditionally concentrated itself around Kota Bharu and the agrarian districts of Tumpat, Pasir Mas, and Tanah Merah. Kelantan's Ulu had once been a region of economic promise for Chinese gold prospectors and nineteenth-century British miners and planters, but the lack of a fertile alluvial plain on which to grow wet rice has meant that the Ulu remains the least populated part of the state. Malaysia's Department of Statistics' Population and Housing Census (2000) listed Malay Muslims who were Malaysian citizens as comprising 94.3 percent of Kelantan's ethnic composition, or 1.2 million individuals out of a total population of 1.3 million. The 2000 census did not include data on the number of Malay Muslims who were not Malaysian citizens in Kelantan. A large number of Malay Muslims from south Thailand work both legally and illegally in Kelantan, primarily on construction projects and in fisheries and restaurants (Dorairajoo 2002). Southern Thai Malay Muslims are also enrolled as students in national and Islamic boarding schools (*pondok*) throughout the state, with some making daily journeys across the border. The spate of violence in the southern Thai provinces of Pattani, Yala, and Narathiwat since 2004 that has left more than 4,000 people dead has led to an influx of Malay refugees into Kelantan, many of whom hold dual citizenship papers and cross the border with ease. A number of Kelantanese Thais are also citizens of both Thailand and Malaysia, a fact not addressed in the national statistics (Horstmann 2002a, 2002b). Dual citizenship is officially illegal in both Thailand and Malaysia, yet rampant corruption and strong patron-client-type ties between villagers and local government officers make its acquisition relatively easy.

The seeming social and political invisibility of the Thai community today is exacerbated by the fact that the national population census, the official classifier of ethnicity in contemporary Malaysia, does not count the Thai as a distinct and separate ethnic group in the country, unlike earlier British surveys. Ethnic groups in the census reports are classified according to a system of ethnic and residential pigeonholing developed by Malaya's nineteenth-century British administrators and subsequently adopted by the post-independence nation-state. According to this rhetoric of ethnic marking, one was Malay, *bumiputera* (the aboriginal non-Malay, such as the indigenous inhabitants of Borneo and the peninsula), Chinese, Indian, or *Other*.[3] Others included Indonesians, Thais, Filipinos, Burmese, Japanese, Koreans, other Asians, Eurasians, and Europeans. Predominantly Buddhist Thais are one of Kelantan's few non-Malay, non-Muslim rural communities and in the 2000 census's *Other* category (for rural-dwelling Buddhist Kelantan residents) they comprise some 10,748 persons, although no formal ethnic category exists to account for this demographic.[4]

Despite their statistical invisibility, many Malaysians know of the existence of the Kelantanese Thai community due to the latter's notorious associations with magico-religious prowess (Gimlette 1920; Shaw 1976; Golomb 1978; Mohamed 1996). They were popularly reputed to be exponents of dangerous sorcery and all sorts of love charms and potions. Malay Muslim visitors from across the country regularly show up in Kelantan's Thai temples to seek out magical practitioners, monk healers, or the sacred ingredients used in the preparation of some forms of Malay magic. They ask the monks for lustral water, sand from the temple grounds, or bits of metal from rusty alms bowls. Well-respected Thai monks and the sacred amulets they produce are much sought after by many non-Thai collectors, in particular the Chinese. A check on Google's search engine in 2010 pointed to more than 3,000 sites listed under the keywords "Kelantan amulet." Most were websites showcasing personal and commercial collections of amulets associated with the famed Kelan-tanese Thai monk, Pho Than Khron. Original Pho Than Khron amulets have market values in the tens of thousands of ringgit, with wealthy buyers coming from Singapore, Thailand, and throughout Malaysia. At the national level, Malaysian visual performances that showcased the "best" of national culture often included dances by representatives of the country's Thai community. These dances were often locally choreographed pieces that were based upon Thailand's standard models of traditional dance. Kelantan's Thai temples are popular tourist destinations and their gigantic statues have set international records. They are written about as "must-see" places in travel guides, online blogs, newspapers, books, and tourist brochures. Even the National Museum in Kuala Lumpur lists the Thai as a distinct ethnic minority in its recent display of kitschy dioramas representing Malaysia's main populations.

Marginality is thus no longer about being small, lackluster, and power-less. Rather it is very much the opposite. The smallness inherent in the con-cept of marginality is what allows members of the community to foreground their agency and create active subjects in themselves by placing their villages on extensive national and global maps. This is in part due to the locatedness of the Kelantanese Thai in a peripheral territorial and political-jural zone. The Thai live on the threshold of two geographical and cultural worlds. Like the residents of the Greek-Albanian borderlands discussed by Sarah Green (2005), they inhabit a "gap." Unlike the Balkans however, Kelantanese Thais are clear as to where they stand ethnically and where they pledge their political loyalties. But their continual attempts to demarcate this points to a deeper confusion of social identities that Kelantanese Thais encounter daily. Boundaries, when created, reassure the community of its own history and sense of belonging in the modern nation-state. But these boundaries are also contested through the myriad movements people participate in. And it is within this strange zone of lucidity and ambiguity, fixity and mobility, encounter and rupture that Kelan-tanese Thais produce their Thainess.

One can visualize Kelantan's Thai villages as inhabiting a Southeast Asian "Balkanic" space. In the face of their inhabitants' clear sense of political iden-tity—they are Malaysians through and through—the process by which this clarity manifests itself emerges from a combination of the social and historical "chaos and confusion" that makes their villages reminiscent of Irvine and Gal's metaphoric description of Macedonia as a "veritable fruit salad" (2000: 63). These are complicated places—Thai communities living beyond Thailand that speak a patois of Thai heard nowhere else on the linguistic map. They hang pictures of the Malaysian king next to those of Thailand's royal family; they are Buddhists, yet many vote into office the nation's Islamic party. They are clear about their origins, but when asked, they cannot recount them or, more interestingly, they find them unimportant. They complain bitterly about Malaysia's ethnic policies and attempt to ape many of neighboring Thailand's cultural practices, but in so doing critique Thailand and express a bitter disdain for it. According to Green (2005), Irvine and Gal's Macedonian (Balkan) salad is "a place that is in between a diversity of powerful places, so that they themselves contain too many differences that are too close and too mixed up together, never resolving themselves into clearly separated entities" (129). Green's brilliant ethnography rightly reminds us that the Balkans are not merely places of disconnect but rather a historical zone of overlapping relationships. Her approach is helpful in understanding Kelantanese Thai productions and articulations of Thainess because it does not deny the fractality of the borderland. Green suggests that it is important for the scholar to "switch back and forth between scales" when studying these indeterminate places and the people living in them (141). In the case of Ban Bor On and Kelantan, this involves thinking through the encounters between history and ethnography.

Before the powerful central Siamese polity of Ayuthaya engaged in political maneuverings in the four northern Malay states (Kedah, Perlis, Kelantan, and Terengganu) in the mid-eighteenth century as a means of reasserting political dominance over what at the time was considered a difficult Muslim hinterland, Kelantan had enjoyed a period of relative autonomy and freedom from direct Siamese intrusion.[5] This was punctured by scattered moments of domestic court intrigue and occasional civil unrest among the Malay rulers (*raja*) and chieftains of Kelantan's various districts, with the neighboring state of Terengganu to the south, and Patani further north (Roff 1974: vi–vii).[6] In 1769, Kelantan and Terengganu came under Ayuthayan suzerainty. Between 1776 and 1800 Kelantan was ceded to a more powerful Terengganu, and by the mid-nineteenth century, Kelantan had become secured into a network of Bangkok-centered vassal polities called *mueang*, each with its own class of indigenous ruling elites. Local Malay titulary rulers were obliged to recognize Siamese political overlordship through the triennial tribute of gold and silver trees (*bunga mas dan perak*) to the Bangkok court.[7] The transference of tribute was done via Bangkok's political representative in the southern port city of Nakhon Sri Thammarat (Vella 1957; Skinner 1965; Marks 1997).[8] In return for their purported allegiance and docility to Bangkok, Kelantan's Malay rulers received Thai titles and military support (Skinner 1965: 19). Siamese military garrisons were stationed at Kebun Mengseta, halfway between the Sultan's palace and the mouth of the Kelantan River in Kota Bharu (Mohamed 1974: 36). The river that formed the state's main trade route between interior and coastal settlements was guarded by a Siamese gunboat at its mouth.

By 1903, Kelantan had become a British Residency under the directives of the Siamese court. This allowed for greater political autonomy for Kelantan's Malay elites, who were now forced to rethink their loyalties to Britain and Bangkok. The seeming calm that cloaked the social-political landscape of nineteenth-century Kelantan belied older Kelantanese Malay articulations of disgruntlement with Siamese overlordship. Shahril Talib (1981: 48) noted that in 1831 the Malay rulers of Kelantan participated in a joint campaign with the leaders of the other Malay states (including Patani) against the Siamese. The failed coup resulted in the Kelantanese ruler having to surrender the fugitive ruler of Patani to Bangkok and pay a fine of 30,000 Spanish dollars and ten *katies* of gold dust to the Siamese monarch (Skinner 1965: 7). Gold dust also had to be paid to the Phraklang, the Bangkok-appointed commissioner in charge of administering the state.

Direct Siamese inroads into the political affairs of Kelantan reached their zenith in the closing decades of the nineteenth century. This was a time when Siam was struggling to secure a new political geography for itself—with the French in Indochina and the British encroaching into Burma and parts of Malaya. At the same time royal secessionist debates arose among jealous relatives of Tuan Long Senik, the Siamese-appointed sultan of Kelantan. In 1890 and again in 1896, King Chulalongkorn (r. 1868–1910) visited Siamese Kelantan in an attempt to visibly clarify and confirm the territory's subordinate status within the Siamese administrative machine (Lim 2009). By so doing, the Siamese state attempted to reassert its hegemony over what was otherwise viewed by the court as a quarrelsome domain (Talib 1995: 42). The distant territories of the Siamese polity were forcibly dragged closer to the center of power in Bangkok while ensuring a certain degree of regional but pro-Bangkok autonomy among their Malay rulers.

On 10 March 1909 the Anglo-Siamese Treaty was signed between Siam's minister for foreign affairs and Britain's chief negotiator in Bangkok. The border agreement emerged out of an earlier secret convention signed between King Chulalongkorn and the British in 1897. In it the Siamese monarch agreed not to cede territory south of Mueang Ban Tapan on Siam's Kra Isthmus to any foreign power. In return, Siam was offered protection by the British should this southern region become threatened by a foreign instigator. The treaty also laid out the geographical boundaries of the political territories of British and Siamese Malaya. Mohamed (1974: 35) wrote that "it was generally understood in London and Bangkok that the signature of the convention implied recognition of Siamese claims to the northern peninsula including Kelantan and Terengganu. Indeed, in the subsequent Boundary Agreement of 1899 which defined the frontier between 'British' and 'Siamese' in Malaya, it was formally admitted that Kelantan and Terengganu were 'dependencies' of Siam." On 6 October 1902, Siam and Britain had signed a treaty in which Kelantan would remain a dependency of Siam. But this was not to last and by 1909 a new political relationship presented itself in the borderlands.

The ratification of the Anglo-Siamese Treaty in July 1909 established a permanent border between British Malaya's Unfederated Malay States (now Kelantan, Terengganu, Perlis, and Kedah) and an independent Siam. This aquatic boundary of a politically uncontested sovereignty was hydrologically mapped at the deepest sections of the Golok River and its Tak Bai (Taba) tributary a year later.[9] Both river divides remain in effect to the present day, albeit with episodic interludes of Japanese and Thai expansionism during and immediately following the Second World War.

Although the newly created border officially separated British Kelantan from Siam's Narathiwat province, it was nonetheless instrumental in facilitating the transfer of people, ideas, and goods between both places.[10] Roads and rail lines introduced a culture of rapid and convenient mobility never before experienced by Kelantanese villages. Metalled roads were laid, linking Kelantan's Pengkalan Kubor border with Palekbang near Tumpat and other market towns in the state. One of the stated conditions of the 1909 treaty was Britain's agreement to loan the Siamese government four million pounds at 4 percent interest to build the southern extension of Siam's railway line, which would link it with the Kelantan rail line (Mohamed 1974).[11] This was done in tandem with the British development of the Federated Malay States Railways (East Coast Line) rail network that had begun in 1904. The railroad bridged not only the Kelantanese border towns of Rantau Panjang and Bandar Tumpat with Siam's southern line but also extended itself south all the way to Singapore. In 1910, the Tumpat–Tanah Merah line was completed, opening up Kelantan's Ulu to rail traffic. By 1921, the market town of Bandar Tumpat was connected via Siam's southern rail line to the west coast state of Kedah and from there to the entire Malayan train system

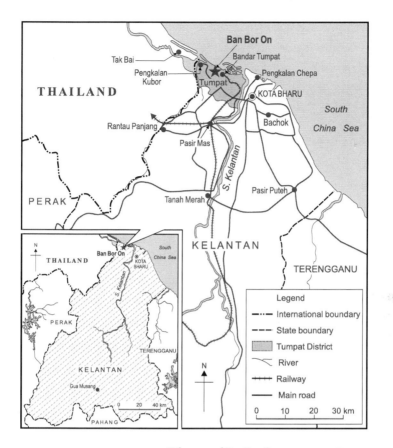

MAP 2. Kelantan and Ban Bor On

(Talib 1995; Mohd. Kamaruzaman 1990).[12] The East Coast rail line was formally inaugurated ten years later in a colorful event that was graced by the British High Commissioner Sir Cecil Clementi and the sultan of Kelantan.

Until Malaya's independence from British rule in 1957 there were twice-weekly passenger train services from Kelantan's Wakaf Bharu and Bandar Tumpat stations to Sungai Golok in Thailand. Train services from Kuala Lumpur to Sungai Golok were stopped in 1978 due to heavy rice smuggling on board the lines. Like the Muslim Cham settlements of the Mekong Delta described by Philip Taylor (2007), Thai villages have always been dynamic locales, even before the development of colonial road and rail networks. Although located at a borderland that has for a long time been popularly stereotyped by locals as remote, traditional, impoverished, and different, Kelantanese Thai villages were and continue to be lively places. Here wealthy Chinese philanthropists from distant cities interact with Buddhist monks and residents to build record-setting Thai and Chinese statues that tower along unnamed roads. Kelantan's chief minister and spiritual leader of PAS, Datuk Nik Aziz Nik Mat, makes regular appearances at Thai temple celebrations, as does a barrage of Thai, Malay, and Chinese men and women, politicians and farmers, smugglers and monks, ghosts and scholars, in search of magic, electoral support, relatives, knowledge, histories, and friends. Identity politics in Kelantanese Thai communities are the complex progeny of a genealogy of encounters that stretch back into the past and project themselves into the future. Although many Thai villages are today cartographically located in Google and WikiMapia images and young Kelantanese enjoy the communicative benefits of Facebook, Friendster, Hotmail, and iPhones, the past is never far from the present. Ancient spirits hover in temples as monks visit with their international friends in cyber chatrooms. Being a part of a nation-state pulls the village into the folds of a postcolonial Southeast Asian modernity bent on a political ideology of development and assimilation.

Old ghosts fade away as their favorite haunts are turned into private housing projects, schools, vegetable plots, shopping malls, and roads. But mobility brings with it new specters. International terrorism, religious fanaticism, drug abuse, and HIV infection are some of the new ghosts that haunt the Kelantanese Thai countryside. Instead of being a part of the natural landscape, like the ghosts of the past, these threats emanate from places far across the international border.

The Village

Located fifteen minutes away from the Malaysian-Thai border, Ban Bor On consists of 128 households. The village is almost entirely ethnically Thai and Buddhist except for a few Chinese residents and a Hindu Tamil family. The latter, however, have Thai kin in the village and most of the Arumugams speak Thai fluently and attend Buddhist services in the local temples. Kelantanese Thai villagers are speakers of the Tumpat Tak Bai dialect of southern Thai. Across the border in lower Narathiwat, the dialect is referred to as the Chehe patois (*samniang chehe*) after the district in Narathiwat where a number of Thai Buddhist villages are found. Some villagers, however, remind me of subtle linguistic variations that mark Ban Bor On's Thai as uniquely "theirs." Long periods of Thai and Malay interaction have resulted in lexical convergences in both directions, with the Kelantanese Malay vocabulary incorporating a number of Thai words and the Kelantanese Thai lexicon including many Malay loan words (Golomb 1978; Mohamed 1989). Younger Tumpat Tak Bai speakers tend to embellish their speech with Malaysian-accented English and popular urban Malay slang and catch phrases just as they do in Internet chatrooms and on their social network-ing sites. The new hybrid language allows one to play with a particular rendition of modernity—one that is global, youthful, vibrant, and distinctively Malaysian, but unquestionably Kelantanese and Thai.

Many Ban Bor On villagers have friends and family living in Narathiwat. The Thai Buddhist villages that border the Tak Bai and Golok rivers in Nara-thiwat far outnumber similar Tumpat Tak Bai–speaking communities on the river's Malaysian bank. Most of Narathiwat's Buddhist villages are located in the district (*amphoe*) of Tak Bai (Taba), although a number are also found further north, in and around Sungai Padi, Sungai Golok, Tanjong Mas, Lamphu, and Ra-ngae.[13] All are easily reached from the Tak Bai border via a good system of modern highways and dirt roads. Taxis, motorcycle cabs, and minivans eagerly await passengers at Thailand's border checkpoints, their drivers calling out to passersby who step out from the white-walled Thai government immigration kiosk into the chaotic scene of the Tak Bai border market. Drivers charge a small fee payable in either Malaysian ringgit or Thai baht for the short trip into Narathiwat's Thai Buddhist settlements.

Asaad Syukri (1971) suggested that there must have been at least 15,000 Thai Buddhists living in the Tak Bai region before the signing of the Anglo-Siamese Treaty. His figures were probably derived from Graham's 1908 report, which listed the number of Thais (Siamese) in Kelantan as 15,000 and the number of temples (*wat*) as forty. W. A. Graham became Siamese Kelantan's first Brit-ish resident in 1902 and his population figures were estimated on the poll-tax returns of some 60,000 men and women and 180,000 children. Robert Win-zeler (1985: 69) noted that Graham's data was likely to have included Thais from villages on both sides of the Tak Bai border, since the present-day frontiers of Kelantan came about only in 1910. Before that, the borders of the Siamese prin-cipality of Kelantan (*mueang Kelantan*) were less clear-cut and included much of today's Narathiwat province as well as Malaysian Kelantan. In 1997 the Thai Buddhist population of Narathiwat's Tak Bai district was approximately 20,000, with twenty temples. Tak Bai's total population that year was tabled at 57,515, the majority of whom were Malay Muslims (Wattana 2000: 21).

Ban Bor On is one of Kelantan's largest Thai villages. It is bordered on all sides by grassy fields, the remnants of once fertile rice lands. Until some thirty years ago, wet rice had been the agricultural mainstay in the village. Rather than grow a single variety of rice, villagers cultivated a number of types with such exotic-sounding names as *khao lok dam, khao nak, khao wa, khao chang, khao son, khao khem thong*, and *khao nang li*. Each rice variety required different amounts of water during the growing and crop maturation phases. Cows and water buffalos were used to till the clayey fields until they were replaced by more efficient mechanical plows. Some villagers also grew vegetables and leaf tobacco on the side, but these plants were cultivated mainly for individual consumption and rarely marketed. Vegetables were usually planted in the off-season between rice crops. The dissolution of Ban Bor On's rice economy and its subsequent replacement with intensive leaf tobacco and, later, market vegetable cultivation was triggered in part by the easy availability of a tastier polished Thai grain brought in from across the border. In 2001, a ten-kilogram sack of Thailand's Rabbit Brand rice sold for about RM35 (US$9.20) at the Bandar Tumpat market, making it more affordable than the Malaysian-grown crop. Thai jasmine rice (*khao hom mali*) was also considered more delicious by residents and kept better than the Malaysian variety. Villagers often complained that Malaysian rice, once cooked, had a tendency to go bad within a day, smelled peculiar, and was unappetizing.

In an attempt to protect a declining local rice industry, Malaysian law prohibits the purchase of rice from Thailand for personal consumption without official approval. Thai rice is only allowed to enter Malaysia's domestic market in bulk via large-scale commercial ventures, and Kelantan's supermarkets and village markets are stocked high with sack upon sack of Thai rice. Although most of the rice is obtained through legal import licensing, rice smuggling across the Thai-Malaysian border is rife. A number of Kelantanese Thai village men work as smugglers, transporting not just rice but truckloads of frozen suckling pigs, pork, alcohol, and live cows. These smuggling circuits, known in Thai as *projeks* (after the English word "projects"), are complex syndicates that involve both Thai and Malay traders, customs officials, and local policemen on both banks of the Tak Bai in close and corrupt collaboration.[14] *Projek* work, despite its obvious hazards, is exciting for many a Kelantanese man tired of run-of-the mill jobs in Malaysia. Successful smugglers can make thousands of ringgit from their nocturnal escapades.

The higher cost of Malaysian rice was the indirect result of Kelantan's experiment with the Green Revolution. New varieties of rice seed were more reliant on a steady water supply than the hardier Kelantanese crop. Heavy pumps were therefore needed to irrigate rain-fed rice fields. The state government's construction of irrigation channels (*tali air*) that cut through the fields of Ban Bor On and the nearby village of Ban Phan Jao was an attempt to produce continually flooded lands that would allow for double cropping and a subsequently larger paddy output. Unfortunately, the undulating topography of the lands in and around Ban Bor On prevented water from remaining in the fields as ground water flowed out and into the canals. The only way to improve the retention of ground water was to mechanically rechannel it from the irrigation canals back into the rice fields. But this was a practice that villagers could ill afford for lack of capital and expertise. Although the initial period of Green Revolution cultivation in the early seventies did see a sudden burst in Kelantan's paddy outlay before the soils began drying up, this success was soon marred by weevils (*maeng koesing*), a problem not encountered in the past. Four-wheeled mechanical tractors—which replaced traditional water buffalo- and cow-driven plows—were required to till the land, as were combined harvesters. These were usually rented from national agricultural cooperatives but were expensive and a financial strain on the average cultivator.[15] Frustrated villagers soon left their fields unattended and the clayey soils dried and cracked, making it impossible for subsequent cultivation to occur. In just a few years, Ban Bor On's once fertile rice lands were transformed into grass pastures of blade-like cogon grass (*Imperata cylindrica*) that provided fodder for cows and buffalos.

Today, Ban Bor On's villagers no longer cultivate rice. Many of the older and middle-aged residents are intensive market gardeners. Wet and dry vegetables such as purple eggplant, chilis, lettuce, red and green leaf spinach, long beans, cucumber, and okra are grown on raised bunds on either individually owned or rented plots. Although most villagers possess their own plots, less well-off farmers may rent plots from landlords or work on them as paid labor. Thai tenant farmers prefer to lease lands from fellow co-ethnics, although in some instances they may work on lands owned by Malays. Rent is paid in cash on an annual basis, usually amounting to about RM100 (US$30) per year. Vegetables are cultivated throughout most of the year with the exception of the monsoon months from late November through February, when the soils are saturated by heavy rainfall and most cultivated crops rot. Enterprising villagers grow more water-resilient varieties during these months, such as hardy water convolvulus, turmeric, and spinach, thereby ensuring a steady flow of income to the local agricultural economy. Expenses are incurred in the purchase of chemical herbicides, fertilizers, and pesticides as well as in repairing farm machinery such as hoses and soil tillers. Although fertilizers can be obtained at discounted rates from co-ops run by Malaysia's Department of Agriculture (Pejabat Pertanian), many farmers prefer to purchase their own inputs, blaming the national co-ops for providing low-quality deals. Seeds are obtained from the previous seasons' crops, ensuring a recycling process that cuts cost. Sometimes traveling salesmen from Thailand enter the village and promote Thai seed and fertilizer to the farmers. Once harvested, the produce is washed, weighed, bundled, and packed neatly in plastic bags for sale to middlemen buyers, a number of whom are also Ban Bor On residents. Truck-driving middlemen resell the baskets of Thai-cultivated vegetables to market suppliers at Kelantan's large wholesale produce centers such as Wakaf Che Yeh, Kota Bharu, and Tanah Merah. The large profits to be reaped from commercial agriculture have led many residents to devote even the smallest garden plots to some form of cash cropping. So widespread is vegetable agriculture in the Thai village landscape that Thais have become synonymous with its cultivation in the popular imagination of many Kelantanese. In fact, one of the differences Ban Bor On villagers spoke of when comparing their community with Tak Bai Thai villages was that the latter *still* cultivated rice (in 2002) and in some villages, *still* harvested the crop using palm-size sickle-knifes (*kaek*).[16] "If you want to see what Kelantan was like in the past, just go to Tak Bai," my Malaysian friends would tell me.

Although rice cultivation was fondly recollected by older villagers, it was also associated with the hardship and poverty of a time past. In his early encounters with the Kelantanese peasantry, Hugh Clifford observed the dismal local rice economy, which he blamed on "primitive modes of cultivation" (Clifford 1897: 37). "We were so poor in those days," was a refrain I heard time and again when I asked villagers to talk about the past. History was about being poor and having to make do with the simple things one had. Rice was always plentiful but everything else was hard to come by. And one could not survive on rice alone. Changing political systems stemming from Malaya's independence and associated transformations in agricultural technologies and village economics brought a newfound wealth in Kelantan's Thai villages.

The influx of new money from urban employment and commercial cash cropping has led to visible displays of increasing affluence in Ban Bor On. New houses are no longer *basa*—hovels constructed from wood, woven bamboo, and thatch—but are impressive cement and marble-floored structures. Almost every household in the village now has at least one color television, a VCR and DVD player, a refrigerator, a hi-fi audio system, and a telephone. Many villagers own cell phones and personal computers, and by the summer of 2009, most of the Ban Bor On community had wireless access to the Internet.

Ban Bor On's residents were and are a fiercely patriotic people. They often display the Malaysian flag in their homes and temples and talk of the country's socio-economic progress in a language of pride and contentment. By the time I entered the village in 2001, most of them, with the exception of a few elderly men and women, were full-fledged Malaysian citizens. A small number were partial citizens and carried with them the dreaded "red papers" (*kradat daeng*) of permanent residence. The papers restrict movement by preventing their holders from applying for passports, acquiring paid employment, or making land purchases.[17]

One explanation provided me by my Kelantanese friends as to why some Thais were given permanent residency status revolved around the way Malaysian bureaucrats defined citizenry based on ethnicity and language. In the post-independence years, the Malaysian government embarked on a program of creating citizens out of the subjects of the British Empire. In these initial exercises, Kelantanese Thais were suspected of being citizens of neighboring Thailand by some Malay government officers unfamiliar with local renditions of history. Special interview sessions were set up in district towns to quiz Thai applicants for citizenship. The Thais were tested on how well they could speak Malay. The ability to speak the new national language was taken as an indicator of one's Malaysian identity. The nervous applicants were forced to face a panel of Malay interviewers who asked them to list the proper names of certain things, ranging from parts of the body to agricultural implements and household objects, in standard Malay. Already stressed by the encounter and unfamiliar with the national "book Malay" (*khaek nangsue*) as spoken in Kuala Lumpur, many Thais failed the interview and were officially deemed not to be true Malaysians and hence not citizens. Thais who had Malay friends in official positions could derive citizenship papers through other means. My mother, for instance, received her identity papers only after her father bribed local Tumpat officials into granting her an identity card. Throughout the years, however, citizenship exercises were held in Kelantan to correct the wrongly implemented policy. Many Thais took advantage of these opportunities to convert their red cards to the blue ones denoting full citizenship. A handful of older villagers either refused to participate in or were oblivious to these exercises and held on to their permanent resident status. The most recent exercise to politically convert the last remaining

Thai permanent residents was held in 2010, some sixty years after independence.

A four-lane road slices through the heart of Ban Bor On. Built by the Department of Public Works (Jabatan Kerja Raya) in the sixties on what was once an older dirt track, the unnamed road is now a major route bridging Malaysia with Thailand. Rickety private-share taxis and noisy public buses traverse the road, as do assorted other vehicles. In the days before the tarred road was constructed, Ban Bor On was linked to Thailand via the Siamese-Malayan railroad and the movement of salt barges and small boats that docked at the now extinct pier behind what is today the village's only gas station. Malaysia's northeastern rail line no longer services Thailand, and the river that once flowed through the village, connecting it with the vast South China Sea to the east, is but a trickle of its former self. Much of the river has been reclaimed and converted into vegetable gardens and orchards. All that remains of Ban Bor On's riverine history is its memory in the names given to residential sections and subsections of the village (*khet*). These include the Chinese Pier (*tha jin*), where Chinese traders once had a small market and sold pork, and the High Bridge (*phan sung*), the site of an old wood bridge that once spanned the village's wetlands.

Marginal Tales

Malaya, like much of Southeast Asia in the nineteenth and early twentieth century, proved to be an exotic location for many an intrepid European adventurer. The region, with the exception of the west coast port cities of the British Straits Settlements (Penang, Melaka, and Singapore), had yet to be "discovered." Throughout Malaya's colonial history, expeditions led by Western adventurers and scientists have regularly set out to map and trace the history, culture, geology, and biology of the peninsula. Malaya's west coast states received the most scholarly interest, due in part to the location of colonial centers on the peninsula's western front. British commercial and industrial development of the west coast enhanced accessibility to the area, igniting the explorer's imagination of the exotic wilderness of an untamed east coast.

Discourses on racial phenotypes saturated early colonial writings on the peninsula as Darwinian social evolutionism and Orientalism took hold in the lecture halls of England's academies. The corpus of classical ethnographic and historical papers that emerged from these early forays into Malayan(sian) Studies was largely published in the *Journal of the Malayan Branch of the Royal*

Asiatic Society (e.g., Rentse 1934, 1947, 1936; Graham 1908; Skeat 1953, Skinner 1878; Winstedt 1935; Marriot 1916; Laidlaw 1953; Clifford 1897, 1938; Annandale 1900). Later postcolonial Malaysian social scientific scholarship worked within an established ethnic paradigm of a Furnivellian plural society. To this day, Malaysian studies continue to remain firmly entrenched in the language of ethnicity, be it ethnography, sociology, political science, or history. Ethnicity has become the hallmark of Malaysian academic writings in the social sciences and is tied in closely with the nation-state's political inability to move beyond the rhetoric of British-imposed ethnic compartmentalization such as is reflected in national policies of affirmative action for the country's Malay majority.

Academic literature on Kelantan has focused largely on the idea of difference. Kelantanese Malays and Chinese have been fascinating subjects of study for historians, political scientists, linguists, anthropologists, and other scholars by virtue of their seeming cultural, political, economic, and linguistic distinction from Malaysia's west coast cultures (e.g., Nash 1974; Kershaw 1977; Roff 1974; Teo 2008, Lee 2006; Carstens 2005). Kelantan was not just a marginal place on the Malaysian map, but it was also academically marginalized in Malaysian studies which continued to focus largely on the west coast. As early as 1908, Graham had already noted Kelantan's difference from the rest of the colony. There was "little information" on Kelantan, he wrote, and what one could come by in the early twentieth century was often at odds with the reality of the times.

The discourse of Kelantan's marginality and geographical peripheralization has been framed by history. Intense periods of British economic and political colonization in the nineteenth and early twentieth centuries had resulted in the large-scale immigration of labor from China, India, other Malay states, and the Indonesian islands to work the west coast's primary and secondary industries, such as rubber cultivation, tin mining, and urban construction. While nineteenth- and early twentieth-century west coast Malaya moved to the beat of colonial economics, Kelantan remained a distant backwater. This did not mean that Kelantan's British administrators did not attempt to develop the state's primary sector. Notwithstanding Kelantan's heavily forested and mountainous interior, physical geography did not hinder attempts at the early development of extractive industries in the Ulu. Gold and tin mining had, until their takeover by the British in the nineteenth century, been the monopolies of Kelantan's local Chinese minority in old alluvial gold-mining towns in the southern interior such as Sokor, Galas, Nenggiri, Pulai, Kampung Dusun Rendah, and Kuala Toko (Talib 1981, 1987). In a paper delivered at the Royal Geographical Society on 27

April 1896, Sir Hugh Clifford recalled his expedition up the Kelantan river via the Galas and Nenggiri and noted how the gold mines in the area "have been worked by both Chinese and Malays for many generations, and a large quantity of gold has been exported" (Clifford 1897: 33).[18] Although Clifford traveled the full length of the rivers and onward to Kota Bharu, he does not mention the presence of Thai Buddhist communities anywhere in the text, preferring instead to focus on the topography and economy of the Galas and Nenggiri watershed, the Malay court, and "the religious fanaticism of the late prime minister, Maha Menteri" (37). This is a typical omission found in both early and later writings on Kelantan. This could in part be due to the general inaccessibility of many Thai settlements that were beyond the typical Galas-Nenggiri-Kota Bharu aquatic route, and the failure to consider cultural variations in a state that was popularly associated with its Malay Muslim inhabitants. The fact that Thai villages often had impressive temple complexes and free-roaming dogs and pigs, which were not found in Malay villages, must have made them curious sights for travelers interested in describing the ethnology of the state. This lack of literary reference to the community points to the historical marginality of Thais in the eyes of early colonial writers.

Contemporary literature on Kelantan continues to work within the standard geopolitical borders of the state. These works pay scant attention to the agency of the people living within them or to the processes of circulation that link communities. Most do not discuss the historical and contemporary influences exerted by Thailand, for instance on Kelantanese politics and culture, and how these influences are reflected upon and made sense of by Kelantanese in their everyday lives. This is the unfortunate fact of Kelantanese scholarship to this day, which continues to see borders as insurmountable obstacles—rather than fluid navigational bridges—that keep the state and its people locked into their own marginality and difference. An exception to this trend of voiceless description is Malaysian historian Sharil Talib's (1983) article *Voices from the Kelantan Desa, 1900–1940*. In the article, Talib discusses the feelings Kelantanese Malay peasants had regarding the rapid economic changes that hit the countryside with the penetration of colonial economies in the early twentieth century. Doing a close reading of petitions, complaints, demands, and poison pen letters, Talib argues that Kelantanese rural dwellers were not voiceless subjects who merely succumbed to the whims and fancies of colonial economics. Through these narrative genres, farmers actively protested the intrusion of the colonial state into their lives, engaging with it and seeking out compensations for their hardships and newfound suffering.

The few English-, Malay-, and Thai-language works on the Kelantanese Thai community have been largely about Thai participation in processes of ethnic interaction in a plural setting, thereby working within the established ethnic framework and salvage ethnography that has come to be closely associated with Malaysian and Thai Studies.[19] In these descriptive and somewhat romanticized writings, the Thai were constructed as a community that clung stubbornly to a set of adaptive cultural strategies that allowed them to maintain their distinct Buddhist identity in a Muslim state. The Thais one reads about in these works are passive individuals inhabiting culturally homogenous rural lifeworlds. In my ethnography I build upon these works of cultural persistence by showing how ethnic and cultural identifications are reflexively produced. This was a shifting and emergent identification, one that thrived at certain points in time and space but hid itself from view in others. Kelantanese Thai identity production is best understood through the "strange bedfellows" of history and anthropology (Tagliacozzo and Willford 2009: 1). History was important in shaping these intersecting identifications and it is this key humanistic ingredient that is missing in the earlier scholarship that objectifies the Kelantanese Thai as voiceless and emotionless ethnographic subjects.

Academic legacies aside, one cannot fault the authors of such works for a dioramic characterization of village life. The inhabitants of Ban Bor On constantly stereotyped their community in essentialized and ahistorical terms to answer my many prying and often annoying questions. Time and again they pointed out to me how "different" they were from the neighboring Malay: "Thais wear their sarong above the ankles, Malays wear it to the feet," "Thai houses are large, Malay houses are small," "Thais are Buddhist, Malays are Muslim," "Thais are staunch supporters of the Federal Party, Malays vote for the opposition," and so forth. What are lacking from the above descriptions are the nuances and subtleties inherent in such comments—tone, comportment, context, and the perennial anthropological question of "why were they saying this?" To answer this question is to look at the community behind the veil of self and academic cultural stereotyping.

The relationship between borders and the people and national processes they encompass has only recently come to scholarly attention. In *Nationalism Reframed*, Roger Brubaker (1996) wrote about how borders were sites of tension for nation-states. Borders, he reminds us, resulted in the production of national ethnic minorities in new nation-states. Nationalism's Euro-American colonial legacy of territorial demarcation forced the separation of once culturally coterminous communities. In short, the state produced new minority and majority populations within disparate and sovereign spaces.

In Kelantan's Thai villages the processes of historical and contemporary circulation move among three main groups—the Thais, the Malaysian nation-state, and Thailand. This nexus also includes people who live in places far removed from the borderlands—urban Chinese from Malaysia's metropoles, Thai bureaucrats in Bangkok, and Kelantanese Buddhist monks in Singapore. Once the diversity of these individuals is brought to the forefront of analytical theorizing, the seeming neatness of the nexus falls apart. Instead of a clear dialogic process involving three objective actors, Brubaker's "triadic nexus" takes on the form of an ever-changing model with tentacles that reach out to and contract from the social and national spaces not included in its original formulation.

Robert Cribb and Li Narangoa (2004) engage with Brubaker's political framework by looking at how borders, homelands, and ethnic minorities interacted in Mongolia, Laos, and Malaysia. Whereas Brubaker's analysis focused on ethnic minorities as demographic marginals in both their host countries and the perceived external homeland, Cribb and Narangoa discussed a reverse situation. Here, the minority population was more numerous in the host state than in its external homeland. Cribb and Narangoa showed how, instead of drawing ethnic minorities into their spheres of influence, external homelands have been quick to dissociate themselves from the minorities in their midst. As a result, the minority ethnic groups have tended to look inward at their own communities in defining who they are.

Brubaker's and Cribb and Narangoa's studies are just two examples of the way social scientists have attempted to understand the position of ethnic marginals in the midst of contemporary nation-states. Like Brubaker's "New Europeans," Kelantan's Thai population inhabits the frontiers of a state and a country that is not Thai. Across Kelantan's international border is a presumed Buddhist homeland—presumed because not many Kelantanese Thais believe Thailand to be a place from which they originate. Culturally Thailand's southernmost provinces are inhabited primarily by Malay Muslims. To many Thai intellectual and bureaucratic elites in Bangkok, the Kelantanese are diasporic Thais. According to a linear discourse of origination based on national Thai historiography, Kelantanese Thais entered the Malay state through a series of migrations in an unknown period of time when Kelantan was "still a part of Siam." To Thailand's cultural bureaucrats, the Kelantanese Thai represent a "lost tribe" of the modern Thai—people who speak an archaic form of the Thai language that has a vocabulary peppered with "royal" words (*kham ratchasap*) derived from old Mon-Khmer. How they got to Kelantan is uncertain. Thai pop historians hazard guesses at migrations out of thirteenth-century Sukhothai, a principality in North Thailand and celebrated in national Thai historical narratives as being the nation's first Siamese kingdom. Although it is undeniable that Thailand's processes of homeland cultural assimilation through the creation and dissemination of imagined myths of origin for Kelantan's Thai villagers in books, articles, and conversations did affect the way some Kelantanese Thais viewed local histories, most continued to regard themselves as distinct from their Thai cousins across the border. To them, like the rural Chinese of southern Kelantan studied by Sharon Carstens (2005), personhood has as much to do with national affiliation, historical and political relationships, and transnational flows as it does with ancestral origins. Kelantanese Thais proudly told me of how they were undeniably Malaysians. They did not need an external homeland to validate their claims to a distinct identity. But, at the same time, they enjoyed and criticized, often powerfully and with heavy doses of cynicism, the standardizing influences Thailand exuded across its borders. Nevertheless they visited Thailand regularly and watched Thai television with gusto. It is this ability to delicately maneuver between both Malaysian political identification and Thailand's cultural assimilation that frames the way Kelantanese Thais produced their Thainess.

Roads in rural Malaysia are rarely ever smooth, except when upcoming elections initiate a sudden resurfacing of potholes. Along the bumpy road the traveler encounters bus stops, rest pavilions, convenience stores, other travelers, police checkpoints, ghosts, dogs, and traders who break up otherwise simple linear flows. Sometimes an encounter forces one to stop, chat, think, or just wait. At other times, it forces one to continue moving, not turning back. Past and present entangle themselves along these routes. Each chapter in this book is punctuated with similar stops, starts, meetings, departures, and movings-on. Voices call out to be heard as history grapples with ethnography. Ban Bor On, like Michael Herzfeld's (1991) Cretan town, is a place of many histories that intersect, mingle, emerge, and dissipate as men and women move through its space. Borders and boundaries loom large throughout the book, materializing in diverse and sometimes dreamlike and troublesome ways. They structure the way people view themselves, their community, and the mobile world of Thainess that they encounter, build up, and tear apart.

CHAPTER 1

Places

KAE CHI (GRANDMOTHER NUN) LOOKED UP AT ME AS WE SOAPED the plates and blue-and-white China bowls with lemon-scented detergent. One of the villagers had tried manufacturing homemade dish-washing liquid soap and had given Kae Chi some samples to test on the temple's crockery. "Thais have always been living here," said the old nun, grinning, exposing a toothless smile and echoing a common explanation I had heard time and again in Ban Bor On. Sensing my frustrated puzzlement, she proceeded to narrate the origin of Ban Bor On as she knew it, all the while balancing her thin frame on a little plastic stool. The "old people" (*khon kae kae*), she said, had mentioned that there had once been a large rock-encircled pond (*bor*) in the area behind the present-day fire station. The fire station (*bomba*) marks the easternmost extremity of Ban Bor On. Beyond the multi-storied building is the Malay community of Kampung Tar, the District Water Office (Jabatan Pengairan dan Saliran), the local Public Works Department (Jabatan Kerja Raya), and the Al-Islamiah Arab secondary school (*rong rian arab*).[1]

Around the perimeter of this pond grew a clump of tall, slender, spiny palms known as *ton on* (*Oncosperma tigillarium*). Only a few of these tall trees remain in Ban Bor On today. Most have been cut down to make way for new and expanding roads, agricultural plots, and private residential developments. The pond was unique, Kae Chi remembered hearing. It never dried up, not even during the hottest months of the year between March and September, and provided a constant supply of cool drinking water for tired travelers along the dirt road that has now become a four-lane thoroughfare. To the Malay villagers living around Ban Bor On, the Thai village was known as Kampung Pauh. The name was derived from a majestic mango tree (Malay: *pauh*) that had once grown next to where the large rest pavilion stands opposite Mae Uan's sundry store in the heart of present-day Ban Bor On. All that remains of the pond and the mango tree today are their fuzzy images in the collective memory of a few of Ban Bor On's oldest inhabitants.

Kae Chi passed away in 2007 at the age of eighty-eight.[2] Born in the Year of the Rooster, Kae Chi had lived in Ban Bor On all her life. She was a constant companion during my time in Wat Nai. We shared the same temple, she in a small and bare cement room near the funeral hall and I in my wooden quarters just behind the temple's main gate. As age crept up on her, she moved out of the temple and back to her home across the road, where her only son, his wife, and their thirtysomething unmarried daughter lived. Here she lived out her final years, greeting visitors, always smiling, and doing simple household chores. I remember Kae Chi fondly, and the image of her small white-robed form hunched over as she tenderly picked weeds and grasses from the temple's sandy grounds every afternoon is etched in my memory. Deep wrinkles wove a complex labyrinth of fine lines across Kae Chi's thin face. Her dark, leathery complexion attested to years spent cultivating rice and vegetables under the tropical sun.

In her younger days she had been an industrious vegetable trader. She grew leafy greens and purchased large green chili peppers from her friend Eh Chum at eighty Malayan cents for a bunch of one hundred. In his 1915 annual report on the state, Kelantan's British Advisor R. J. Farrer noted with curiosity the daily travels of Kelantan's market traders. Of these mobile villagers he writes:

> There can be no doubt that the native of Kelantan "eget aevis," the flocking of the "orang darat" (up-country people) to the daily markets does not imply cash. They bring their produce (sometimes of incredibly small value for extraordinary distances) and sell it, and then only have the cash to buy what they require. At one market, I found a woman who carried 40 Lbs of betel leaves 6 miles in order to sell it for twice what it cost her, her gross profit, before deducting a market charge of nearly a penny, was 12 1/2 cents (say 3 1/2 pence) with which she would buy her luxuries before trudging home again! (and this is not a single outstanding case). (Farrer 1916: 2)

Travel was thus about more than just gaining large profits. Like the religious and secular pilgrimages described by Simon Coleman and John Eade in their book *Reframing Pilgrimage* (2004), travel, to the Kelantanese villager, was about the trip itself and the enjoyment received from the experience of journeying, trading, and moving. Kae Chi traveled a lot in her lifetime. She had been to

Thailand many times to go sightseeing, perform pilgrimages at various temples, and visit her brother in Narathiwat. Villagers who knew her from her days as a feisty vendor recollected how she would delicately balance bamboo baskets of garden produce on her head each morning as she briskly walked along the dirt track that led from Ban Bor On to the Kelantan riverbank at Palekbang. On some days she would take the train from the Tumpat station to the now-defunct Palekbang stop. From here, she would hire a Malay boatman for twenty British Straits Settlements cents to ferry her across the wide watery expanse that separated the district of Tumpat from Kota Bharu. The boatman charged an additional fee of ten cents per basket of produce carried aboard the vessel. Once on the opposite side, she continued her journey on foot to the large market in the center of the bustling town, where she sold her chilis at a twenty-cent profit per hundred.[3] These daily journeys began in the cool morning hours before the blazing Kelantan sun made walking barefoot unbearable. Kae Chi returned to her village at nightfall. Sometimes she and her friends made dangerous trips into Narathiwat's dense forests, braving bandits and wild animals to harvest jungle fruit like the velvety black *lok kanyi* berries for sale in Kelantan's markets.

Once upon a time, as starstruck young lovers, Kae Chi and her husband had entered into a powerful romantic pact. As the final act of matrimonial devotion, they vowed to dedicate the rest of their lives to the Buddhist monastic order and never remarry should one of them pass on. Thus, upon her husband's death, Kae Chi shaved her head and eyebrows and donned the white garb of the celibate Mae Chi.

Kae Chi emphasized that Thais had been living in Kelantan since the vague and immemorial past, an indigenous periodization of temporality known simply as *tang raek*—the initial period. *Tang raek* has no beginning and no end. It is not associated with any circumscribed historical event or with ancestral myths of migration from Thai Buddhist settlements in what is today Thailand. In his 1993 study of a pseudonymous Kelantanese Thai village to the south of Ban Bor On, Mohamed Yusoff Ismail noted a similar disregard for historical origins amongst the village's inhabitants. Ban Bor On's villagers prefer to emphasize inter-village mobility when speaking of times past rather than grand narratives of colonization or immigration on a more national scale. They spoke of people moving between settlements rather than emerging from specific places. These stories are framed within a common context, that of the production of borders between villages, traditional polities, and modern states. Although Kershaw (1969), Golomb (1978), and Mohamad (1980/1981) did document immigration stories of Thai settlers entering either uninhabited or Malay-occupied lands from Thai Buddhist polities to the north, these stories were minor reflections of larger place-making strategies in the Kelantan flood plains. The everyday histories Kae Chi and others in Ban Bor On spoke of referred to traditional and contemporary patterns of movement and non-movement that had been shaped by a changing border and a shifting cartography.

Kae Chi shared the temple with an elderly gentleman named Lung Piak. No one knew Lung Piak's real age. When I asked him how old he was, he claimed to be one hundred on some days and ninety-something on others. His voice was soft and sometimes it was difficult to make out what he was saying. His story of Ban Bor On's initial settlement differed from Kae Chi's in its emphasis on movement; Kae Chi's tale had been one of stasis. But these were local movements, from one Thai village to another, and not grand migrations.

Lung Piak stayed in the room adjacent to mine and I would see him every day. He was a tall and slender man who was always dressed in a short-sleeved shirt and slacks unless he was alone in his room, when he would do away with the shirt. Across his boney chest were faded tattoos in an indigo hue. The tattoos were a sign of magical potency and masculine bravado. Many men in Ban Bor On and other Kelantanese Thai villages sport tattoos. Most are cabalistic patterns featuring sacred letters in old Khmer. A few are more secular creations. Popular tattoos among many young men are the Thai words for "mother" (*mae*) and "father" (*pho*) inked on the upper arms or on a corner of the chest. The tattoos reinforce the cultural importance of parents in Kelantanese Thai kinship. I was reminded many times over that one's parents were one's personal Buddha and that filial piety was a sacrosanct virtue.

Each morning, as the heat of the sun made movement tiresome even for Wat Nai's mangy dogs, which sought out precious spots of shade under the temple's coconut and mango trees, Lung Piak and I would sit on the verandah of our quarters. He sat on a decaying rattan armchair and I on the cooler green cement steps. We stared out into the sandy vastness that was the temple's courtyard, sometimes in silent contemplation and at other times talking about days gone by and people who no longer lived.

Lung Piak had once been a wealthy rice mill owner. His mill was the only one in the village and signaled the beginning of a new agricultural technology that was to change the daily lives of all residents. But years of gambling, the decline of the rice economy, and conniving relatives had reduced him to destitution, and the once well-to-do man now lived as a pauper off the generosity of the temple's monks. Villagers shook their heads as they saw Lung Piak saunter uneasily back to the temple from the Malay-run coffeeshop in Kampung Tar every morning. He had fallen down a number of times but he never relented on his morning coffee. His gait was peculiar. Lung Piak always walked with his body leaning forward as if he was about to fall face down onto the ground. One could hear him from a mile away as he dragged his rubber flip-flops across the sand.

On days when his illness did not make him weak and forgetful, Lung Piak liked to talk. He recounted many stories, including how Ban Bor On's ancestral inhabitants had been men and women forced out of the nearby settlement of Ban Kao by disease. This was not a movement of choice but of necessity. As evidence for his out-migration theory, Lung Piak pointed to the large number of Ban Bor On residents who possess parcels of rice land in Ban Kao and to the intimate kinship ties that bond the residents of both villages. Many Kelantanese Thais still regard Ban Kao, an old community a short drive from Ban Bor On, as the oldest continuously inhabited Thai settlement in the state. Where these first settlers had come from was not important to Lung Piak. Local oral histories place the origin of Ban Kao's inhabitants in the village of Ban Trat, on the opposite bank of the Ban Kao tributary. Although Ban Trat had once been a thriving Thai wet rice–growing community, its inhabitants were forced to leave their homes due to increasing salination in the fields. New and fertile rice land was found in the present-day site of Ban Kao and Thais have been living there since. Legend has it that a temple once stood in Ban Trat but was abandoned when the villagers left. Today, the village of Ban Trat consists mainly of Malay households, including only five Thai families, all of whom participate in the religious services of Ban Kao's temple.

What mattered most to Lung Piak was not the unilinear history of habitation and migrations, but rather the fact that Thais, regardless of their village of residence, had been living in the fertile Kelantan plains since *tang raek*. Lung Piak believed that pioneer migrants from Ban Kao had first established an intermediary village on the plateau between Ban Bor On and Ban Kao that they called Ban Din Sung (the Village on Raised Land). At present Ban Kao, Ban Din Sung, and Ban Bor On are still primarily inhabited by Thai Buddhists, and all maintain elaborate temples. All three villages come under the jurisdiction of the Malaysian electoral district of Terbak, with its administrative center in the market town of Bandar Tumpat.

The pride with which stories of Thai ancestral situatedness in Ban Bor On were narrated by people like Kae Chi and Lung Piak speaks of the relationship villagers have with various perceptions of the past. In Ban Bor On history is never far from the present. Memories that have a select emphasis on particular historical moments—some real, others not so—shape the way villagers talk about their community. Even Ban Bor On's modern topography of tarred roads, brick houses, and invisible Internet communication lines is contextualized within the historical geography of a much older village that maintains intimate social and ritual associations with nearby Thai settlements.

Ban Bor On's population, like most Thais in Kelantan, did not engage with the British colonial industries of tin, rubber, or gold extraction that began in the Ulu in the nineteenth century.[4] Until the early 1970s most villagers grew wet rice, supplementing their income with vegetables, fruit, domestic animals, and homegrown leaf tobacco (*bekau fan*). Rice was primarily for personal consumption—to trade in rice was considered unethical to Thais. If market trading was done, it was often in commercial vegetables. The nearest market was in the town of Bandar Tumpat, and it was here that villagers met Thais from other settlements and the majority Malays, who for the most part avoided entering ethnically hostile Thai villages. Bandar Tumpat was a commercial, social, and administrative hub that included local government offices, wealthy Chinese merchants, foreign residents, and an exciting and hedonistic nightlife.

Bandar Tumpat's commercial success resulted from the town's strategic position at the confluence of the Kelantan and Golok rivers and at a place where major international connections could be made by sea. Goods and raw materials from Kelantan's southern hinterlands were transported by boats along Kelantan's major rivers, which flowed out into the South China Sea. Bandar Tumpat's naturally deep harbor made it a perfect zone for colonial port development. From here, goods were exported to Bangkok, Singapore, and throughout the peninsula via steamers. The decline of the shipping industry since the 1960s due to changing water levels, increasing sedimentation, and the underdevelopment of colonial extractive industries has made Bandar Tumpat a sad shadow of its former bustling self. Remnants of its earlier ethnic and cultural cosmopolitanism remain in the form of handsome two-story wooden shophouses that line the town's paved roads; British-, Malay-, and Chinese-style mansions; a Hindu temple; a Chinese shrine house (*bio*); a lighthouse; and a Sikh residential compound with its own *gurdwara*.[5] The boundaries between Ban Bor On and Bandar Tumpat are unclear unless one looks at land maps. To some Bandar Tumpat begins after one crosses the rail tracks. Thai villagers have been going to Bandar Tumpat, known simply as *lad* (the market), for as long as they can remember.

1.1 Old and new shophouses, Bandar Tumpat

In the past, these visits were primarily for trade and commerce—many Ban Bor On farmers sold vegetables in the Tumpat market—or to visit with friends and acquaintances in the town. Today Bandar Tumpat serves Ban Bor On's residents' commercial, social, and administrative needs. They go there to pay their electricity bills at the state post office, visit clinics, purchase prepaid calling cards for their cell phones, go to Internet cafes, bring their children to kindergarten, buy groceries, do their banking, eat at the Chinese- and Malay-run coffeeshops, make land transactions at the District Land Office, buy hardware and bird cages, learn to drive, rent cars, and get styled haircuts. From Bandar Tumpat's rail and bus station Ban Bor On villagers make their way not only across Kelantan but also across the country and beyond, in search of work, friends, family, and the excitement of new opportunities.

One of the common points in Kae Chi and Lung Piak's recollections of the Ban Bor On of *tang raek* was the village's association with Bandar Tumpat. Until the early seventies, monks from Wat Nok, Ban Bor On's other temple, would walk through Bandar Tumpat's streets as part of their early morning alms round (*juen bat*), stopping at Thai and Chinese houses and shops to receive offerings of rice and cooked food. The monks were invited to walk through the town by a wealthy Tumpat Chinese philanthropist (*tauke*) and close friend of the then Kelantanese ruler, Sultan Ismail (r. 1920–1944). Known to Tumpat residents as Datuk Kaya Budi after the honorary title (*datuk*) bestowed upon him by the sultan for his goodness of character (*kaya budi*), Datuk Kaya Budi, whose given name was Wee Kwee Theow, had received the royal title after presenting the sultan with a large bungalow that the Malay ruler subsequently turned into his Tumpat palace. Fluent in Thai, Malay, and Chinese, Datuk Kaya Budi was an intermediary between the British municipal council of Kelantan and Tumpat's Thai population. He was a strong supporter of Wat Nok's abbot Pho Than Daeng and his clergy.[6] Although his body was laid to rest in a cemetery in Kota Bharu's Chinese district, the *datuk*'s family continued to look to Wat Nok as its familial parish. Today his descendants still visit the temple, making annual offerings to its monks in memory of the man and clan who had been so instrumental in shaping Thai, Chinese, and Malay relationships on the Kelantan frontier.

The history of Ban Bor On is intimately associated with that of Bandar Tumpat. Ban Bor On residents remember the Bandar Tumpat of the forties, fifties, and sixties as an exhilarating place. Their reminiscences of a happy time gone by are often juxtaposed against the dullness of the present town, with many lamenting that "nothing ever changes in Tumpat." Back in its heyday in the fifties and sixties, Bandar Tumpat boasted two cinemas that screened the latest Hindi, Malay, Hong Kong, and Hollywood movies. On evenings when there was no movie playing, the theater held Malay shadow puppet and traditional Mak Yong dramatic performances lasting many nights on end. Bandar Tumpat was abuzz with social clubs, gambling dens, and brothels. In the days of high imperialism in the state, British officers would relax at the Tumpat Club with local Chinese and Malay aristocrats. Datuk Kaya Budi was at one time vice president of the esteemed club. Today the only nocturnal stirrings in the market town are one or two small coffeeshops that serve late-night snacks of rice, instant noodles, a hamburger or two, and Indian pancakes (*roti canai*) eaten with curry. Otherwise Bandar Tumpat's streets are silent, the dank wooden shophouses that line the roads are boarded shut, and few, if any, people walk along the dimly lit streets.

Bandar Tumpat is the largest town in the district of Tumpat. Each state (*negeri*) in Malaysia is divided into a number of administrative precincts called *jajahan*. *Jajahan* are subdivided into yet smaller units of *daerah penggawa* (*daerah* for short) that are made up of electoral districts (*mukim*), which are in turn made up of villages (*kampung*). Thirteen of Kelantan's twenty-four primarily Thai villages are found in the *jajahan* of Tumpat. Consisting of only 169.5 square kilometers, Tumpat is one of Kelantan's smallest districts, with some 75 percent of the *jajahan*'s land use area devoted to agricultural activities. The *jajahan* of Tumpat is composed of seven *daerah penggawa* covering a total of 30 *mukim* and 57 villages. According to 1998 census reports, Thais accounted for 6,535 individuals in the Tumpat district, whereas Malays numbered 105,153 persons and Chinese only 1,914 persons.[7]

For a long time, Kelantan's village communities remained cut off from one another. Foot paths and raised paddy bunds linked neighboring settlements in a complex grid of local trails, but these were often hampered by dense tropical jungle. Although some villagers such as Kae Chi were avid long-distance travelers and traders, most Ban Bor On residents saw mobility as one of the defining characteristics of an exhilarating modernity. Modernity was about movement and road building. The past, *tang raek*, was for the most part about a relative situatedness and localism. It was marked, as Kae Chi reminded me, by slow, tiring, and at times dangerous movements through the rural and natural landscape. Tarred roads, and, since the 1970s, electricity, were a sign of the times. They accelerated the speed of movement in, through, and across local, national, international, and ideological spaces, making mobility a central aspect of life and identity for everyone.

Roads

Kelantan's Thai villages are cut up by large asphalt-laced roads (*thang minyok tar*) and smaller paths (*thang iad/thang nai ban*). Where tracks met with the larger roads, a *wang gela* or crossroad formed. Asphalt roads were built by the state's public works team, usually under the directives of the Public Works Department. Villagers could request that a free government-tarred road be constructed in their village if they required one. All that was needed for a road to be built was proof that a marked track (*rizab thang*) of some sort had been formally indicated on the British-derived land grants villagers held.[8]

The construction of paved roads was part and parcel of colonialism's *mission civilisatrice*. Roads tied up distant parts of the colony to its administrative center and brought the culture of the metropole, with its policies, laws, and economies, into the hinterlands of the colony. In colonial Kelantan, roads linked the Ulu's mining settlements with the port towns of Tumpat and Kota Bharu, between which raw materials and other amenities were transported back and forth. So important was road building to the practice of colonialism that annual British state records devote substantial sections of their reports to the detailing of road works, often listed under the heading of "communications." Unfortunately little research has been conducted on the social history of road works in Kelantan, despite its predominance and significance in shaping processes of mobility and early economic and social development in the state.

Intensive road works in Kelantan were put in place by the Colonial Office's Public Works Department (formed in 1903) in the middle of the twentieth century. Metalled and tarred thoroughfares soon replaced the footpaths that had spread across the state, opening up once-isolated villages to the increasing colonial presence. By 1904 there were already roads in Kelantan's more prosperous trading centers such as Kota Bharu and Bandar Tumpat. Mohd. Kamaruzaman (1990: 58–59) noted that Kota Bharu was already linked to the outskirt districts of Banggol and Gunong—the latter being close to the Thai settlement of Ban Arey in 1904.[9] Writing in the early years of the twentieth century, Graham observed that there was already an eight-mile road linking "the village of Tumpat" with Kota Bharu (1908: 57). The first major road to be built by Kelantan's Public Works Department was a trunk road that led from the state capital to the southern Ulu region, the economic heart of the rubber and mining industries. By the 1930s, Kelantan was crisscrossed by 233 miles of road (Talib 1995: 117). Some fifteen years earlier, the southern district of Pasir Puteh was linked to Kota Bharu via a coastal road that allowed for ease of travel, and hence political control, into one of Kelantan's more troublesome districts and the site of the anti-British Tok Janggut rebellion of 1915. Later road works were built around the Pasir Puteh and Ulu Kelantan trunk roads (ibid.: 116). Today Kelantan, like all other Malaysian states, is a complex tapestry of large and small highways. Roads continue to be widened, resurfaced, and tarred. Roadways now span the Kelantan and Golok rivers, linking Bandar Tumpat with Kota Bharu, Tanah Merah, and Thailand at various entry points across three causeways.

Roads are important in the everyday lives of Ban Bor On's residents. They bring a few young Ban Bor On women to the duty-free shops in Pengkalan Kubor at the Thai border for work each morning and to the Chinese-owned coffeeshops in Kota Bharu, where older women work as kitchen hands, cooks, and waitresses for Chinese employers. Their bilingualism in Thai and Malay (and for some, Mandarin and Hokkien), coupled with the unspoken allure of the female body, make them ideal candidates for these positions. Agricultural produce from Ban Bor On's fertile gardens are hauled in trucks along these roads to markets all over the state, a practice that has historical antecedents in the traditional vegetable trading grid Kae Chi and others participated in in the past. The road leading from Ban Bor On to Bandar Tumpat once hosted an active streetside market where Thai, Chinese, and Malay traders mingled and haggled.

Pilgrims travel along these roads as they move among Kelantan's twenty Thai temples to attend Buddhist celebrations. Roads also bring Thai visitors to cities across the Tak Bai and Golok rivers and onward to temples along the Lao and Myanmar borders. As air transport is too expensive and inconvenient for many villagers, overland routes linking Kelantan with Thailand are the preferred means of movement for most villagers when heading across the border. Roads brought villagers to Bangkok's Grand Palace, where they paid their last respects to King Bhumipol Adulyadej's mother in 1995 and his sister in 2008. From the unnamed road in front of Wat Nai, villagers travel to far-flung provinces in Thailand such as Chiang Mai in the north and Nakhon Phanom on the banks of the Mekhong River. Their perceived cultural identification as Thais was linked to these road adventures that stretched the community beyond the comfortable confines of local bordered spaces.

Road meanings take on different significance throughout the day. In the wee hours of the night, when the burden of traffic lightens up along Ban Bor On's main thoroughfare, rice smugglers zip by in unassuming vehicles in a desperate attempt to reach Kota Bharu with their loot without encountering police checks. The road at night becomes transformed from a zone of sacrality—pilgrims, monks, and Buddhist ordination parades traverse it during the day—to one of danger and contraband under the yellow glow of government street lights. Sometimes these "rice projects" (*projek koesan*) turn into exciting high-speed car chases when waiting policemen give chase.[10] Wat Nai's strategic location along the road has made it a primary site for police stakeouts. During my stay at the temple, it was not uncommon to see police cars parked discreetly behind the temple's walls as their officers lay in wait for unsuspecting smugglers. Reckless driving by the smugglers has led to a number of accidents along the road. Villagers turn up in large groups to watch the commotion and gather up the sacks of rice strewn along the road by nervous smugglers in their last-minute efforts to dispose of the evidence.[11]

In the early morning about an hour before the sun rises, when the village is blanketed in a cool darkness, the road's sacrosanct nature returns once again.

Ban Bor On's monks walk silently along the roads at dawn as part of their alms round. From the main thoroughfare, they fan out in pairs onto the smaller paths that cut deep into village residential space. As the sun slowly rises over the horizon, a new day begins in Ban Bor On. The chickens are always the first to rise and crow noisily as if communicating with one another across village space. Sometimes the strange loud whooping cries of the night jar—a small brown bird villagers call *nok khi khran*, the "lazy bird," due to its supposed preference for walking instead of flying—pierces the dew-laden air. School children in their pressed uniforms, town workers, and farmers make their way along the road, sometimes on foot, sometimes on bicycles and motorcycles, and sometimes in cars, trucks, and buses, to their respective destinations. A lone potbellied pig waddles by the side of the road scavenging for food, only to disappear into the shrubbery. Ban Bor On is, after all, a Thai village.

A smaller two-lane branch road leads directly from the village to Bandar Tumpat. Another branch road leads from the main thoroughfare to Ban Phan Jao and from there onward to Ban Khok Phrao and Ban Jai. Wat Nai and Wat Nok sandwich this recently tarred road, which for a long time had been just a long wooden bridge (*phan jao*) built and maintained by Wat Nai's monks over a wet and muddy pond. The water hole (*phlak*) had been formed by the trampling of cow and water buffalo hooves as farmers brought the beasts to and from the rice fields every day. By the mid-1970s, the pond had dried up and the obsolete wooden bridge had been dismantled, taking with them a precious slice of Ban Bor On's past.

Like most roads beyond Kelantan's towns, Ban Bor On's village roads are unnamed. Addresses are listed as part of postal centers and not as places alongside roads. Once one reaches Kota Bharu and the larger towns these roads become named zones and borders and the sites of shops, schools, hospitals, eateries, and gas stations. Black-and-white signboards placed strategically along the road announce to travelers the name of the district and village one was entering. There was no sign to welcome one to Ban Bor On or to bid one farewell. Visitors knew they had entered the Thai village by virtue of the visual and aural indicators of Thainess that pervaded the sensory roadscape: colorful Buddhist temples, wandering pigs and dogs, roadside stores with Thai names such as Wilai Restaurant and Somchai Stationery, the sound of Thai pop music that wafted out of living room windows, beer cans in trash heaps along the road, and the absence of the sheep and goats that mark many a Malay Muslim settlement.

Roads are places steeped in locality. Like the international border, the road imprisons and releases. Kelantanese Thais in recollecting the past often spoke of how people walked frequently in *tang raek*. Nowadays, they said, one relies on some form of vehicular transport to get to even nearby destinations. They spoke of the road as a living place, one that was born of national development and grew as the state government widened it. Roads were about progress, both economic and social, but they also created unhappiness as roadworks forced villagers to part with sections of their private lands and gardens in the name of national development. In short, roads were a material manifestation of the mobility that structured the everyday lives of those who relied on it.

In her study of the paved road in the Portuguese village of the Alto Minho, Joao de Pina-Cabral (1987) noted that peasants associated the road with a negative perception of modernity marked by the breakdown of traditional face-to-face community relations. In rural Minho, observed Pina-Cabral, social order was calibrated according to a popular belief in an unchanging "pastness." This sense of local history was linked to peasant experiences of a past that was marked by socially repetitive events (such as processions, Mass, self-help systems, funeral practices, and bread making) that involved spatial units including the household, the hamlet, the parish, and the borough. Paved roads passing through the Portuguese settlement disrupted the natural flow of these ordered events and resulted in the instability of peasant identity. Roads imposed a new concept of linear "national" (standardized) time on the repetitive temporality of the peasant's worldview and were seen by many villagers as both convenient and socially disruptive transport capillaries.

Similarly, Sharon Roseman (1996) complicates the picture of roads as tropes in strategies of indigenous history production. She notes that in the Spanish Galician village of Santiago de Carreira, collective memories abound regarding the 1964 construction of the paved road that linked the once-isolated settlement with the provincial highway system. Unlike the negative imagination of the road as a socially disruptive national project, Galician villagers admired their road and associated it with modernity and economic development. But to them, the road was not the result of a top-down imposition of political and economic order by the Spanish state, an idea that contradicted official elite discourses on the meaning of road building. Rather, villagers fondly recollected how they constructed the road themselves through "the sweat of their voluntary labor, and with the help of draft animals and tools that they lent to the project" (Roseman 1996: 837). The road was, therefore, a physical and valued manifestation of village tradition as remembered by residents in the stories they told about their communal participation in voluntary labor. Like Pina-Cabral's road in the Minho, the paved highway to Santiago de Carriera symbolized the villagers' subjective experiences of the past and the traditions contained within them. Similarly the Thai villagers of Ban Bor On, with its unnamed trunk road, combined local experiences of the past with contemporary identities based on movement and marginality. Theirs was a past that was intimately associated with common perceptions of rootedness in the settlement, the Kelantanese state, and, since 1963, the Malaysian nation-state.

Roads, although linking settlements with towns and cities, also disrupt the stability of rooted boundaries. They facilitate motion but also foreground stability in place. Herein lies the conundrum of Ban Bor On's identity as a situated locale on the hinterlands of Malaysia. Roads are arteries along which *tang raek* is captured in the present. These arteries penetrate the borders of the village, exposing them to the nation-state's ideologies of governance, citizenship, and belonging. Roads in Ban Bor On are not simply symbols of change; they also mark traditional patterns of movement and non-movement that villagers see as an integral aspect of their Thainess.

Roadside Thainess

A short walk from Wat Nai along Ban Bor On's trunk road, past the well-stocked Somchai Stationery Store, is Pho Chum's recently renovated two-story residence. In front of the emerald-green painted structure with its large stainless steel water tank runs a narrow slip of land that once belonged to my grandmother, Koe Pui, who had inherited it from her grandmother. Many years ago, my grandmother sold the plot to the elderly Pho Chum and his wife for a small amount. I remember her telling me that it made more sense that way since the land was directly in front of Pho Chum's home and his grocery store. It was also too narrow for profitable fruit or vegetable cultivation so there was no real point in holding on to it. Near Pho Chum's is the large blue-and-white gated compound of the Malaysian government's Drugs, Customs, and Excise Unit (Unit Pengesan Dadah, Kastam dan Eksais Diraja). The unit stands at the far end of a narrow paved track that also serves as the unit's driveway. This part of the village is called *soi ma*—dog lane—after the hounds kept by customs officials as sniffer dogs. Like the fluttering green PAS and dark blue Barisan Nasional flags that fly high over the village during election months, the customs' quarters bring bureaucratic Malaysia into its most distant hinterlands. The Malaysian-Thai border is a problematic frontier, one that needs the constant policing of the unit as smuggling and contraband circuits cross it with ease. Occasionally customs officers seize cattle from cross-border animal thieves. The retrieved bovine loot is penned up at the far end of the complex's grounds, where they await resale in auctions.[12]

One needs to be careful when walking along Ban Bor On's main road (map 3). Traffic zips along it at top speed in both directions. There are no traffic lights, and the narrow, sandy patch of land by the side of the street is not much of a sidewalk. Small businesses hug both sides of the road that links Ban Bor On with Kota Bharu in one direction and with the Thai border in the other. In 2001 and 2002 these included three restaurants serving Thai food, an egg supplier, a number of vehicle (primarily motorcycle) repair garages, hair salons (two of which also serve as dressmaking shops), a couple of grocery stores, a bakery, a defunct cookie factory, a signcraft business, a large furniture factory, and a lumber-trading establishment. Traveling toward the Pengkalan Kubor–Tumpat T-junction, the road leaves Ban Bor On and enters the district of Ketereh with its large medical center. The center is actually a complex of buildings, containing a small hospital, clinics, and residential units for doctors and nurses. The hospital is often packed with villagers from the district who are treated there before being sent for specialist consultation in the state capital. Nearby are a cluster of three schools: two primary (*sekolah rendah*) and two secondary (*sekolah menengah*). Mandarin-medium Chong Cheng is very popular with Thai and Chinese parents, with some classes composed almost entirely of Thai children from Ban Bor On and surrounding villages. Ketereh primary school and Pengkalan and Sri Terbak secondary schools teach classes in Malay according to a national syllabus.

On the opposite side of the road from *soi ma* is a three-story building that serves as a hotel. Managed by Phi Nuat and his Thai-speaking Chinese wife, Ban Bor On's only hotel charged guests a reasonable RM50 (US$14) a night for a simple bedroom. Phi Nuat had had big plans for his hotel. He had anticipated transforming the building's uppermost floor into a fancy seafood restaurant at which beautiful girls from Thailand, and perhaps from Russia, would be waitresses. Caucasian waitresses with their blond hair and blue eyes, laughed Phi Nuat, would be such a novelty in the village that they were sure to attract customers to his restaurant. That restaurant never materialized and the hotel remains empty for most of the year, save for the occasional visitor. Phi Nuat's wife runs a hair salon from the front of the establishment, and recently a small minimarket was set up next to it.

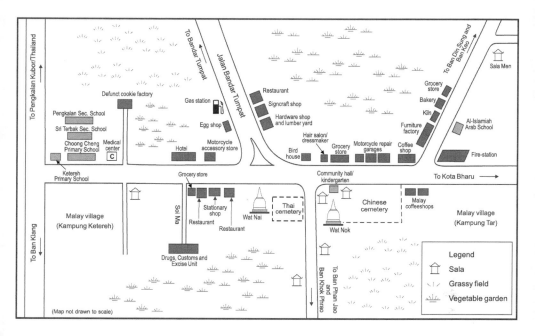

MAP 3. Ban Bor On and environs

Bird houses (*rang nok*) are a common feature in Kelantan's built environment today. A few years before I moved to Ban Bor On in 2001, an uncommunicative Chinese couple—no one in Ban Bor On seemed to refer to them by their names—had purchased a pair of newly constructed row houses along the road opposite Wat Nai and a stone's throw from Mae Uan's sundry shop. The couple chose to live in one of the houses and converted the other white-walled structure into a nesting site for swiftlets, whose edible nests fetch large returns when sold on the international Chinese gourmet food market. This was not the first time that local entrepreneurial Kelantanese had attempted to benefit from global Chinese gastronomic demands: it was the latest in a series of supplementary income fads to hit Kelantan's Thai villages. In the late 1990s, Thai villagers began catching toads by the hundreds, which, when dried, were believed to be a possible cure for cancer. The toads were sold to Chinese buyers who then exported the amphibians to Taiwan and Hong Kong, where they would fetch exorbitant prices. Then there was the tortoise meat trade. Tortoises began disappearing from temple ponds, rivers, and just about anywhere the reptile poachers could get hold of one. Tortoise hunting did not last long and soon villagers had moved on to the next moneymaking venture—raising miniature bantams for chicken shows that took Kelantan and neighboring Terengganu by storm in the late 1990s. Bantams, known locally as *ayam srirama* or Lord Rama's chickens, after the noble protagonist of the popular Hindu Ramayana epic, were soon replaced by the colorful flowerhorn (*cichlasoma*) aquarium fish believed by some Thais and Chinese to be magnets for good luck and wealth. Today, interest in raising flowerhorns has gone the way of the rarely seen bantams and tortoise- and toad-hunting; Ban Bor On's villagers eagerly await a new global trend to stir their community.

Like most Thai villages in Kelantan, Ban Bor On is marked by the presence of rest pavilions (*sala*) set up alongside its main road. These are places where villagers gather during festivals, ritual occasions, and social celebrations. Certain *sala* in the village have become meeting points for young men in the evenings. During election campaigning, *sala* become hubs for party politics, their plain pillars plastered with posters, flags, and banners of either the federal or Islamic party. Pavilions also serve a more practical function. On a day-to-day basis, they are stops for buses and taxis. Constructed by private individuals, some *sala* are very old and have forgotten histories, such as the one on the opposite side of the road from Mae Uan's sundry shop, while others are more recent creations. Most are built in traditional Thai architectural form, open on all four sides and shaded with a gabled roof. Older *sala* are elaborately embellished structures of burnt clay tiles decorated with interesting cement figures in the shape of dragons, owls, and various fantastical beasts. *Sala* announce the invisible cultural borders of the Thai village to pedestrians and motorists. The roadside *sala*, like other material markers of Thai identity along the road—noodle shops, dogs and pigs, Buddhist monks on their alms rounds, and temples—are ethnic speed bumps in an otherwise culturally neutral national roadmap.

Unlike the *sala*, street signs are put in place by the state. One cannot miss Ban Bor On when traveling along the road. Two large white road signs inscribed with bold black letters and smaller milestone markers announce the perimeters of the *mukim* of Terbak. One sign is placed near Manee's restaurant, where one arm of the Ban Bor On road heads in the direction of Bandar Tumpat. Another sign is found next to the impressive blue and yellow *sala* in front of Doctor Chan's mansion in the westernmost corner of Ban Bor On. Yet another black and white "Terbak" sign is found in front of Mae Uan's store, in what is possibly the social center of the village. The signs seem to map the village, drawing invisible boundaries around it and defining it as the *mukim*. In reality, however, the signs refer only to the mukim that also envelopes nearby Thai and Malay settlements

1.2 A *sala* by the road

in a larger government-defined topography. Ban Bor On is not Terbak but has become it in the eyes of travelers moving along the road.

On drawn maps, the borders of places are clearly demarcated as dotted lines and colored patches. On the ground these cartographic borders are invisible. In their place stand road signs, milestone markers, pavilions, and temples. I was often perplexed by where village boundaries began and ended and by how villagers seemed to know exactly where personal and fenceless plots of farm-land were separated from other cultivated plots. Maps and land grants clearly indicated the perimeters of places, but these were rarely resorted to in everyday stories about specific locales. Sometimes there was a marker, an indicator of an invisible border — a tree here, a rock there — but in most cases, the perimeters of place remained in the imagination of its moving inhabitants.

In these geographical imaginings, road signs and dotted lines seem not to matter. Thai social actors pointed to simpler but no less important indicators of Thainess as cultural space. For instance, on the back of Phi Sung's motorcycle one day, he told me that Thai houses belonged to Ban Bor On and that the Malay ones were built in the adjacent Malay settlements. Malay houses were generally smaller than Thai ones and Phi Sung pointed out to me the architectural variants between Thai and Malay houses. Similarly, dogs and pigs sauntered through Thai settlements but never Malay ones. Their paw and hoof prints demarcated ethnic zones in the soft sand.

Ban Bor On, like most large Thai villages in Kelantan, is subdivided into a number of residential groupings called *khet*. There are five *khet* in Ban Bor On. These are the *khet* of Ban Tok (the western village), Ban Thung Kha (the village of the field of cogon grass), Ban Hua Phan (the village at the head of the bridge), Ban Klang (the central village), and Ban Ok (the eastern village). Each *khet* includes some twenty households clustered close to one another. Monks from Ban Bor On's two temples receive their daily alms from residents living in a particular *khet*. By walking along paths through a *khet*, the monks silently and symbolically trace out the otherwise unmarked geography of the *khet*, thereby constructing a sacred topography that links the village to its temples. All the households that support a temple through using it as their ritual focus, regardless of their *khet* affiliations, are part of the local congregation (*lek wat*) of that temple.

Constant movement occurs within and throughout the world of Kelantan's Thai settlements, between *khet* and roads, villages, and towns. Recent anthropological theorizing has concluded that cultures comprise a confusing array of emergent practices that form sites for the everyday expression and experience of boundaries. Places come about and are transformed by social agents who engage with and across them as part of physical and ideological circuits of movement. By participating in a series of tangled flows, social actors (the anthropologist included) are able to produce and narrate their own experiences and whims about locations, histories, and personhood, often in contrast to the rigid and essentialized imaginations of the state and its representatives. In short, the emergence of Ban Bor On as a situated Thai place in a modern Malaysian nation-state is the product of a complex web of overlapping and intertwined travel practices of cultures and people en route. A good example of this cultural lacework between movements and boundedness can be seen in the way Ban Bor On's villagers publicly celebrate their Thainess through the noisy spectacle of ordination parades (*hae nak*).

Parades occur when young men are to be ordained as monks, usually just before the start of the three-month Theravadin Lenten period known as *phansa* from August to mid-November. Although some men prefer to keep their ordinations simple and quiet affairs, without the noise and visual glamour that constitute the key components of a traditional *hae nak*, many families do enjoy the color and boisterousness of a parade. *Hae nak* parades travel along Ban Bor On's main road. They usually begin at a blue-roofed *sala* located about a kilometer from Wat Nai. Repaired many times, the antique *sala* still sits at the crossroads of a side road that links Ban Bor On's main highway with a smaller road that emerges from behind the district fire station. Referred to simply as the "road behind the fire station" (*thang lang bomba*), this one-lane asphalt track links Ban Bor On with the Thai villages of Din Sung and Ban Kao. A few small businesses line the route, including Na Di's sundry store, a wood furniture factory, a disused kiln, and a bakery. A short distance away is the Al-Islamiah Arab School. As the roads lead away from Ban Bor On, the village's commercial landscape is soon replaced by houses, tall trees, and vegetable plots.

Just as Adeline Masquelier's Route 1 in the Niger "endows the past with a tangible, and at times frightening immediacy" (Masquelier 2002: 830), the road behind the fire station and its small *sala* allows Ban Bor On's residents to experience their past in a Malaysian present. This is not the painful history of colonial exploitation that Masquelier's Hausaphone Mawri relive through the dissemination of narratives of evil spirits and frightening road accidents, but rather a positive imagination of a sacred ancestral temporal space. And ancestors proved that the villagers belonged to the place that on the maps and road signs was clearly labeled simply "Terbak."

From its physical form one would not think that the pavilion from which Ban Bor On's ordination parades begin is a sacred place. Shaded by trees, the *sala* looks like any other pavilion one sees along Kelantan's roads. Empty beer cans, cigarette butts, and plastic drink bags litter the area around its wood base. The *sala*'s recently repainted pillars bear graffiti that are a telltale sign of the place's living associations with Thainess. Etched deep into the wood are a mismatch of Thai letters interspersed with cartoon-type figures and the rough outlines of long-horned water buffalo skulls—an iconographic representation of Thailand's rock band Carabao, an all-time favorite among many of the young men in Kelantan's Thai villages.[13]

The *sala* marks the site where ancient cremations once took place for Wat Nai's abbots (*pho than*). No one can remember who these abbots were or when they were cremated. These were powerful men by virtue of their Buddhist morality and possibly unmatched magical skills. Their legacy lives on in the form of a bevy of unnamed invisible spirits known generically as *chao* that now hover around the *sala*. Some time long ago, in the murky past that makes up much of

Ban Bor On's *tang raek*, elaborate funerary towers (*men*) were built in the vicinity of the *sala* to house the wooden coffins of these *pho than* before cremation. No one can recall the exact spot where the cremations took place. When I was to be ordained as a monk in 2002, Tok Nai Suk, a ritual specialist who was always involved in ordination procedures, accompanied me to the *sala*. A mat was laid out on a shady patch of ground near the pavilion and I was asked to prostrate myself three times while kneeling. Tok Nai Suk informed me that I was paying homage to the actual site of the ancient cremation pyre—currently a tangle of trees, shrubs, and dense undergrowth.

Sala men, or *pho than men* as the pavilion is called by residents, is one of many spirit-inhabited nodes that define space in Ban Bor On. Spirits are everywhere. They live in the large trees that line Wat Nai's old cemetery, and the miniature temple-like shrine houses are the abode of individual *khet* spirits. Spirits dwell in the village's fields, at crossroads, and in old ponds. But modernity has insinuated itself into the village through the destruction of some spirit locales. Tall trees were felled to make way for road expansions and housing projects, dark paths illuminated by bright street lamps, and paddy fields turned into vegetable gardens. The conversations I had with my friends revolving around stories of tutelary *chao* and the more sinister and malicious *phi* were often animated and exciting discussions. Everyone enjoyed retelling the stories they had heard about these strange beings or the spooky encounters they had had with them either directly or indirectly. Some spoke of having seen the beings themselves, often in the form of black shadowy figures perched high in the trees or of strange orbs of light floating through the night sky. The road behind the fire station was ripe with spirits—sacred *chao* near the *sala* and the more terrifying giant *phi* just down the road as one approached the temple of Wat Din Sung.

During one of our conversations on the topic of spooks and other things that go bump in the night, Pho Di pointed out to me that the decline in *chao*-inhabited sites in the village was a result of modern education. He argued that Western science and notions of rational logic taught in Malaysia's government schools had impacted the younger generation of Ban Bor On inhabitants. Children were now part of a new village geography marked by paved roads and power lines. They were no longer terrified of the spirits, and this had inadvertently led to the latter's decline and disappearance.[14]

But these ancient beings never really disappeared. Western modernism, with its focus on changing conceptions of rationality and reality, had undoubtedly affected the Thai villages through a history of encounters with the global technologies of education, the mass media, and so forth. Yet, modernist ideas, as Hansen (2007) and Blackburn (2010) have noted for Cambodian and Sinhala Buddhist epistemologies, were framed within native lifeworlds. In Kelantan, the ghosts and spirits of an ancient but undated past persist, albeit in a transformed context. They live on in the stories people tell. *Thang lang bomba* is a haunted zone that, as one story had it, was inhabited by a monstrous ghost that was so large that cars could pass through its legs as it stood naked astride the road. Then there are haunted temple buildings and their mischievous ghostly inhabitants who played tricks on unsuspecting monks. In the case of the ordination pavilion, the continued retelling of stories about the site's sacredness maintains it as a symbolic dwelling place for spirits. Even though offerings are no longer placed for their appeasement and the pavilion is now colonized by a new type of spirit — the motorcycle-riding young men of Din Sung — the spirits remain present. "I still lift my hands in a respectful *wai* [gesture] when I pass by *sala men*," admitted Mae Nyai, Pho Di's wife, who had been listening to our conversation. To her, as to many other Ban Bor On residents, *sala men* is still the residence of mystical *chao*. And it is the *chao* that give villagers a sense of historical locatedness in the Muslim state.

Sala men combines the past with the present through its association with the cremations of Wat Nai's former abbots and the contemporary ordination of young men into the monkhood. For a long time all men who were to be ordained as Buddhist monks at Ban Bor On's two temples were brought to *sala men* to be ritually dressed in the white robes of the Buddhist renunciate before they were paraded to either Wat Nai or Wat Nok for the ordination ceremony proper. From *sala men*, the procession snaked its way to Wat Nai, traveling along the road behind the fire station and bringing with it not only the boisterous cheer of the parade's revelers but also a moving sense of pride in an indigenous and located past.

Local history, Lorraine Gesick (1995) pointed out in her analysis of the southern Thai myth of Lady White Blood (*nang lued khao*), is grounded in the perpetuation of memories associated with place. As a sacred node from which many ordination parades begin, *sala men* links the contemporary village and its inhabitants with a sacred memory of an unquestioned Thai Buddhist presence in the area. By traveling along the parade route, Ban Bor On villagers reproduce a narrative of Thainess that is powerfully rooted in memories of place. Parade participants symbolically legitimize their cultural affiliations to the Thai villages in which they live through the ritual placation of the spirits by the monk-to-be

1.3 The *sala men*

during the ordination ceremony. And they publicly announce this affiliation during their lively parades along the asphalt thoroughfare.

Hae nak are examples of "meta-movement" (Coleman and Eade 2004: 18). These are not simple journeys to be studied in and of themselves, but complex patterns of circulation that package subjectivity and history. Meta-movement, according to Coleman and Eade, is "the combination of mobility itself with a degree of reflexivity as to its meaning, form, and function. Thus . . . pilgrimage can provide opportunities to reflect upon, re-embody, sometimes even retrospectively transform, past journeys." Parades, like pilgrimages, materialize the reflexive experiences of their participants in a moment of ephemeral visuality. In Ban Bor On, ordination parades are short journeys that showcase not only Thainess to all who care to view them but powerful and unspoken discourses of ethnicity and their associations with national narratives.

The ordination procession begins at *sala men*, usually in the early afternoon after the villagers have had their lunch, and passes the Malay houses and coffeeshops of Kampung Tar before eventually entering Wat Nai, through its large and elaborate gateway. Both Malays and Thais form the audience of these performances. They sit in the coffeeshops along the route, stare out of house windows from behind lace curtains, and look on from the cars, buses, and motorcycles that have been forced to slow down to make way for the onslaught of Thai revelers. Through their participation in the parade, Thai social actors call attention to cultural differences between themselves and their Malay Muslim neighbors. They break the social taboos of Islamic decorum, openly consuming alcohol and dancing in public. From their smiles and laughter, it is clear that these men and women enjoy the public celebrity their performances elicit. They have the power to stop traffic and move at their own pace. There is no need for police approval, as ordination parades have been going on since time immemorial, my friends reminded me. There has been a tacit understanding between Kelantanese Malay police officers and the Thai revelers that overrides government bureaucratic procedures on road safety and usage. Not only are they resurrecting the historical legacy of an ancestral Thai Buddhist homeland in Kelantan, but participants in the parade are also demonstrating both to themselves and to the non-Thai viewers what Thai marginality and agency are all about.

Ordination parades anchor the modern village in a distant but local past. In Ban Bor On, the parade's association with *sala men* and hence with an ancestral Thai presence in and around the villages of Din Sung, Ban Bor On, Ban Phan Jao, and Ban Kao carries with it political significance as well. On this secular level the parade is a visual platform on which to publicly assert not only one's marginality—being different and distinct from the Muslim majority—but also one's pride in being Malaysian. As my Thai friends constantly reminded me throughout my months in Ban Bor On, on my subsequent visits, and during our online conversations, they were Malaysians to the bone. It was inevitable, they argued, that they would share some cultural features with their Buddhist counterparts across the international border. Thais had always been living in the area, they said, and were, for the most part, not the descendants of immigrants from the Thai nation-state, as some Malaysian politicians and Thai academics mistakenly believed.

One of the most memorable spectacles of Thai patriotism to the Malaysian nation-state I experienced in Ban Bor On occurred during Malaysia's Independence Day celebrations on 31 August 2002. When twentysomethings Ta Roen and Ta Thit had their ordination parade that day, some of the participants took the opportunity to explicitly demonstrate a Kelantanese Thai sense of national and state pride in a highly spirited manner.[15] In line with the playful exuberance of the parade, a man by the name of Eh Khrai wrapped himself in a large Malaysian flag and danced his way to the temple to the accompaniment of Thai songs

1.4 Ordination parade

played by the *klong jao* band. We clapped and laughed, cheering him on. The truck on which the two initiates sat was decked, not only with the usual colorful cloth streamers and strings of jasmine buds, but also with stripped Malaysian flags and red Kelantan state flags. Thainess, the float seemed to proclaim, had its foundations in a modern Malaysian state. As we sang and danced to the latest in Thai folk and rock hits, spirited Malay cries of "Merdeka! Merdeka!" (Independence! Independence!) were raised by the Thai parade participants and the flags waved vigorously. The shouts elicited similar responses from the Malay onlookers and recalled a past national narrative when Tunku Abdul Rahman, Malaysia's first prime minister, raised his clenched fist in 1957, announcing the emergence of Malaysia from a legacy of British imperialism. The black-and-white image of the historical episode is screened on television, appears in school history textbooks, and is constantly referred to in the contemporary political rhetoric of Malaysian leaders. Convoys of motorcycles and cars honk their way along Ban Bor On's main road each Independence Day, their passengers waving the Malaysian flag energetically as they move through the settlement. Ta Roen and Ta Thit's ordination added a potent ethnic twist to the festive performances of patriotic fervor.

Ban Bor On is a situated place. Villagers think of it as a place where mobility and stasis overlap. On the one hand villagers like Kae Chi remembered moving through the village and into Bandar Tumpat and beyond. On the other hand, they compared these antiquated travels on foot with the speed of movement that has come to signal road culture in the village. There is an ambivalence here that symbolizes the way Kelantanese Thais speak of their Thainess. For every attempt at locating an encounter through a recollection of movement, there is a subsequent non-encounter. Thainess in the village is a combination of the intense lucidity of an imagined history and the uncertainty of contemporary self-definitions.

On the ground, Ban Bor On is outlined by black-lettered road signs and Thai-style bus stops, its borders explored and traversed by dogs, vehicles, parades, and ancient spirits. Buses 19 and 43 ply the main road in front of Wat Nai, their dirty exhaust pipes pumping black fumes into the air. The buses make a circuitous loop from Kota Bharu to Bandar Tumpat and then, after a short stop at Bandar Tumpat's old terminus, journey back to the state capital again. Most of these yellow-and-white, Indian-manufactured Lata buses have large advertisements plastered onto their sides, transporting the world of market capitalism deep into Kelantan's countryside. In 2001 one such ad I could not help but notice was pro-duced by the Tourism Authority of Thailand. In bold bright letters against a plain black background, it announced "Amazing Thailand: Paradise at Your Doorstep." Thailand was indeed at the doorstep for many Kelantanese. The international border at Pengkalan Kubor was only a twenty-minute drive away and many Kelantanese visited the country regularly. The slogan was part of the Tourism Authority of Thailand's attempts to increase Malaysian tourists in Thailand and part of a wider global campaign at constructing Thailand as an "amazing" tour-ist destination, one that was filled with surprises at every turn. Buses 19 and 43 brought Thailand into Ban Bor On. But this was not a new social phenomenon. The Thai polity had been affecting local perceptions of Kelantanese Thai person-hood even before the construction of the political border at the Tak Bai river. In chapter 2, we continue our journey through the past and present by making our way to the end of the trunk road. The Buddhist country has been instru-mental in molding the direction in which Kelantanese Thais move and the way in which they interpret their journeys. But it has also prevented movement. Its well-policed borders halted and displaced mobility, not only in terms of physical travel but also of ideological shifts. Practices of mobility in Ban Bor On rest upon the historical and political entanglements people had and continue to have with Thailand and Malaysia. Thainess is the result of an emotive combination of cultural rootedness and geographical locatedness that occur when people encounter these entanglements on the peripheries of the state.

CHAPTER 2

Gaps

KHUN DI WAS THIRTY-FOUR YEARS OLD WHEN I MET HIM IN 2001. He had been a monk at Wat Nai for some nine years and was now the elderly abbot's personal secretary and next in line for abbotship. That evening I found Khun Di sitting comfortably on a swivel chair in front of his favorite desktop computer in Wat Nai's green-carpeted computer room. Phi Nuat sat cross-legged on the floor in front of him. During the day, Phi Nuat worked at his air-conditioner repair shop on the outskirts of Kota Bharu. At the time he was also working on setting up his hotel-cum-seafood restaurant adjacent to his parents' yellow-walled house by Ban Bor On's trunk road. Phi Nuat's father was a famed love magician, well known throughout Kelantan's Thai villages for his skills in magically manipulating the affections of the heartbroken, the depressed, and the angry. A steady stream of clients, largely Malay Muslims and Chinese, visited the old man hoping to secure magical potions or to ignite romantic flames where there were none. After work Phi Nuat played soccer with other members of the Pauh Football Club (known locally as Pauh FC), Ban Bor On's very own soccer team, of which he was captain. The members of Pauh FC were all Thai and drawn from different segments of the village's male population. Anyone could join the team — all that was required was an interest in playing and the discipline to attend the informal practice sessions.

Ban Bor On was not the only Thai village to have a soccer team. Many of the larger villages had organized teams that met annually for various friendly leagues and competitions. Pauh FC, however, was well reputed for having secured the most wins to date, and the team's ribbon-decked trophies took pride of place in the glass showcase of Wat Nai's communal hall and on the long, paper-strewn table set up along the dusty edge of the temple's basement computer room.

Khun Di and Phi Nuat sat discussing an upcoming soccer tournament at the Thai village of Ban Klang. A short drive away from Ban Bor On, Ban Klang is Kelantan's largest Thai settlement. The match was to be between eight Kelantanese Thai teams and a visiting team from a university in Songkhla, Thailand. After agreeing on a list of the seven players to represent Pauh FC, Phi Nuat announced with a hint of satisfaction in his voice that he had finally decided on a logo for his team. This issue had been on Phi Nuat's mind for quite some time. I had heard him complain many times that his team, despite its skills on the field, lacked a logo—a necessary symbolic representation of sporting professionalism and a powerful rallying marker with which team members and their supporters could identify.

Phi Nuat sketched out his proposed design on a piece of paper. It was composed of two concentric rings with the larger outer circle representing a soccer ball. The inner circle was divided into halves. One half was decorated with the red Kelantan state flag and the other half, the red, blue, and white tricolor of Thailand. Phi Nuat looked at us and smiled. He seemed proud of his artistic endeavor. Khun Di and I exchanged uneasy glances. It was obvious from his expression that the monk felt uncomfortable with the proposed idea. In his typical soft-spoken manner, Khun Di noted that even though the idea in itself was a good one and very creative, the use of Thailand's national flag was something that bothered him. "The Kelantan flag is all right, but people could wrongly associate us with Thailand [*prathet thai*] if they see the Thai flag on the logo," he pointed out. I nodded in agreement. "We need something else to represent the Thais of Kelantan [*khon thai lantan*]," Khun Di added excitedly. We tossed around a number of possibilities, roughly outlining alternative designs on pieces of scrap paper. Khun Di and Phi Nuat agreed that whatever image was to be used as a team logo, it had to be a symbol that did not have real or construed affiliations with the Thai nation-state but was a strong and distinct signifier of a local Malaysian Thai identity. Khun Di suggested using the spired design of a *nura*'s crown.[1] But the classical *nura* dance drama, although performed primarily by Thais in Kelantan and southern Narathiwat, seemed "too cultural" to be on a soccer jersey. "It would have worked nicely if it was for a cultural troupe or something. But it just doesn't seem right for a soccer team," laughed the soccer captain. Other ideas included a mythical gryphon (*nok khrud*) ("too closely associated with Thailand's national symbol"), a Buddhist wheel of law ("too Buddhist"), and Kelantan's state animal, the barking deer ("already adopted by the Persatuan Bolasepak Cina Kelantan [Kelantan Chinese Soccer Association]").

Just then, Phi Thong, another member of Pauh FC and a good friend of Phi

Nuat's, bounced into the room in his signature green track pants and yellow T-shirt issued by the Kelantan Chinese Soccer Association. "Hey! Thong, so what should we use to represent Kelantanese Thais? Any ideas?" asked Khun Di, his voice brimming with enthusiasm. To the unexpected question, Phi Thong responded in his typically witty manner, "Why, a pig, of course!"

"A pig, not a bad idea," I mused silently to myself. Although articulated in jest, Phi Thong's porcine suggestion can be read in powerful ethnic and cultural terms. Pigs and the consumption of pork are visual signifiers of a Thai Buddhist presence in a cultural landscape where strong Islamic mores continue to place a taboo on pigs. Kelantanese Thais are well aware of the Islamic avoidance of pigs (and to a large degree dogs as well), although no Thais I spoke with could locate the reasons behind this avoidance in orthodox Islamic terms. In order to maintain social harmony, some Thai villagers living in the midst of larger Malay Muslim communities avoid raising pigs or dogs so as not to offend their non-Buddhist friends. Even the smell of pork being cooked could be deemed offensive if it wafted into unsuspecting Malay nostrils, and villagers carefully avoided preparing and consuming the much sought-after meat when in the presence of Muslims.

Pigs used to be raised by many households in Ban Bor On, and though housed in pens they were often allowed to wander through the village scavenging for food. Of late pig-raising has been on the decline in most Thai villages, in part due to the easy availability of farm-raised pork smuggled from Thailand's border markets. Many Thai villagers, however, continue to swear by the taste of locally farmed pigs. Thailand's commercially raised pigs are much larger than the local pot-bellied variety and fattier due to growth hormones and a controlled vitamin-enriched diet. Pork is heavily consumed during Thai social and ritual events. Buddhist prohibitions on killing, however, have meant that many Thais do not slaughter their own pigs, preferring instead to buy butchered meat. For their everyday needs, villagers buy pork from an enterprising middleman who gets the meat from the only market in Kelantan that has licensed the sale of pork. The meat is wrapped in sheets of newspaper so as not to attract the attention of Malay Muslim passersby. Mae Uan's grandson also travels across the international border to Sungai Golok daily to purchase vegetables, fruit, and other Thai produce which his mother then resells at an inflated price at their roadside stall. Pork is often on the menu in Ban Bor On and the young man regularly takes orders for the meat. Although rare, the occasional swayback hog can still be seen waddling through the public spaces of the village in the early hours of the morning, symbolically tracing out the circumference of a mapped non-Muslim residential zone (Kershaw 1969; Golomb 1978; Yusoff 1982).

More prevalent than pigs in Thai villages were the mangy dogs that traversed the roads scavenging for scraps and territory. The mutts often became the victims of traffic accidents or late-night shootings by representatives from the Animal Control Unit. The unit aimed to control the stray dog population, which was deemed an eyesore and source of disease by the state. Thai villagers condemned the state government's culling of its dog population, both on Buddhist grounds and because many of the dogs shot were, in fact, privately owned and registered pets. To many a Thai in Ban Bor On, the culling of dogs, especially pet dogs, was viewed in ethnic terms. "Malays kill Thai dogs," they quietly complained, although the ethnicity of the shooters was never really known. For some Thais, the state's late-night shootings were seen as an unfair and cruel imposition of cultural values on the Thai community and were a painful reminder of Thai marginality at the hands of a Muslim majority, who, despite being on affable terms with the Thai minority, occasionally did express their unease at certain aspects of Thai social and cultural life. Malaysia is, after all, a Muslim-majority country—my friends used to remind me—and to many Malaysian Muslims, dogs were polluting animals and therefore were treated with disdain.

Phi Thong's pig suggestion was hilarious and we had an enjoyable time attempting to design soccer logos using pigs, mangy mutts, and soccer balls. One logo we came up with had two pot-bellied pigs kissing a soccer ball. "They have to kiss it," insisted Phi Thong as we roared in laughter. On the ball between the pigs' snouts sat a typical Ban Bor On canine—skinny and diseased. But the pig idea remained exactly that—an idea. It was, in reality, impractical, dangerous even, since as Phi Thong and Phi Nuat admitted, the design would seriously offend the religious sensitivity of Muslim players with whom Pauh FC occasionally played friendly matches. Although they occasionally joke about the Muslim "other," Kelantanese Thais are largely on good terms with their non-Thai neighbors and celebrate the inter-ethnic harmony at both the state and national levels.

By the end of our meeting, nothing had materialized by way of a soccer emblem. The other ideas conjured up included a mango tree (after the Malay name of the village), a Thai long drum (*klong jao*), and elephants. Phi Nuat eventually settled for a depiction of an elephant sitting on a soccer ball, which I was tasked to redraw neatly before deciding whether to print it on the jerseys. The elephant, Phi Nuat said, has a dual significance. It is an animal held in high regard by Thai Buddhists and also closely associated with the visual identity of the village. Before he was born, the Buddha's mother had dreamt of a white elephant entering her womb. The Thai elephant's close association with Buddhism and Brahmanism has been celebrated in art, literature, and mythology. One of Ban Bor On's most prominent floats during the annual Loy Krathong parade in November is built in the form of a large white elephant holding a lotus bud in its trunk. Each year before the parade commences, the elephant float is taken from its wooden shed at the back of the temple and placed by the temple's ordination hall. Here the heavy wood and papier maché creation is placated with food offerings — sugar cane, coconut, betel, sweets, and various other foods — by one of the village's magical practitioners, who also sits on the elephant's back as the float is paraded through the streets of Bandar Tumpat. In 1959, when the late Na Bong built Wat Nai's gateway, he too used an elephant as a motif for the temple space. Na Bong crafted a pair of four-headed elephants — representing the vehicle of the Hindu god Indra — and perched them high on both sides of the gateway. Since then, Wat Nai's main gate has been called the Elephant Gate by both Thais and Malays.

It was only through thinking about the possibilities for a team logo that we realized how difficult it was to pinpoint a common visual marker of what it meant to be Kelantanese Thai without offending neighboring non-Thai/Buddhist sensibilities and without bringing Thainess into the political arena of national symbols emanating from across the border. How could one be Thai without associating oneself with the Thai nation-state? Was this even possible or was it just a figment of the diaspora's imagination? Tired and frustrated at the seeming impossibility of choosing a modern yet meaningful indicator of a historically rooted local identity, we decided to stick to the elephant on a soccer ball.

I walked back to my small room by the Elephant Gate, musing over what had just transpired. Why had it been so hard to generate a common and emotionally charged portrait of Thainess when it was so visibly present in the community? Ordination parades, rest pavilions, stories of ancestral settlement and magical spirit beings, the taste of fermented fish sauce, temple festivities, and dogs and pigs colored my life in the village. Yet it seemed impossible to come up with a particular personification of this experience. Henk Nordholt's observations on the formation of national space in Indonesia (1997) are an interesting case in point. In Indonesia national space is created through the manipulation of "outward appearances" (clothes, photographs, landmarks, street names, postage stamps, etc.) by its citizenry. But symbols of national identity are spatially and temporally situated. They make sense only when displayed in the context of the national imagination and they return to their inherent and intangible ambiguity when pondered over outside the boundaries of the nation. Thus the difficulty in selecting a marker of Thainess that did not carry the burden of Thailand's national rhetoric and that was also sensitive to the multicultural world of a largely Muslim-run Malaysia.

To many Ban Bor On residents, the very word Thainess (*khwam pen thai*) did not make sense. Villagers rarely used the phrase when speaking of their ethnic and cultural identity. Instead they would often just shrug their shoulders and smile. "We are Thai, after all [*rao khon thai bueh*]," they would say matter-of-factly to one another as if expecting the listener to know exactly what they meant. And most people did know what this *after allness* meant, but they had a hard time articulating it in simple terms. In part, the difficulty of constructing Thainess as a theoretical and historically situated model of Thai cultural essence—a "we-self" in Thongchai Winichakul's term (1994)—in Kelantan is due to the multiplicity of meanings that the idea elicits. Trying to come to grips with the "after allness" of Thainess was an attempt to peel away the tight and powerful layers of Thailand's cultural influence that shape the ordinary lives of Kelantanese Thai villagers. The question that begs answering, as Khun Di, Phi Nuat, and Phi Thong came to realize that cool October evening, is whether it is possible to construct a simple symbol to represent an indigenous and creative agency that is unquestionably Thai yet divorced from Thailand's hegemonic influence. How was one to be Thai without having Thailand breathing down one's neck?

Social actors often use space as a site for articulations of cultural distinction. The problem of the soccer logo emerged from our attempts to anchor the perimeters of an ethnic and cultural space that were, in practice, ambiguous and slippery. It was not that Ban Bor On's soccer team lacked key identity symbols. Yet each symbol when carefully thought through called attention to the difficulty of materializing culture and its associations with tradition, history, and modernity in the margins of states. The obsession with seeking out a visual marker of Thainess for Khun Di and the soccer players points to a deep-seated concern Kelantanese Thais have with what they feel is their community's social invisibility. In order to decipher the concealed gaps that have been at the forefront of Kelantanese Thai concerns with self-definition—Thainess—it is necessary to return to history and explore the social and political production of ethnic invisibility in the north Malaysian borderlands.

A Space of Gaps

The development of the colonial border and its rail and road works affected the way marginality and its cultural correlate, Thainess, was constructed in Kelantan. Transport networks made some groups of sojourners more visible than others to the colonial administrators, who consequently bypassed and inadvertently marginalized those who did not participate in the colonial culture of immigration. For instance, the active transborder participation of Kelantanese Thai villagers in the Malay and Thai market economies of lower Narathiwat and north Kelantan is not mentioned in most official histories of Kelantan's development as a colonial state.

Thais traveled through the state and moved back and forth across the British-Siamese frontier, but no colonial records seem to have recorded their movements. Local Malay and Thai historical treatises focus on the political and social maneuverings of the Malay elites in the state's administration, leaving a question mark regarding the position of the Thai minority in Kelantan. Where were they, one wonders? The nineteenth-century Pongsawadan Mueang Kelantan, a Siamese-authored chronology of Kelantan's dynastic history, is similarly silent on the state's non-Malay minorities (Wyatt 1974). Likewise, the Hikayat Sri (Seri) Kelantan, a Malay treatise of the state's chronicle compiled in the early twentieth century, does not mention Thai Buddhists living in Kelantan. Notwithstanding these omissions, Thais had played important social, ritual, and political roles as village headmen, magical practitioners, court entertainers, monks, retainers, and members of the sultan's royal entourage by the nineteenth century. Because their social engagement with Malay politics has largely been overlooked in historical literature, Kelantanese Thais have often been marginalized in Kelantan's state production processes. Given that Thais were traditionally active players in Kelantan's socio-political scene, one thus needs to ask how these gaps in the record of encounters emerged in the first place.

Victorian ethnology was a prime mover in territorial discussions surrounding the production of bordered British space in the colonies. Britain's treaty negotiator, Ralph Paget, had used a racial and cultural card in his negotiations with Siamese officials regarding the transfer of Kelantan, Terengganu, Kedah, Perlis, Setul, and Patani to the Crown. Simply put, the British were to control the Muslim principalities and the Siamese had jurisdiction over so-called Buddhist territories. The ethnological argument on territoriality was similarly mapped out by Strobel, the general advisor to the Siamese government, with whom Paget had entered into informal discussions just prior to the consolidation of the 1909 treaty. Paget's use of ethnicity in defining the perimeters of British administration, however, came under criticism from Strobel. Strobel's reaction was articulated in relation to the inclusion of the west coast border state of Perlis in the cession and did not concern Kelantan. Strobel had written to Paget a year before the treaty was signed, expressing his concerns over the latter's interpretation of the ethnic frontier:

> If that is to be the game, I think we had better abandon the negotiations at once. I am having sufficient difficulty with the King of Kedah and am not prepared to go further than the three states I originally named. . . . *There are considerable settlements of Siamese in Setul, and it might not be possible to include that state.* . . . As for Patani it is out of the question, as the Siamese Government will never consent to its cession. [Strobel quoted in Mohamed 1974: 54, emphasis mine]

What then of the "Siamese" on both banks of the Tak Bai tributary with whom many Kelantanese Thais were trading on a daily basis in crowded village markets, and with whom they shared kin and cultural alliances? Interestingly enough, only W. A. Graham, the first Siamese-appointed British advisor to the government of Kelantan in 1902, noted the visible presence of the "Siamese" (referring to local Tumpat Tak Bai speakers as opposed to central Thai–speaking immigrants and officials of the Bangkok government) in Kelantan in his 1908 travelogue. He observed:

> The Siamese in the State number 15,000. They live in chiefly the coast districts, in villages apart from the Malays, where they follow their own religion and customs unmolested. They are well behaved and prosperous. The Siamese of Kelantan are chiefly the descendants of settlers from the northern parts of the Peninsula, but there are also several villages near the coast the forebears of the inhabitants of which came from Siam proper, accompanying the Siamese general Phaya Pitsanulok, on a military expedition some sixty years ago, and afterwards being left behind to keep the peace between Kelantan and the neighboring state of Sai. [Graham 1908: 20]

Furthermore, Graham counted forty Buddhist temples in the state (33).[2] It was thus unlikely that their presence went unnoticed in the territorial politics of

Bangkok, Kota Bharu, and London. Strobel had earlier cautioned that Setul's large Siamese population could complicate the picture of British rule in the northwestern corridor of the peninsula. The French ethnologist Jeanne Cuisinier, who studied Malay and Thai performing arts in Kelantan in the early 1930s, similarly noted the Thai Buddhist presence in the state. In a lecture delivered to the India Society in 1934, she wrote: "But a single pagoda with a dozen monks and a dozen devotees would be enough to keep alive old Siamese customs [in Kelantan]; and there are many pagodas" (Cuisinier 1934: 43).

Local Thai Buddhist histories from the Tak Bai region tell of the community's presence as a politically important minority in the frontier zone some thirty years before Cuisinier's travels in Kelantan. Wat Choltarasinghe (Wat Chehe), which hugs the banks of the Tak Bai on the Thai side of the border, had been used as a bargaining tool by the Siamese government in the ethnological and cultural strategizing between the Siamese and British administrators (Wanipha 1992: 89n).[3] The British had desired to secure a Malay and Muslim political-cultural environment separated from the Siamese Buddhist social world to the north. Although Tuan Long Senik and his state councilors in Kelantan were instrumental in encouraging British administration in their home state as an alternative to direct Siamese rule, the motivations for such a move were many. Primary among them was the desire for Kelantan to fly its own flag, and to ensure the genealogical reckoning of Malay rulership (Talib 1995: 58). It is probable that such animosity, coupled with the much feared and detested behavior of the Siamese commissioner and his soldiers, made Kelantan's Malay elites adamant about creating a bounded Malay polity for themselves that was removed from Siamese ethnic and cultural trappings. Similarly, Siamese officials worked within a national discourse of the ethnic polity where everyone within Siam's borders was *ideally* Siamese.

Siamese negotiators, in line with an argument proposed by King Chulalongkorn, readily pointed to the location of Wat Chehe on the banks of the Tak Bai as the furthest extremity of a Thai Buddhist cultural outpost. Unlike temples in the vicinity, Wat Chehe's massive ordination hall, with its multi-layered roof and heavy square pillars, was constructed according to nineteenth-century central Thai aesthetics and resembled similar buildings in Bangkok's royal temples built during the reign of Rama III. The interior walls were covered in murals detailing not only scenes from the life of the Buddha but also fascinating aspects of everyday life in Tak Bai.[4] Siamese bureaucrats argued that should Wat Chehe (and hence the Tak Bai region of lower Narathiwat), with its characteristic Thai form,

2.1 Wat Chehe, Narathiwat

be situated within Britain's Unfederated Malay States, which were predominantly a Malay and Muslim cultural environment, the temple would be subject to the laws and possible discriminatory practices of a non-Buddhist Muslim state.

Wat Chehe is an important temple for both Kelantanese and Tak Bai Thais. It was for a long time the center of the ecclesiastical examinations (*nak tham*) for monks from the lower Narathiwat-Kelantan region, as well as an important pilgrimage site. By constructing a political discourse of cultural conservation that purposely failed to consider the other twenty temples on the British bank of the river, Bangkok's Siamese authorities effectively secured the northeastern corner of what was once Siamese-ruled Kelantan as part of a newly imagined Siamese and, more important, Buddhist state based on central Thai ritual and aesthetic conventions.[5]

The demarcation of the international border by British and Siamese forces along ethnic and cultural divides shaped discourses of geopolitical difference at the local level. These discourses were imagined by Kelantanese Thais using a rhetoric of ethnic difference. That colonial Kelantan was a Malay-ruled principality (*mueang khaek*) was powerfully entrenched in the collective memory of Ban Bor On's older villagers. Kelantan was a sovereign space politically removed but territorially linked to Siam via the Tak Bai and Golok rivers. Crossing both rivers brought one into *mueang thai*, a Buddhist kingdom under the guardian-ship of a Theravadin monarch. "If you look carefully when the river is calm," Kae Chi pointed out, "you can actually see the area where it divides in half between *mueang thai* and *mueang khaek*." Although inhabiting politically disparate territories, the Malay and Thai residents of both polities were for the most part on friendly terms with one another, and before the national symbols of bordered sovereignty restricted easy movement across the river, people traveled across it freely. When speaking of the pre–World War Two period in Kelantan's history, some Ban Bor On residents recall fondly how Malays and Thais were caring intimates, while other villagers speak of a more sinister period of Malay-Thai animosity that mars the past. There seems to be no agreement as to whether the past or the present was better in terms of ethnic cohabitation. This nostalgic reflection of the past as a period of both intimacy and violence is juxtaposed against similar views of the present. Contemporary Kelantan is often spoken of in a language of increasing Islamic fundamentalism and national policies of Malay privilege that has led to occasional tensions between Malays and Thais. On the ground however, relations remain cordial.

The feeling of marginalization many Kelantanese Thais have today reflects their historical position within what was, until 1957, a colonial state. Shamsul Amri Baharuddin (1999) stated that it was Victorian Orientalist knowledge produced by nineteenth-century British administrators that categorized different ethnic groups according to a reified pattern of stereotypes and ethnological typologies. Colonial epistemologies imposed objectified biological, social, cultural, and linguistic differences on Malaya's subject population so as to better understand, probe, and manage the diversity of the colony. These newly created subjects and bordered identities were separate and distinct, thereby preventing the ambiguity of overlapping categories.

Such a practice was not unique to Malaya.[6] Bernard Cohn (1996) observed similar exercises in British India. The plurality of colonial society and the ethnic boundaries it produced and celebrated were subsequently ossified through public education and other forms of legislative practices that Cohn termed "officialising procedures." Through the dissemination of these procedures into the everyday lived realities of the subject population via census reports, birth and death certificates, identity cards, taxation records, and land-holding enactments, the colonial bureaucracy managed to extend its hegemonic grip over all aspects of public life in the colony. Ethnic pigeonholing was subsequently adopted by the independent Malaysian government and its ruling Malay bureaucrats in the form of "authority-defined" identities (Shamsul 1996a). The formal top-down imposition of authority-defined identities for all Malaysians existed alongside an "everyday-defined" social reality, that is, the contextually located identities social actors defined and experienced for themselves. In Ban Bor On, both authority-defined and self-ascribed identities overlap and intertwine. Everyone I spoke with unquestionably acknowledged themselves as Thai (*khon thai*) both officially and informally. As with Shamsul's analysis of the social categories "Malay" and "Chinese," Malaysia's national definition of what constitutes "Thai" is a perplexing and often contested issue. The lack of a fixed colonial typology or phenotype for Thai Buddhists in the state has exacerbated the problem of contemporary Malaysian ethnic classification. The latter relies on the British-derived constitutional definitions of Malaya's three main ethnic groups: "Malay," "Chinese," and "Indian." British annual reports and censuses of population counted "Siamese" as an ethnic group within Kelantan. But the term itself carries both political and cultural associations and makes no reference to spatial origins. Were the Siamese in the colonial records Siam's citizens or were they locally born and bred British subjects?

In contemporary Malaysian political rhetoric, who is Thai remains unclear. The community constantly bickers over the labeling of its ethnic community. Some call for the official standardizing of Malaysian Thai ethnicity as "Siamese" — an older British designation to distinguish them from Thai citizens. Others argue for use of the term "Thai" to refer to Malaysian Thais, saying that there is clearly no confusion when it comes to issues of national identity. This interesting fact brings to task Ryoko Nishii's contention that, within the bordered perimeters of the nation-state, "old ambiguities are less tolerated and less useful, as there is little play in the borders of modern states" (2000: 197). In her ethnography, Nishii observed how Thai-speaking Muslims (Sam Sam) in Kedah were redefining their ethnic categorization to fit into the reified molds provided by the Malaysian state. By abandoning the Thai language in place of Malay, Kedah's Sam Sam constructed themselves as ethnic Malay, thereby eradicating their historical marginality and cultural peripheralization in a polity that constitutionally defined Malays as Muslims who spoke the Malay language. In Ban Bor On, ethnic compartmentalization matters, as it is a national indicator of social personhood and it shapes one's access to the various privileges administered by the Malaysian government. The social ambiguity of peripheral ethnicities in national borderlands is tolerated by the nation-state and, in fact, reproduced by it through the lack of a specific official ethnic category.

In today's Malaysia the ethnic categories of "Thai" and "Siamese" are often interchangeable. The birth certificates of children born to Thai parents list them as either Thai or Siamese, but this ethnic category is subsumed under the larger category of "*dan lain-lain*" (and all others) in national censuses and other official records. For Kelantan's Thai, local-level bureaucrats such as nurses, teachers, hospital workers, and government clerks further complicate the national ethnic profiling process, as each person seems to have his or her own definition of who a Thai or a Siamese is. The social perimeters delimiting authority-defined identities are, as Shamsul observed , blurred realities. The issue of Thai ethnicity in Kelantan is a complex one without a clear solution in sight, but has at its base the social invisibility of the community in the eyes of the state's colonial administrators.

This fact was pointed out to me by my friends one afternoon in Wat Nai. It had been raining the whole day, a prelude to the northeast monsoons that smash the Kelantan coast every year from November through February. Khun Tam, Khun Sung, Khun Nyai, Khun Di, and I sat in the wood- and zinc-roofed *sala* in front of the temple's kitchen, watching the rain come down and form small creeks in the sand. The rain confined us, preventing us from leaving the dry shelter. I took the opportunity to ask the monks how Thai ethnicity was defined in Malaysia, since I had heard conflicting views on this from various villagers. According to the brothers Khun Sung and Khun Tam, a person's ethnicity (they used the authoritative Malay term *bangsa* here instead of the less formal Thai *chat*) was determined by one's name. Simply put, a Thai was someone whose ethnic identity was officially acknowledged through the use of typical "Thai-type" last names or the Malay appendages "son of" (*anak lelaki*) or "daughter of" (*anak perempuan*) in individual given names.

Most Thais in Kelantan have a composite of names, for instance, Suchart Nartsuwan a/l (*anak lelaki*) Eh Dam. In this case, Suchart is the given name and Nartsuwan the last name (*nam sakun*). Sanskritic-sounding first and last names like Suchart's have been popular in Kelantan since the 1960s, with increasing penetration of Thai cultural standardization via the mass media, cultural ambassadors from Thailand in the guise of missionary monks, teachers, soldiers, tourist arrivals, and so forth. In this example, Eh Dam is the given name of Suchart's father and it recalls more traditional Kelantanese Thai names that were derived from colors, days of the week, or visible character traits. *Dam* means "black" in Thai, in possible reference to the infant's tanned complexion. Villagers born before the Thai-ization process of the 1950s and 1960s tend to have no last names.

Hence my mother is merely See Luan a/p (*anak perempuan*) Chao Chan. She does not think she has a last name and no one in her family could recall having one.

Almost every Ban Bor On villager I met had a standard Thai-type last name that is supposedly derived from one's patriline. My younger interlocutors spoke of how "all Thais had *nam sakun*." They spoke of it as a defining feature of their cultural identity, distinguishing them from all other ethnic groups in the country. In their understandings of naming procedures, the *nam sakun* was primordial rather than historically produced. In practice, however, many individuals had only recently created their last names, especially when patrilineal surnames had been lost, forgotten, or never existed in the first place. In recent years all that was required to be officially categorized as Thai in Malaysian state records was for one to have a *nam sakun* that was registered as a legitimate patriname when the child was born and that appeared on the child's birth certificate. In some instances, the *nam sakun* has replaced the "son of" and "daughter of" appendages, especially among the youngest generation of Kelantanese Thais. Most Kelantanese Thais, however, still maintain the "son of" and "daughter of" indicators of paternity on all official government correspondences (Abdul Rahman 2001: 80). It is not uncommon to find younger Thais that have a Thai *nam sakun* last name followed by the more traditional Malay "son of" and "daughter of," as the example of Suchart demonstrates.

Interestingly, despite its preeminence in the everyday culture of the village, the use of the patrilineal *nam sakun* was a recent invention in Ban Bor On. *Nam sakun* began appearing in Kelantan in the 1950s with the increasing standardization of Kelantanese Thai culture along the lines of Thailand's national cultural models. "We did not have *nam sakun* in the past. People only began having them after I had children. It was pretty recent," laughed Kae Chi when I asked her about the history of this important symbol of Thainess in Kelantan. A number of older residents admitted that some people did have preexisting *nam sakun*, mostly if they had emigrated from Thailand, where surnames have been a necessary template of modernity, citizenship, and belonging since the reign of King Chulalongkorn. Students enrolled in schools in Thailand were obliged to have a *nam sakun* as a mark of a full Siamese citizen. Thailand's increasing bureaucratization of Kelantanese Thai culture through the development of temple schools and the influx of missionary monk-teachers from Bangkok meant that the everyday world of Kelantan's Thai villagers was, by the 1960s, suddenly burdened with a barrage of administrative forms required during student registration and ordination procedures. These forms, called *bai samak*, were prepared in Kelantan by the state's local Thai intelligentsia but modeled on similar ones used in Thailand. All forms included a space for one's *nam sakun*. Villagers without patrilineal surnames thus had to create one through a process of borrowing or invention. A common method used in constructing these "Thai-sounding" *nam sakun* was to merge two or more first names to form a single longer name. Ta Yong hilariously described it one evening while massaging Mae Nyai's swollen arm: "I am a Suksawat. My grandfather's name was Suk and, well, maybe my great-grandfather was Wat. Therefore I am a Suksawat." I complained that I did not know my maternal grandfather's *nam sakun*, unlike everyone else in the village. In response Ta Yong joked, "Your grandfather is Chan. His father was Daeng. Maybe you are a Chandaeng?"

The afternoon rain did not let up. I continued my conversation with the four monks. Since there were no clear parameters for Thai ethnic classification in Kelantan, each person hazarded his own interpretation. Khun Sung recalled his good friend from the southern district of Pasir Puteh, a large man by the name of Chao Duek. In all social contexts Chao Duek defined himself as Thai, but he was officially categorized as Chinese in Malaysian state records. Although both his parents considered themselves ethnically Thai, he had been given a Chinese name, including a Chinese-type surname (*sae*), at birth. Why this was so Khun Sung did not know, although the interchanging of Thai and Chinese names was a common practice among Thais in the northern Terengganu village of Ban Khok Prong—where Chao Duek came from—with its mixed Thai and Chinese populations. Sensing my increasing perplexity, Khun Sung recollected his own case to complicate further what was already a confusing situation. At birth, he had been given the name Ah Teng a/l (*anak lelaki*) Eh Toh by his parents. Although Ah Teng was a common Chinese name in Malaysia, he was officially classified as a Thai (Malay: *bangsa thai*) because of the incorporation of the "son of" category on all formal documents bearing his given name. In an extreme and candid instance of authority-defined ethnicity gone wrong, Khun Sung told me that his sister's young daughter was officially a Punjabi although neither her father nor mother was of the northern Indian ethnic group. "How then did she end up being a Punjabi?" I asked curiously. Answering in a manner that was both serious in its implications and lighthearted in its sheer ridiculousness, Khun Sung replied that the little girl's name, Valerie Mei-Ling, must have sounded Punjabi to the Malay clerks at the registrar of births office.

Khun Nyai, who had been quietly listening to Khun Sung's lively explication of the complexities of ethnic category formation in Malaysia, was quick to take him up on the issue. He argued that a child's ethnicity depends not only on the officers in charge of the registration process but also on the parents who give the child the name. Sometimes parents fill in birth registration forms incorrectly, a fault that if not fixed immediately becomes a permanent part of one's ethnicity. And ethnicity, once ascribed by the state, is impossible to alter.

Mobile Personhood

Unlike the stubborn staticity implicit in official categories of ethnicity and naming, the everyday self-ascribed identities of Ban Bor On villagers are more malleable. They are based upon narratives of difference and similarity. At some moments, this social definition of Thainess was articulated as the opposite of being Malay. "Thais are everything Malays are not," was a sentiment of social binary exclusionism I heard expressed in Ban Bor On constantly. Malay villages were dirty, Thai ones were clean; Malay girls were easier to date, Thai girls were more difficult; Malays detested pork, Thais could not do without it; Malay villages were low-lying and hence prone to annual floods, whereas Thai villages were built on elevated land; and Malays wore their sarongs to their ankles but Thais preferred shorter sarongs. So reads the list of stereotyped cultural differences shaped by ethnic oppositions.

In other contexts, however, cultural differences were downplayed, and Thais and Malays were seen as culturally—although not religiously—similar. They enjoyed many similar foods (with the exception of pork), had many of the same agrarian lifestyles, shared common linguistic terms, and for the most part enjoyed each other's company. Muslim Malays were friends with Buddhist monks and Thais sought out Malay magical healers, many of whom used Thai-derived spells in their curative practices. Thai magical practitioners also maintained an esoteric corpus of incantations, many of which included Malay and Arabic vocabulary. This strong co-ethnic social identification has been noted by a number of scholars in their analyses of Kelantanese Thai society (Kershaw 1969; Golomb 1978; Mohamed 1980, 1990a, 1990b, 1993a; Horstmann 2002a, 2002b). The superficial similarities between both groups could also account for the invisibility of the Thai community in colonial writings on Kelantan, as early travelers and explorers paid more attention to Kelantan's Malay Muslim majority. "I preferred living with Malay housemates," Ta Rien informed me, as he remembered his college days in the southern state of Johor. "They are very similar [culturally] to us and, unlike the Chinese, they do not look down on us Thais," he added. His only grievance was that he had had to give up eating pork when at home so as not to offend his Muslim friends.

During a study-skills and motivational seminar for Thai students held at Wat Kao, Na Chao Lai, a prominent member of the Kelantanese Thai Association (Persatuan Thai Kelantan) who had political ambitions of being Malaysia's next ethnic Thai senator (he has since given them up) gave a speech in which he declared that Thais and Malays were not different.[7] The assembled audience of Malay school teachers, teenage Thai students and their parents, and political representatives from the youth wing of the Barisan Nasional Party listened expressionlessly as he ranted on about how, "in Kelantan, the Thais and the Malays are only differentiated based on [who wears] the *songkok* and *kopiah*."[8]

On a less formal but equally poignant level, Kae Chi once told me a story of ethnic complementarity. Her tale pointed to indigenous understandings of ethnic and cultural identification in Kelantan's Thai villages based upon distinct occupational niches. Her eyes lit up and she smiled as she recounted the story of ancestral harmony.

> Thais and Malays have this story. They both believe that Malays (*khaek*), Thais (*thai*), and Chinese (*jin*) were once siblings (*phi kab nong*).[9] The Thai was the eldest child, the Malay was the second, and the Chinese the youngest. Since he was the youngest and thus the most pampered, the Chinese was given his father's business acumen. Therefore you always find Chinese as successful traders. They own a large number of shops in the town [*lad*]. The Malay was given boats to fish with. The Thai was given paddy lands. This was how it was originally. Everyone lived harmoniously. The claim that one ethnic group [*chat*] is better than the other is a recent phenomenon.

The federal government's *bumiputera* (lit., sons of the soil) scheme, which had since the early fifties celebrated Malay indigenism by providing Malaysian Malays with increased economic opportunities and governmental assistance, widened the cultural rift between Thais and Malays.[10] Since they did not consider themselves the descendants of immigrants, having lived in Kelantan since the pre-1909 period, being officially denied the full benefits of the *bumiputera* scheme irked them. This was coupled with the continuation of the Malay Reservation Enactment, which made it hard for Thais to acquire land from Malay sellers.[11] To many Ban Bor On residents, Kelantan's political environment was both frustrating in its unequal distribution of ethnic empowerment and culturally threatening in its increasing Islamicization and the latter's associations with global radicalism. The discourse of an increasing Islamic fervor in Malaysia began in the late seventies with the success of the Islamic Revolution in Iran. It was visualized in the 11 September 2001 attacks on New York's World Trade Center, which Ban Bor On residents watched intensely over Thai television channels, and continued through the 2000s with a narrative of Islamophobia and terrorism.

Notwithstanding their feelings of discontent over the *bumiputera* scheme in general, a number of Thais I spoke with noted that national policies of Malay exclusivism did have their advantages. Even though they are not officially categorized as *bumiputera*, Kelantanese Thais pride themselves on certain benefits that they are privy to within the *bumiputera* package. There is, in other words, some acknowledgment of the situatedness of the community, and the Kelantanese Thais are guaranteed a place in the national ethnic imagination of indigenism. This includes loans for purchasing houses and the ability to participate in *bumiputera*-only bank investment schemes. When the investment projects (Amanah Saham Bumiputera) were opened to Thai participation in the early eighties, many Ban Bor On villagers took immediate advantage of it. The high rates of return that the *bumiputera* bank schemes yielded allowed many Thais to amass even greater economic wealth. This was translated into increasing displays of conspicuous consumption and greater disposable income, reflected in the large brick mansions that have become synonymous with Thai villages.

Thais who applied at local banks for participation in the *bumiputera* investment schemes had to present to the bank officials documentary evidence of their ethnicity as Thai (or Siamese). In this instance, the category of "Siamese" was used to distinguish Malaysian Thais (called *oghe sie* by Kelantan Malays) from Thailand's Thais (*oghe thai*). When speaking in Thai among themselves, however, Kelantanese Thais never referred to themselves as Siamese but rather as "Thai" (*khon thai*). The uncertain nature of ethnic labeling for Kelantan's Thai population in a nation-state where social pigeonholing was the norm means that one's official identity has to be authoritatively proven through evidence from a variety of bureaucratic sources (Abdul Rahman 2001: 80). To the bank staff issuing loans, one's ethnicity was garnered from three sources: one's birth certificate, one's parents' identity cards, and a written statement formally acknowledging one's Thai ethnicity from the village headman. Khru Chang of Ban Klang, who had been in charge of issuing this unofficial document of Thainess to would-be investors, told me that its Malay phrasing followed a standard format. The document mirrored Malaysian constitutional definitions of Malayness through equating ethnicity and religion with the practice of custom. The statement reads: "This letter ascertains that the following person(s) are Siamese, adherents of the Buddhist religion and followers of Siamese customs [*adat istiadat Siam*]."

This ambiguous production of a distinct and bounded Thai/Siamese ethnic category by both Kelantanese Thai and Malaysian state agents and its corresponding affiliations with the maintenance of village identity and national policy achievement must be seen in relation to the development of the international border and the subsequent production of citizenship. The 1909 treaty territorially differentiated Narathiwat Thais from their Kelantanese cousins along the constructed frontier. Being positioned so close to the international boundary and constantly engaging with and across it—a process facilitated by the development of transborder market economies, public transport, Internet and new media communication, and transportation lines—allowed Ban Bor On residents to experience and produce narratives of Thainess that effectively circumscribed their community even more through a process of spatial and cultural demarcation.

Hinterlands

Border towns are confusing places. Despite being the furthest reaches of state hegemony—spaces of confinement and national demarcation—these liminal zones are often sites of intense cosmopolitan social interaction. International borders are materialized in the bodies of uniformed customs administrators, money changers, and form-fillers. They forge themselves as physical sites of spatial and political transition in the faded signs of welcome and goodbye, posters of what to fear—wanted terrorists, AIDS, the flu—and what to embrace— sandy white beaches, handwoven mats, bird cages, large gilded Buddhas, smiling faces, beautiful wood palaces, and intricate traditional Malay kites. All the while drab panopticon-like immigration buildings manned by stern-faced officers welcome, threaten, and disgust travelers.

No discussion of the Kelantanese Thai ethnoscape can neglect the role of such frontier towns in molding the way villagers think about themselves, the state they live in, and the history they constantly produce. Politically, Kelantan ends at the Pengkalan Kubor waterfront. This is a hot and dusty place. Small food stalls line the sides of the road near the massive immigration complex, offering for sale a variety of rice and curry dishes, brightly colored sugar-laced drinks, fried snacks, and plastic toys. Flies, cats, sheep, and goats make their way around these stalls and the trash by the side of the road, as do Malay cab drivers, weary shoppers, and the occasional sweat-drenched backpacker. The coastal air is always stale and heavy and seems to blanket the market town with an overpowering stench that is both salty and fishy—the smell emanating from the polluted Tak Bai river and the fisheries' processing plant adjacent to the immigration complex. Along the sides of the road are smaller Malay- and Chinese-owned sundry shops and ticket booths advertising bus tickets to various destinations throughout Kelantan and Malaysia in bright florescent letters. A taxi stand and unsheltered bus depot allow travelers to move easily from Pengkalan Kubor to Tumpat, Kota Bharu, and beyond.

Pengkalan Kubor is a place of encounters. Here people often meet their friends during the comings and goings of shopping adventures in Thailand and at the border's Duty Free Zone (Zon Bebas Cukai). The zone is a 6.4-acre fenced enclosure housing a market and small shops stocked high with a menagerie of made-in-Thailand products, including large plastic-wrapped Winnie the Pooh plush toys, football jerseys, imitation denim, colorful plastic mats, and stainless steel pots of every possible size, that spill out of the shop and onto the pedestrian walkway. Opened in 1990, the popular shopping haunt is administered by the Royal Malaysian Customs. Not everyone comes to Pengkalan Kubor to shop for food and home appliances. Some come for more nefarious reasons. They hire motorboats to illegally cross the river after the immigration checkpoints have closed for the day at 6 pm. Once in Thailand, they partake in Tak Bai's notorious nocturnal scene of run-down bars, prostitution, and for some, drugs. Through their experiences of rice smuggling, sex, vacation tours, shopping excursions, pilgrimages, familial visits, and other forms of cross-border movement that starts and ends at Pengkalan Kubor, Ban Bor On's inhabitants expand the space of the borderland and the meanings Thailand and Malaysia hold for them. Moving through these spaces—legally and illegally—forces Ban Bor On residents to reflect on what it means to be ethnically and culturally Thai but politically Malaysian.

Pengkalan Kubor was, for a long time, a sleepy Malay fishing village known to Thais as Tok Luang. Malaysia's booming economic prosperity transformed Tok Luang into a bustling market catering to a clientele from both Thailand and Malaysia. Across the river on the Thai side of the border is the sprawling chaos of

2.2 View of Tak Bai from the river

Narathiwat's Tak Bai (Taba) market, where on Fridays many Kelantanese Thais flock to stock up on rice, fruit, vegetables, Thai pop magazines, toiletries, and imitation designer-label clothing.

The journey from Pengkalan Kubor to the Thai market town of Tak Bai takes about five minutes on small passenger ferries. Long-tailed boats — so named after their long, motorized "tails" — zip up and down the murky river, bringing travelers to various locations along the Tak Bai coast. A newer and larger Tak Bai ferry service is jointly operated by the Thai and Malaysian governments and allows for cars, motorcycles, and trucks to crisscross the river in both directions, enhancing networks of international trade, tourism, and communication for both countries.[12] Villagers can now drive to each other's settlements, transporting their vehicles on the ferry's wide rusty platform amid the jostle of heavy hand-drawn wooden carts stacked high with Thai and Malaysian produce. Today it is common to see minivans and motorcycles with Narathiwat license plates parked at wedding feasts and temple fairs throughout Kelantan. Through attending these social events Narathiwat and Kelantanese villagers reassert their ancestral kin ties with one another, taking apart the boundedness inherent in the national border and replacing it with a common experience of cultural affiliation.

According to some Ban Bor On residents, their village's proximity to the international border, coupled with a new, historically unmatched economic affluence, has inadvertently led to its moral and physiological contamination. Young men would jokingly tease one another about their sexual exploits in the brothels of Tak Bai and Sungai Golok. Malaysia's—and in particular Kelantan's—strict Islamic laws surrounding codes of feminine decorum and the sale of alcohol have prevented Pengkalan Kubor from becoming associated with the bar and prostitution culture that thrives along the Thai border. Until the recent bomb attacks on bars and hotel nightclubs in Sungai Golok by purported Islamic separatists, many young Ban Bor On men flocked to Tak Bai and Sungai Golok for an inexpensive slice of Thai hedonism. Girls were cheap here, my friends reminded me. Those with more money to spend head to the hotel discos and bars of urban Sungai Golok. Here the sex trade is more cosmopolitan and caters to a larger clientele of wealthier Malaysians from across the country. Tak Bai is more provincial and its tiny bars are considered by many Kelantanese Thais to be "not as exciting" as those of Sungai Golok. But drinks, women, and, for some, drugs were cheaper in the hinterlands and many a Ban Bor On young man ventured to nearby Tak Bai to satiate a desire for paid sex not attainable in Kelantan. Prostitutes from all over Thailand enter Kelantan via the Pengkalan Kubor crossing; a number find employment as waitresses (*dek serp*) and hostesses (*pelaye*) in the seafood restaurants and late-night coffeeshops decorated with blinking Christmas lights that have mushroomed in Kelantan's Thai and Malay villages. Here they entertain a clientele comprising primarily urban Chinese entrepreneurs and younger Kelantanese Thai and Malay men—the same men who often make the nocturnal journeys into Tak Bai. Some have married local Thai men and accompanied their husbands back to their Malaysian villages. Sexual promiscuity on the part of many Kelantanese Thai men has resulted in an explosion of AIDS-related deaths in the villages in the past ten years. The real threat of the disease has led many Ban Bor On men and women to view Thailand and its citizens with a certain fear. The young men who succumbed to the disease and whose funerals I attended time and again were popularly believed to have been stricken by the virus during sexual escapades in Tak Bai and Sungai Golok. Some were rumored to have transmitted the disease to their innocent wives, thus spiraling the physiological contagion into Malaysian bodies. Crossing the border was risky and, if one was not careful, deadly.

The border that emerged with the signing of the Anglo-Siamese Treaty created a zone across which illicit movements have flowed, including those of viruses, criminals, and prostitutes. Thailand has been constructed by Ban Bor

On residents as a corrupt space of disease, danger, and hedonism. This negative stereotype of the nation across Tok Luang is not new. For a long time, Ban Bor On and other Tumpat residents have looked at Thailand as an area rife with crime and banditry. Murderers, bandits, and gang leaders, fearing arrest from the Thai/Siamese police in the nineteenth and early twentieth century, often sought solace and new identities in Kelantan. Kae Chi noted the movement of criminals in both directions when she observed that felons from the southern Tak Bai villages of Phron escaped to *mueang khaek* to avoid prosecution in Siam. Many settled in Tumpat villages, where they married local women. A number of Ban Bor On lawbreakers also sought safety and new identities for themselves in Narathiwat. Today, the criminals of old have been replaced by fears of a new kind of villain—southern Thai Muslim terrorists with Al-Qaeda connections were rumored by some of my interlocutors to have training camps in Kelantan's dense rainforests. The narratives of fear and contagion that taint Ban Bor On's borderland are, however, balanced by more positive images of traveling monks, relatives, friends, and pilgrims who move into and out of both Thailand and Kelantan via the Tok Luang and Golok borders.

The ease of movement across the Tak Bai tributary for both Malaysians and Thais means that social and ritual events in Thai villages in Narathiwat and Kelantan now include more participants than there were in the pre-border period.[13] Until the spate of terror attacks on soldiers and civilians in Narathiwat, Yala, and Pattani beginning in 2004, Buddhist festivals at temples in both Narathiwat and Kelantan, such as the annual *kathin* celebrations in November, were elaborate, large-scale affairs attracting crowds of thousands from distant communities. Kelantanese Thais looked forward to these events months in advance, anticipating the exciting entertainment—concerts, shadow puppet performances, and traditional dance drama revues—that were an integral part of large temple fetes. These cross-border flows are facilitated by the popularity of Tumpat Tak Bai radio broadcasts on Thailand's southern radio station, such as the early morning *Hua Rung Luk Thung*, which serve as aural noticeboards for the announcement of Kelantanese and Narathiwat community events. Telephone lines have extended into every Thai village across the borderlands, making communication easy between what were once distant and socially isolated settlements. Since 2004, however, my friends have expressed fear of attending these celebrations. "You never know what may happen," they warned me. Monks, in their bright saffron robes, seem especially afraid, as they believe themselves to be easy targets in a war that they claim was violently opposed to all symbols of the Thai Buddhist state. Temple festivals in Narathiwat are now much quieter affairs, especially during the evenings, when Malaysians and locals alike, fearing for their safety, avoid the public events.

Ban Bor On villagers remember the past as a time of social isolation. Temple festivals did not attract numerous villagers from faraway communities the way they do today. Attendees at these fetes usually walked from nearby villages and camped at the temples for the duration of their visit. Temporary encampments called *koethom* were built out of wood and thatch by the temples' helpers for the weary travelers. Each *koethom* was a self-contained unit and comprised men, women, and children from a single village. Larger festivals required a greater number of *koethom*, as more visitors showed up from different communities. Travelers cooked their own meals in their *koethom* compound, supplementing their diet with what was provided by the host temple (which was often just jars of fermented fish sauce and some curry). Poor travel infrastructure between Thai villages coupled with large tracks of forested land between settlements made moving tedious and dangerous. People feared not only wild tigers and elephants but also the bandits and hoodlums who stalked quiet travel routes. The complications posed by travel made the places beyond the village seem even more distant and strange.

The riverside border with *mueang thai* at Pengkalan Kubor was half a day's journey by foot from Ban Bor On along the dirt trail that was later to be widened and paved over. The border could also be reached via the muddy embankments that snaked through paddy fields. Village accessibility improved after the Second World War. Roads were built and their metalled arteries expanded into government-sponsored rural development programs. Better policing in Thailand's deep south since the eighties has slowly but surely minimized the earlier obstructions and challenges to travel.

Like the smugglers, prostitutes, colonial administrators, and itinerant merchants described earlier, Buddhist monks regularly and frequently move across both banks. Their present-day and past travels are usually part of inter-temple circuits that connect the temples of Kelantan and southern Thailand in a complex network of sacred and educational nodes. Today, as in the past, it is common practice for monks to leave the comfort of their home villages to reside in temples further away. At Wat Nai in 2001, for instance, only three of the nine monks had been born in Ban Bor On. The others came from Thai and Chinese communities in Terengganu, Tanah Merah, Kota Bharu, and Semerak. One reason for the constant flow of monks was the excitement that the new experiences of travel afforded. This was coupled by a ritual need among abbots to maintain fully staffed temples of at least five monks each.[14] Abbots often requested that temples with an excess of monks redistribute their religious manpower to temples with fewer monks, a practice that continues in Kelantan to this day.

Monastic education was an important determinant in structuring these early inter-temple mobilities. For a long time Kelantanese Thai monks had to travel to temples in lower Narathiwat, Patani, and Songkhla in order to sit for the Bangkok-set *nak tham* (Buddhist doctrine and history) and Pali (*parian*) examinations.[15] In 1948, the west coast state of Kedah, with its large Thai community, hosted the first in a series of yearly *nak tham* examinations in British Malaya. Phra Wijaranayanmuni, commonly referred to by his titled name of Chao Khun Khron, the chief monk (*chao khana rat*) of Kelantan at the time, initiated the study and teaching of *nak tham* in Kelantan a year later. Having *nak tham* classes in Kelantan instead of southern Thailand slowed down the movement of Kelantanese monks across the border for study. The first person involved in teaching these classes in Kelantan was a local Bang Rim Nam monk, Phra Maha Chan Kesaro, who was later to succeed Phra Wijaranayanmuni as the chief Monk of Kelantan and the second Phra Wijaranayanmuni of the state. The examinations were conducted at Wat Bang Rim Nam, where Phra Maha Chan was abbot until his death in 1992. Today, most Thai temples in Kelantan hold their own *nak tham* classes for monks and interested laypersons, the latter usually comprising teenage boys and girls. Monks who have completed all four years of preliminary Thai education in Kelantan's monastic school system teach the evening and weekend *nak tham* classes. Different temples in Kelantan are listed as venues for the centralized examinations, with each temple hosting *nak tham* examinations for three consecutive years.[16] Exams are held every February, the scripts obtained from Bangkok and brought to Kelantan by monk representatives of Thailand's national ecclesiastical examinations board (*mae kong tham sob sanam luang*).[17] The role of the Bangkok monks in the *nak tham* examinations remains highly symbolic, as the actual teaching and grading of the papers lies primarily in the hands of the Kelantanese. They represent the moral agents of the reified Buddhist Thai nation-state and the official standardizing body of Theravada Buddhism across a community of Thai Buddhists worldwide.

Even after the formation of the international border in 1909, Wat Tuyong on the outskirts of Patani town and Wat Chehe in Tak Bai continued to serve as preparatory centers for Kelantanese Thai monks sitting for these standardized exams. Many Kelantanese monks ended up residing in these temples for long periods even after taking the exams. Here they would engage in Buddhist study while savoring the much sought-after freedom of travel, a luxury that lay villagers could ill afford, having been tied down to the rigid demands of the agricultural cycle. Some monks traveled further north to temples in Songkhla and Phuket and to the stupa of the Great Relic (Mahathat) in the center of Nakhon Sri Thammarat province, where they lived for many years before returning to Kelantan. The late Lung Chu, once a noted magical practitioner well-versed in the arts of shamanism (*phi jab*) and astrology (*du duang*), told me that two Kelantanese Thai monks had founded temples in Songkhla. Wat Chaimongkhol and the nearby Wat Phetmongkhol in the center of Songkhla town were established by the monks Chai and Phet, respectively. Pho Than Chai hailed from the village of Din Sung and Pho Than Phet from Ban Bor On. Both had gone on wandering expeditions (*thudong*) in Siam much earlier and decided to establish temples out of what had once been small monastic shelters. A few Kelantanese Thai monks even made it to Bangkok, the religious and political heart of Thai Buddhism in the nineteenth and twentieth centuries.

Monks from across the Tak Bai river also moved to Kelantan, sometimes taking on abbotship in Kelantanese temples. Ban Bor On's Wat Nok was established by a monk named Daeng who hailed from the Phron region of southern Narathiwat. The temple had two successive abbots from Phron, although a senior monk who was born in Ban Klang holds the position today. Wat Nai has also played host to a large number of monks from Siamese-ruled Patani, most of whom originated from the province's Khok Khwai district. A number of these men remained in Ban Bor On after leaving the monkhood and married local women.[18]

The famous nineteenth-century monk and mystic, Luang Pho Pok Loh, was originally a Malay Muslim by the name of Pok Loh (Uncle Abdullah). Uncle Abdullah had converted to Buddhism after making a vow out of fear of being attacked by a tiger he encountered on a path. According to a small booklet (undated) sold at the Narathiwat temple he supposedly built up, Luang Pho Pok Loh was born in the Malay village of Tasek in the Tak Bai district. He was ordained as a monk on 29 May 1874. As a forest monk, Luang Pho Pok Loh traveled extensively throughout the southern Thai peninsula, reaching even Nakhon Sri Thammarat, where he paid homage to the Mahathat relic. He is believed to have traveled south to Kelantan and is listed in the text as having passed away there. No one I spoke with in Kelantan seemed to know where or when this happened.

Kelantanese Thai temples continue to be staffed by monks from various parts of Thailand. The influx of Thai citizen monks into Kelantan proved a headache for the local Malaysian monastic community as the Malaysian abbots attempted to exert disciplinary control over the highly mobile Thai citizen population. Reports in both the Thai and Malaysian press of Thai citizen monks cheating laypeople of their money in bogus magical rituals and begging illegally on the streets of Malaysian towns and cities have tarnished the reputation of Thailand's monks among many Kelantanese. Unlike the revered figures of the past, today's mobile Thai citizen monks are treated with a degree of suspicion and their moves are carefully monitored by Kelantanese temple abbots. Kelantanese also spoke of how they had heard both as rumors and in the Thai media that some monks from across the border had been arrested in Thailand for rape, having sex with corpses, indulging in sorcery, and tax evasion. Monks found guilty of such activities are subject to monastic discipline and sanctions, including jail terms and expulsion from the monastic community.

Contemporary Kelantan's rising cost of living has meant that very few economically active Thai men are engaged in the full-time agricultural pursuits of their forefathers. Most work long hours in Kota Bharu and other urban centers across Malaysia. Free time is deemed precious and something that can only be savored in the monkhood, where material pursuits are temporarily put on hold. When I asked my monk friends at Wat Nai and Wat Nok why they moved about so frequently, even if it was just to Kota Bharu to have lunch at Ramu's Curry House or Pizza Hut, they replied that the time they were spending in the monkhood represented the only opportunity they would have to satiate their wanderlust. Besides these short city excursions, many young Kelantanese Thai monks also participate in the network of vacation tours to Thailand organized by local temples and entrepreneurial-minded laypersons in collaboration with temples in Narathiwat and Thai tour agencies.

So powerful is the desire to travel (*pai thieow*) that some Kelantanese and Narathiwat monks have become regular tour organizers. Their coach excursions to various provinces in Thailand are often held over Malaysian national holidays (the two-day Chinese New Year break in January–February being especially popular) so that villagers employed in non-agricultural jobs can go as well. Usually costing no more than RM250 (US$84) for a seven-day sightseeing package, these are affordable and popular vacations for many Ban Bor On villagers and often their only opportunity to experience the Thailand that lies beyond the southern border provinces. Wealthier and more adventurous villagers make trips further away. Some have gone to Sri Lanka and India as part of pilgrimage tours to historical Buddhist sites, though tours to faraway locales are few and far between when compared to the more common Thailand getaway packages. Kelantanese monk tour organizers often work with tour operators in Narathiwat in shaping their itineraries. Tours frequently include visits to local Buddhist celebrations and pilgrimage sites, with travelers spending nights in temples along the way thereby saving on the cost of hotel accommodation. Not all the places visited are of a religious nature. Ban Bor On residents who had gone on these tours often recalled fondly how at Kanchanaburi, about an hour's drive west from Bangkok, they were accommodated on a raft floating on the Khwae River: the chief attraction not so much the raft or the scenic beauty of the natural landscape, but the onboard disco at night. The younger monks jokingly complained to me that as monks they could not participate in the lively atmosphere, even while their fellow travelers danced the night away. Participation in these tours, or *rombongan*, as they are called by Ban Bor On residents (using the Malay term for an organized group), allows monks and lay tourists to consolidate a sense of village identity that is framed within the mobile experience of encountering. The movement generated by the journey beyond Ban Bor On's borders makes travelers more aware of their social identity as different from that of Thais from other Kelantanese villages, and from that of the Thai citizens they met on their adventures.

Mae Dam is a friendly, curly-haired woman who used to live next to Ban Bor On's only gas station. By 2008, she had moved to Penang to be with some of her grandchildren and to seek medical treatment for an eye infection. She returned to Ban Bor On occasionally and her house was always abuzz with the chatter of family members. Mae Dam was an avid traveler. She went on tours to Thailand about once a year before deciding to devote herself to being a full-time nanny to her eight grandchildren. She had been one of Ban Bor On's leading tour organizers, working in close association with a relative who lived in Narathiwat. Together they planned *rombongan* tours to Thailand using itineraries provided by Narathiwat travel agents.

When I arrived at her house one morning in 2002, its sandy compound shaded by fruit trees and a large fragrant *dangnga* bush, Mae Dam was surrounded by her squealing grandchildren. They tugged noisily at her batik sarong, waiting eagerly for the fried fish balls she was distributing. Once the children had been given their treats and the din had died down, we sat on the stone bench in front of the house to talk. I told her of my interest in *rombongan* tours. She smiled and eagerly showed me the pictures she had taken of her many visits to Thailand, explaining the significant ones as I flipped through the thick album. Mae Dam pointed out that although different Thai villages organized these tours, participants preferred to travel with their own village groups. "It is just us Ban Bor On people. You see, if we went [on a tour] with people from Ban Klang or Ban Kao it is unlikely that they would look out for us as we do for each other."

By "looking out for each other," Mae Dam was referring to the practice of mutual care and concern that villagers exemplified en route. These included ensuring that everyone was on the bus before it departed or buying meals and snacks together. As Mae Dam put it, strangers rarely assisted one another, even if they were from Thai villages in Kelantan. What was most salient to sociality and camaraderie was one's connection to the inhabitants of any one village rather than the imagination of solidarity based upon a shared culture and feelings of marginality defined by politico-jural locatedness in a contemporary state. Hence, coming from the same village and adhering to the unstated principles of mutual assistance was an important means of patterning one's social identity as a member of the Ban Bor On collectivity.

Travel across the border creates opportunities for connection and social interaction. Interactions between Thais from Thailand and local villagers are always interesting encounters, as they allow Ban Bor On villagers to perform and celebrate a cultural identity for themselves that is simultaneously similar to yet different from that of their non-Malaysian counterparts. It is an identity that plays with the very ambiguity that living along the border permits. Nowhere was this more evident than in the long, drawn-out interactions between formal representatives of the Thai nation-state—academics, monks, journalists, and elite members of Bangkok's standard Thai-speaking bureaucracy—and Ban Bor On villagers.

I experienced this interaction directly during a meeting I attended between members of Thailand's bureaucracy and Wat Nai's abbot in September 2002, which was held in the abbot's living quarters (*mae tek*). On one side of the wide room with its polished wood floors was a private sitting area where Pho Than Di had his favorite lazy chair and watched soccer and Thai boxing matches on a large flat-screen television. On the opposite side of the room, in front of an old and elaborately carved wooden wall panel decorated with stylized Thai and Chinese motifs of angels, bats, and butterflies, stood the altar. On its many shelf-tables were myriad old and new Buddha images as well as pictures and statues of Thailand's various Chakri kings. Next to the main altar was a smaller one on which were set life-size statues of Wat Nai's two former abbots.

I did not know of the meeting until I received a text message from Khun Di asking me to come to the *mae tek* immediately. There was an urgency in his message that made me nervous. At the time I had been a monk for no more than three weeks, and I entered the abbot's quarters only to participate in rituals or to meet with the abbot about a matter of importance. I hurriedly twisted my bright orange robes tightly, swinging the long cloth over my left shoulder and tucking the loose end neatly under my arm before heading to the large building, unsure of what lay ahead. "Had I offended the abbot?" I asked myself, thinking of all the recent occasions when I might possibly have rubbed him the wrong way.

Women and older men were seated on the floor along the sides of the room. They exchanged small talk in hushed tones. I smiled at them and they smiled back, palms pressed together in a greeting of respect to members of the religious community. In the middle of the room sat Pho Than Di on a pink cushioned settee, with Khun Di by his side. I clasped my hands and bowed down before the senior monks. They returned the greeting without a bow and asked me to join them on the couch. On the floor in front of us, with their legs tucked to one side in a manner of politeness, were four men and one woman. Unlike the Ban Bor On villagers, most of whom sat cross-legged at the far edge of the room, the visitors from Thailand positioned themselves directly in front of the abbot. They were respected guests and thus treated with the formal and distanced reverence Ban Bor On residents reserve for non-intimates. They wore neatly pressed long-sleeved dress shirts and slacks and seemed oblivious to the presence of the staring villagers around them. They spoke only standard Thai—Thailand's official patois based on the central Thai dialect. Khun Di introduced me as someone who was researching the history and culture of the Kelantanese Thai community. He informed me that the visitors were from Princess Maha Chakri Sirinthorn's administrative office in Narathiwat. The Thai princess, the eldest daughter of King Bhumipol Adulyadej, had originally thought of visiting Ban Bor On as part of her annual tour to Thailand's southernmost provinces. Royal tours were carefully planned and coordinated activities involving many people from both sides of the border, and the princess's tight schedule had made an imminent visit impossible. So she had sent her representatives to the village instead.

Khun Di had been told of the visit by the palace officials only on the day itself. His immediate response after informing the abbot of the news was to ask the students in Wat Nai's Thai school to clean their dust-filled classrooms because the "representatives of the Princess were coming to see their school."

The students proceeded to spread the word to their parents and, somehow, through a process of miscommunication, a large number of parents and their friends turned up at the temple to meet and greet the Thai princess.

The bespectacled man who sat on the floor directly in front of us and who did most of the talking was the deputy director of Narathiwat's Royal Office. He asked the monks a number of general questions regarding the ethnology and history of the Kelantanese Thai. "How many Thai people live in this village? What do they do for a living? How old is this temple? Do the Thais here watch Thai television?" and so on.[19] The questions constructed the Kelantanese Thais as an ahistorical and seemingly self-contained community. The dynamics of encounter, of travel and movement, and of the confusing inter-ethnic negotiations that go on every day in a changing hinterland seemed oblivious to the Thai bureaucrats. What was interesting was the response the questions elicited. The abbot and Khun Di spoke mainly in the Tumpat Tak Bai dialect, inserting standard Thai tones into some words and phrases so as to ensure that the man understood what they were saying. Using Kelantanese Thai also allowed the monks to do away with some of the stifling formality of an interview in a non-native dialect. It lightened the encounter. But by speaking Kelantanese Thai in the face of Thai officialdom, the monks were inadvertently but powerfully constructing borders of difference for themselves.[20] Language defined a sense of Kelantanese Thai localism that resisted Thailand's national linguistic and cultural hegemonies. Thailand could enter the temple through its standard Thai–speaking representatives, but it was prevented from monopolizing the meaning of Thainess for the Kelantanese.

Using the Tumpat Tak Bai dialect meant that Pho Than Di and Khun Di had to constantly explain their answers. This process of lexical translation was always met with cheeky grins from both monks and looks of confusion from the palace representatives. "We also say *rue bin* and not *khrueng bin* [to refer to airplanes]. Also, the word for wedding is *likah*, not *taeng ngan*," laughed Khun Di. Earlier Pho Than Di had pointed out how Tumpat Tak Bai–speakers used the word *kin* (to eat) to refer to both drinking (standard Thai: *duem*) and smoking (standard Thai: *sup*). The officials smiled and nodded in polite agreement.

The questions that the deputy director asked seemed to revolve around a common theme, that of how *Thai* the Ban Bor On residents *really* were. It was a narrative of Thainess I had heard asked many times before, whenever Thailand's academics or government officials visited Kelantan. The Ban Bor On villagers I spoke with never suggested the political agenda of their Thai visitors, although

Khun Di was a little more reflexive in his remarks. To these Thai citizens, the local and Malay history of Kelantan and its borders were subsumed beneath Thailand's national discourse of a shared culture that stretched beyond the current confines of national territory and produced diasporic citizens around the world. Finding out how *Thai* the Kelantanese were was a means by which to reassert a powerful sense of cultural patriarchy over what were viewed as Thailand's lost sheep. It was an attempt by the Thai nation-state to manage and make sense of its cultural diaspora without incurring the wrath of the Malaysian state. Yet in speaking Kelantanese Thai, Pho Than Di and Khun Di resisted this national myth of a politically framed definition of Thainess.

The meeting that afternoon played two hegemonies against each other—that of Thailand over "all Thais everywhere," and that of the successors to the British colonial state toward a minority in their midst. Charles Keyes (1995: 144), echoing Thongchai Winichakul's earlier work (1994), pointed out how the mapping of the Siamese state's perimeters in the nineteenth and early twentieth centuries had led to an obsession among the Bangkok elite with seeking out connections with people who inhabit the newly sovereign territory. In part, this national rhetoric of classifying "who were the Thai" was a reaction to French colonial doctrines of race and territory in French-ruled Indochina. In the Siamese case, race was closely correlated with linguistics. Thus, people who spoke languages in the Tai linguistic family were a part of the Thai national imagination even if they were separated by sovereign borders. And it was this historically constituted definition of cultural kinship that brought the standard Thai–speaking bureaucrats to Ban Bor On that warm afternoon.

The large number of Ban Bor On residents who had gathered at the temple to greet the Thai princess and Khun Di's excited attempts at ensuring the cleanliness of the school pointed to the reverence with which many Malaysian Thai villagers regard Thailand's monarchy. By visiting the temple the palace officials symbolically incorporated the villagers into a national Thai Buddhist history, albeit one that was mired in confusions and paradoxes. Ban Bor On's Thais became a museum piece representing some of the nation's most distant cultural denizens. One needed to understand them to find out about their histories of migration rather than of stasis, and about their associations with Thailand both in the past and present. These were unimportant issues to most villagers, as it was beyond reasonable doubt that they were first and foremost Kelantanese and secondly Malaysian. Thailand factored into the picture only as an afterthought and as a possible source of a revered but at times terrifying inspiration.

Ban Bor On's villagers, including Pho Than Di and Khun Di, were active agents in producing their own understandings of what constituted their ethnic and cultural identities. To them, it was the local distinctiveness achieved from experiences of living apart from the modern Thai nation-state that was crucial in shaping who they were, their Thainess. The villagers expressed this as a story of historical and linguistic difference from Thailand. This discourse resisted the hegemony imposed by the standardizing practices of the bureaucratic Thai state in terms of Buddhist culture and linguistic affiliations. The villagers spoke of themselves not as cultural and ethnic minorities but as true Malaysian citizens, bemoaning the fact that they were denied many of the privileges accrued to Malaysia's *bumiputera*s. It was this proud association with Malaysia that made them consider themselves different from the Thais of Thailand and from which the perennial question of national ethnic labeling emerges. The development of markets and infrastructure in Tak Bai and Pengkalan Kubor increased the exposure of Kelantanese Thais to the national culture of Thailand, and shaped local stereotypes of the Buddhist polity and its people. Through locating themselves along dynamic frontier zones of national and cultural space, the people of Ban Bor On produced a reading of Thainess that in essence contested their feelings of marginality and social invisibility.

Ban Bor On can be thought about in various ways. It is a place of fixity, lucidly defined by its mapped location on a geopolitical grid at the extremities of Malaysia. It is also a discursively constructed place that exists in the imagination of its residents—a place that has "always been here"—not the product of ancient migrations and diasporic moments from Buddhist polities to the north. Nonetheless, local-level discourses celebrating the historical movements of people between villages on both sides of the frontier allow for the dismantling of narratives of a static enclave of Thai ethnic and cultural identification. The seemingly dislocative histories of place that Kae Chi, Lung Piak, and others talked about objectify the village in very real terms. These histories of locatedness continue to be creatively reproduced in the contemporary Kelantanese Thai village in the way men and women talk about their encounters with Thailand and its border.

The lives of Ban Bor On's residents cannot be disentangled from the cultural and political chaos of mobility that affects their community. The messiness of ethnic and cultural self-definition is pillared upon the fact that to Thailand and Malaysia, the Kelantanese Thais live in a place far removed from the centers of national cultural production. Their marginality makes them socially invisible, yet their discernible engagement with the metanarratives of governance and citizenship places them clearly in the view of bureaucrats and politicians. In attempting to make sense of this maze of shifting social and personal identifications that collectively constitute Thainess in the village, it is necessary to return to the unnamed roads, railway tracks, and gravel paths traversed in the previous chapter. When we take our gaze away from the large players of identity production and refocus on what is directly around us, we notice that the marginality of the village — its existence as a "gap" between two powerful sovereign worlds — is in actuality a strange and unsettling misnomer.

CHAPTER 3

Forms

EVERY EVENING, EXPRESS TIMURAN (THE EASTERN EXPRESS)
leaves Singapore's one and only train station for the thirteen-hour journey north
to Bandar Tumpat. The sleepy Malaysian town is served by two other train lines.
The daily Express Wau and the weekend-only Express Kenali—the latter named
after Tok Kenali (1870–1933), one of Kelantan's foremost Islamic theologians—
link the station with Kuala Lumpur.[1] Being both affordable and comfortable
despite the frequent delays, Keretapi Tanah Melayu's (Malayan Railways) fully
air-conditioned coaches are some of the most popular modes of long-haul travel
for Kelantanese.

If it is on schedule, Express Timuran will reach the Tumpat plains by eight in
the morning. The district of Tumpat is a picture postcard of Malaysian rurality. It
is marked by the shady greenery of vegetable gardens and wide rice fields interspersed with clumps of tall bamboo, fruit orchards, and shady coconut groves.
Running parallel to the train tracks are the dirt paths along which pedestrians,
cyclists, and motorcyclists travel. Brown and white Malayan cows, smaller and
leaner than their American cousins, graze lazily among flocks of white cattle
egrets in the fields. Occasionally a grey water buffalo comes into view. Once
used as beasts of burden to plow fields, water buffalos are now rarely raised by
villagers, who prefer mechanical harvesters to work the rice fields. On its way
to its final stop, the morning train passes yellow-domed mosques, old wood
residences, and newer houses of brick and wood, with their ocher zinc roofs
held up by the quaint cement Greco-Roman–style columns that are so popular
in east-coast Malaysia.

A few minutes from Bandar Tumpat's little station, Express Timuran chugs
by two large Thai temples. Glimpses of these majestic complexes punctuate the
foggy morning landscape. Kampung Kulim's Thai temple, Wat Bot Ngam, faces
the rail tracks just past the Wakaf Bharu station. Built in 1965 on the site of an

old cemetery in a Chinese village, the temple's handsome ordination hall (*bot*) brilliantly reflects the rays of sun that bounce playfully off its mirror-laced ornaments. Designed by an architect from Thailand and taking nine years to complete, the building resembles similar structures constructed across Thailand and modeled on a standard Thai national aesthetic that draws its inspiration from classical central Thai temple art. There is nothing distinctively "Kelantanese" about the building's facade and one could easily mistake it for a temple in Bangkok. Hidden from the passenger's fleeting view is the larger-than-life statue of Phra Sayam Thewathiraj. Constructed of cement and painted dark brown, this sword-bearing divinity was created by Siam's King Rama IV (Mongkut), who imagined him as the guardian spirit of a newly bordered and sovereign Siamese polity in an age of high colonialism in Southeast Asia. Thailand's national deity stands in a quiet corner of Wat Bot Ngam and proves an interesting juxtaposition of ritual and political meaning in a Thai temple situated within a Chinese village in a Muslim Malaysian state. Smaller red-roofed shrines housing images of popular Taoist deities dot the sacred precincts of the temple. Like most rural Chinese throughout the Kelantan plains, Kulim's residents profess a syncretic religion that combines Thai Theravada Buddhism with indigenous Chinese beliefs and practices.

Just after passing Wat Bot Ngam, Express Timuran goes through a tunnel and emerges on the periphery of the Thai village of Din Sung. Wat Din Sung's main gateway and its enormous three-story multipurpose hall tower over the surrounding trees and smaller buildings, and the temple's older preaching hall comes into view fleetingly. The building was constructed in the shape of a traditional Thai pavilion resting on a replica of Thailand's swan-headed royal barge, the Suphannahong. Mistakenly called the Dragon Boat by some Malaysian and Singaporean tourists, this colorful structure is surrounded by an algae-filled moat and fenced in by two intertwining *naga* serpents. From here, the train slows down as it crosses the rail lines over the unnamed road leading from Ban Bor On to Bandar Tumpat, and within minutes it pulls into its final stop.

The production of imposing Buddhist monuments such as Din Sung's swan barge and multipurpose hall on Mecca's Verandah has to be seen in relation to a new politics of place, identity, and encounter along the Malaysian-Thai frontier. Kelantanese Thais inhabit a space that has historically been a contact zone between the Thai Buddhist state to the north and the traditional Malay polity with which the Thais have aligned themselves. The colossal statues and buildings one sees, not just as images from train windows but all over Kelantan today, are not only symbols of this interactive dimension but also newfound material expressions of a grandiose Thainess for the community of local builders.

Kelantan's temple monuments are modern nodes in an old circuit of cross-cutting movements. The statues engineer a series of mobile encounters around them. They envelope a variety of people from different backgrounds ranging from backpackers to the most senior of Buddhist monks, Malay politicians, ethereal terrorists, Chinese businessmen, and Thai bureaucrats. The monuments make vibrantly visible a small ethnic community that has been thrown aside in colonial and later national practices of state demarcation and consolidation. Kelantan's Buddhist statues and monuments stand as an indigenous and creative testimony to the meeting and mixing of peoples and their cultural and political ideologies. Through building and then talking about their creations, Kelantanese Thais reflect on both their own historical experiences and their position as cultural and ethnic marginals in Malaysia.

Driving through Ban Bor On one cannot miss Wat Nai's imposing fifty-foot-high Walking Buddha statue, plastered with thousands of tiny gold mirror mosaics that were purchased in Bangkok by Tok Nai Suk. The elegant statue, its flame-shaped finial piercing the clear Kelantanese sky, was completed in 1996 after ten years of construction. The statue stands on a three-tiered cement base smoothed over with marble slabs. From the topmost tier, one has a spectacular view of Ban Bor On and its surroundings—the temple's murky turtle pond, the rutted road leading to Ban Phan Jao in the distance, and far off on the horizon, the tops of the remaining old *ton on* trees that once grew in abundance in the village and from which the village got its name.

Tourists flock to the temple daily. They are mostly ethnic Chinese, hailing from the urban towns across Malaysia and Singapore. Wat Nai's other day-trippers include Thais from across the border and distant villages in Kelantan, Malay urbanites from Kuala Lumpur and beyond, and tourists from places as far afield as the Netherlands, Australia, Switzerland, and Japan. All crane their necks as they walk around the statue, marveling at its immensity. For these tourists, visits to the temples are often part of larger itineraries that brought them to Kota Bharu's handicraft villages, the pristine beaches along the eastern shoreline for which Kelantan is famous, and for some, the cheap shopping found along the Thai-Malaysian border at Rantau Panjang.[2] A number of tourists also cross the border into Sungai Golok to savor Thailand at its hinterlands—cheap food, massage parlors, and an exciting nightlife.

Chao Iat was responsible for building the statue. The self-trained artist and

3.1 Buddhist colossi, Ban Klang

sculptor was skilled at constructing buildings and statues in classical central Thai form. Wat Nai's Walking Buddha is a replica of a similar one found in a temple in Thailand's Nakhon Pathom province. The original statue is a fifty-two-foot-high bronze image cast by the famed Italian sculptor and academic Silpa Bhirasri (Coraddo Feroci, 1892–1963) in 1957 to mark Thailand's celebration of the twenty-fifth century of Buddhism. The original image, like its Wat Nai copy, represents the Buddha in mid-stride, his left hand raised slightly, fore-finger and thumb forming a gentle circle. Bhirasri and Chao Iat's creations are modern interpretations of the famed Walking Buddha statues of thirteenth- and fourteenth-century Sukhothai sculpture considered by some Thai art historians to be masterpieces of the local sculptural form.

The immensity of Wat Nai's Walking Buddha shapes the way visitors experience space in the temple. Rarely do they venture beyond the shadows of the giant statue to explore the other areas of the monastic complex. Once the prayers are said by the pious and the necessary photographs taken on cameras and cell phones, the travelers return to the comfort of their vehicles, protected from the sweltering heat that reflects off the tarred road and the sand around it. The buses and cars then depart, speeding off to unload the tourists at yet other temples with giant statues, often ending their journey in front of Wat Klang's ninety-nine-foot-high Sitting Buddha. Throughout my stay in Wat Nai, I met many curious out-of-towners who asked me for directions to temples with enormous statues. It was not long before I had committed to memory route maps to Wat Phra Non, Wat Klang, Wat Din Sung, and Wat Khok Phrao. The most recent monumental statue to be added to the inventory of giant cement images of the Buddha stands in Wat Nak, in the southern district of Bachok, some two hours' drive from Ban Bor On. The 108-foot-high statue of a standing Chinese Amitabha Buddha is the second impressive creation for Kelantanese artisan and sculptor Chao Jim. Hailing from the village of Ban Klang, Chao Jim first built the majestic Sinic-inspired Wat Klang Buddha. "I hear they are even installing an elevator in the statue," chuckled Khun Rien as we stared in amazement at the scaffold-enveloped image one evening in 2005. When we revisited Wat Nak in 2008, the entire statue was plastered with tiny white mosaics. The statue stood on an open lotus flower on whose huge petals were tacked sheets of yellow paper bearing the scribbled names of Chinese donors who had contributed financially to its construction. Years earlier, Wat Nak had already set a record for having the longest "dragon wall" in the state. The temple's encompassing wall, built in the shape of two scaly green Chinese dragons, measures 595 feet long. The monsters meet head to head, eyes bulging and fangs exposed, at the temple's main entrance.

The first Kelantanese temple to begin building massive Buddhist images was Wat Phra Non in the village of Ban Pho. Situated along the main Tumpat–Pasir Mas road some twelve kilometers north of Kota Bharu, Wat Phra Non's 130-foot-long Reclining Buddha is the longest of its kind in Southeast Asia. Work on the statue began in 1977 and was completed some ten years later. Today Wat Phra Non is one of Kelantan's most-visited tourist attractions and it is featured in the state's travel guides and tour itineraries. Together with Kota Bharu's colorful central market, the statue is a photographic icon of the northeastern state. The large number of tourists that visit the temple each day has spurred an informal economy along its periphery: enterprising Ban Pho residents have set up stalls selling photographic film and snacks—cold drinks, rice salad (*khao jam*), spicy green papaya salad, and fresh coconut juice. Wat Phra Non is such a well-known landmark on Kelantan's tourist map that some of my friends at Ban Bor On used to tease me about it. Since I do not look Thai, they would often jokingly refer to me as "the lost white person on his way to Ban Pho," when introducing me to fellow intimates. Sweat-drenched Caucasian backpackers are a common sight along the road leading to Wat Phra Non. The temple is not easy to get to by public transport and guidebooks warn that the nearest bus stop is about four kilometers away. Tourists do "get lost" as they wander the roads looking for the sleeping colossi. The large statues at Wat Nai, Wat Khok Phrao (with its massive Chinese-styled statue of the Bodhisatva Kwan Im), Wat Klang, and Wat Phra Non have all been featured as places of interest in Kelantan by Lonely Planet's *Malaysia and Singapore* guidebook, which many budget travelers use to navigate their way around the country on a shoestring budget. Sometimes the younger monks at Wat Nai would cheekily refer to their afternoon nap as them "going to Wat Phra Non," since they too were "sleeping monks" (*phra non*), as the Reclining Buddha image is called in the Tumpat Tak Bai dialect.

Subsequent construction projects in Kelantan's Thai temples can be divided into two categories: monumental buildings (including ordination chapels [*bot*], temple doorways [*sum pratu*], kitchens [*khrua*], preaching halls [*rong tham*], schools [*rong rien*], and open-walled pavilions [*sala*]) and religious statutory. Wat Kao's gold-and-blue, three-spire gateway, for instance, is believed to be the largest of its kind in the state. One of the motivating factors for the gateway's size was that tour buses could enter the temple in a grand manner. So heavy was the temple's gateway that it collapsed under its own weight at least once during the construction phase. In order to stabilize the structure, its designer, Na Chao Phi—who by 2010 was suffering from a bout of several health ailments, including diabetes—was forced to compromise on the height of the pillars holding up the spires. The final product is one of sheer magnificence but it lacks the slender elegance of its original form. Villagers marveled at it while quietly critiquing its stumpy and heavy feel.

Wat Ban Phai's new ordination hall in the village of Ban Phai in the southern district of Pasir Puteh is an immense structure, the largest of its kind in Kelantan. Its chief architect was Chao Jim, who is presently one of Kelantan's most sought-after traditional Thai artisáns. Unlike older craftsmen such as Na Chao Phi and Chao Iat, Chao Jim represents a new age of artisanry in Kelantan. He derives inspiration for his projects from national Thai renditions of traditional art. His work is heavily influenced by the central Thai art patterns and designs one finds on computer programs, CD-ROMs, and art manuals sold in Thailand. Despite the exorbitant fees he charges, Chao Jim's handiwork is very much in demand among Kelantanese monks intent on building Thai-type structures in their temples, and he often has two or more projects going on simultaneously.

Less spectacular than Wat Ban Phai's richly ornate ordination hall is Wat

Nai's recently renovated kitchen complex. The structure, with its rows of stainless steel sinks, was built upon what had once been the temple's old wood kitchen. The new kitchen, completed in 2003, is believed by villagers to be the largest temple kitchen complex in all of Kelantan, and they proudly emphasize this point time and again during conversations about the Kelantanese Thai building craze.

The building of larger-than-life statues and record-setting monuments like kitchens and gateways is nothing new in the artistic history of Theravadin societies. Early South and Southeast Asian Buddhist polities such as Pagan, Anuradhapura, Ayuthaya, Sukhothai, and Nakhon Sri Thammarat were sites for the production of Buddhist colossi that not only demonstrated the kingdom's power and the ruler's devotional piety but also served as visual displays of their supporters' immense store of merit. The tradition of building big did not stop with the onset of colonialism and nationalism in the region but rather took on a new significance, one where size celebrated the nation-state and its ideologies. In 1966, work began on the twenty-four-meter-high statue of the Sitting Buddha at Wat Khao Kong, a temple in Narathiwat's Lamphu district and a stone's throw from the Tak Bai border. The statue, built in the northern Thai Chiang Saen style, was completed in 1970 and stands as a golden beacon of Thai Buddhist cultural identity in Thailand's predominantly Muslim south. The statue received a large part of its construction funding from a Thai government bent on securing the politics of Buddhist nationalism along the Muslim frontier. In Kelantan, a different social and political landscape presented itself. Instead of receiving state support and financial assistance, Kelantanese temples had to raise funds for construction themselves. Whereas Thailand's giant statues carry powerful political and religio-nationalist significance, Kelantanese images and buildings are laced with the political flavor of ethnic marginality.

Not all the statues and monuments that have been built on the Kelantan plains are of Thai artistic derivation. Many, such as Wat Nak's white-tiled Amitabha Buddha and Dragon Wall and Wat Khok Phrao's Kwan Im (Guanyin) statue, are primarily Sinic representations with little or no Thai artistic accents. Gargantuan Chinese statues built across the Kelantanese Thai religious landscape point to an ongoing process of ethnic and cultural negotiation in contemporary Kelantan. The materiality of the statues and buildings mediate between local Thai social actors, Chinese economic players, and the Malaysian state. In order to understand this complex process of Thai ethnic affirmation through an engagement with mammoth Chinese-style religious forms it is necessary to pay attention to the way in which the Chinese community interacts with its Thai counterparts in Kelantan.

Sinic Universes

According to Malaysia's Population and Housing Census for the year 2000, ethnic Chinese, or people who claimed to be Chinese, comprised a total of 49,067 persons or 3.7 percent of Kelantan's total population. Social scientists researching Kelantan (for example, Kershaw 1969, 1981; Winzeler 1985; Dollah 1987; Golomb 1978; and Mohamed 1993a, 1993b) have traditionally divided the state's Chinese population into two distinct "sectors": rural and urban. Kelantan's rural Chinese, known to local Thai speakers variously as *jin ban* (village Chinese), *jin bok* (rural Chinese), *jin ni* (local Chinese), or *jin thai* (Thai-ized Chinese) are old communities of primarily Hokkien speakers who share many cultural and linguistic affinities with their Thai and Malay neighbors. In the south of the state in and around the district of Gua Musang, rural Chinese communities are mostly of the Hakka dialect group. Gua Musang's Chinese villages have been isolated from developments in the northern floodplains by a generalized inaccessibility due to Kelantan's mountainous and densely forested interior, which until the nineties had been pinpointed by the Malaysian state as a hotbed for communist rebels. Sharon Carstens (2001, 2005) noted that by the late-1980s, the communist threat had in effect ended and road and highway developments in Kelantan linked Gua Musang with the larger urban centers of Kota Bharu, Kuala Krai, and the Sungai Golok border. The area soon experienced an increase in Malay villagers in search of better economic opportunities and Thai citizen migrant workers who came to work on cocoa and rubber plantations. More Chinese men also began visiting brothels in Sungai Golok, which was now a mere three hours away. Although a small number of these Hakka speakers have married Thais from the north, there has been minimal inter-ethnic interaction between the southern Hakka and the Tumpat Thais. A substantial number of rural Hokkien-speaking Chinese also live in Kelantan's northern Thai villages, and older residents are often conversant in Thai. Some rural Chinese communities living far from the main centers of Thai population in the Tumpat and Pasir Mas districts do not speak any of the southern Chinese dialects but converse only in Kelantanese Malay.

Kelantan's urban Chinese (*jin mueang*) are usually Mandarin or Cantonese speakers who trace their ancestry to more recent waves of immigration from nineteenth and twentieth century China and other parts of the Malay peninsula.[3] In reality, however, the divide between the two groups is blurred (Teo 2003). In his ethnography of ethnic interaction in Pasir Mas, Robert Winzeler (1985: 21) noted that some of these so-called "urban Chinese" have also migrated into rural areas and taken up agricultural lifestyles or the small-scale market trading traditionally associated with their rural cousins. Similarly, a large number of village-based Chinese have moved to Kelantan's towns in search of work and education, leading to "mutual acculturation and assimilation between the two Chinese sectors" (ibid.). Katsue Takamura (2004) observed that many Chinese schoolchildren living in villages close to the Rantau Panjang–Sungai Golok border spoke a variety of Chinese dialects and shared much of the common Mandarinised culture of their urban peers. To these children, cultural inspiration came not only from the more established Hokkien communities in the countryside but from a global image of *Chineseness* defined by the Mandarin and Cantonese mass media in Hong Kong, Taiwan, and Malaysia's urbanized west coast.

The close associations shared between the Thai and the urban and rural Chinese were partly structured by the syncretic nature of traditional Kelantanese Chinese belief systems, which incorporated elements of popular Taoism with Thai Theravadism and Sinic Mahayanism. Many Chinese have been active participants in the ritual life of Thai temples, attending ceremonies and festivals with their Thai friends and neighbors. Many are also important financial supporters for the Thai Buddhist institution. Thai temples and monk lodges (*samnak song*) have been built in Chinese villages across the state and staffed by ethnic Thai and Chinese monks. Although most Kelantanese Chinese villagers worship at shrines (*bio*) dedicated to Taoist deities as well as at Thai temples (*wat*), the Chinese rarely place the same degree of social and ritual obligation on a man's ordination into the Buddhist monkhood as do their Thai neighbors. Many Chinese who do embrace the saffron robes do so for short periods of time—from a few days to a week or month—as part of vow fulfillments (*buad bon*). This is unlike their Thai counterparts, who see ordination as an integral part of ethnic identity consolidation and an important rite of passage for all men. Thai men often do spend a few months in the monkhood, usually during the four-month Theravadin Lenten period. A few Chinese men have, however, remained in the monkhood for long periods of time, with some even succeeding to the abbotship of Thai temples.[4]

Thai monks have always been mobile individuals, a characteristic observed by scholars of Theravadin societies in the Thai world (Tambiah 1970; Davis 2003; Tiyavanich 1997; McDaniel 2008). A number of Kelantanese Thai monks have been regular visitors to Chinese settlements not only in the state but throughout Malaysia, where they are often invited to officiate at funerals, housewarmings, and weddings, embellishing the otherwise Chinese-centric occasion with Thai Theravadin flair. Monk travels increased in frequency and expanded in scope during the fifties and sixties as improvements in road, rail, and, eventually, air transport opened up Kelantan to other parts of Malaysia. It was during this period of heightened mobility that Kelantanese Thai Buddhism was introduced to Chinese urban centers across the Malay peninsula, including Penang, Kuala Lumpur, Johor Bharu, and Singapore, through the auspices of its monk representatives. As more Chinese from beyond Kelantan became aware of the existence of temples in the state, Chinese religious tourism in Kelantan began to boom. It was not long after that certain Kelantanese Thai temples began to encounter a steady influx of Chinese pilgrim-tourists intent on visiting the home ground of the Thai monastic leaders they had met or about whom they had heard miracle stories. Many of these monks were popularly associated with sacred curative powers, divination, and magical amulets, which were much sought after by Chinese devotees and collectors.

Thais also participate in Chinese religious and social activities, although their numbers pale in comparison to the Chinese who attend Thai ritual events. Religious celebrations at Taoist shrines in Bandar Tumpat and Kota Bharu, including the popular birthday celebrations of Kwan Im (Guanyin) and Ma Chor, the southern Chinese goddess of seafarers, attract a number of Thai participants and worshippers. In a less ritualistic setting, the annual Lantern Parade organized by the Tumpat chapter of the Malaysian Chinese Association (MCA), the ethnic Chinese wing of Malaysia's Federal Party, sees a small group of Thai participants each year. The parade begins at the MCA headquarters and Mandarin kindergarten in Bandar Tumpat before snaking its way along the town's main roads. When I took part in the parade in August 2002 it was led by a pickup truck decorated with colorful paper lanterns. Behind the truck walked the kindergarten children and their mothers, all of whom held lit lanterns. The Thai mothers walked with their Thai friends behind the Chinese participants, forming what seemed like an ethnic contingent of sarong-clad women in an otherwise distinctly Chinese event.

The rise in the number of Chinese visitors to Kelantan's Thai temples, coupled with a new money economy and the ethnic agenda of the Malaysian

3.2 Chinese divinity

government since independence, has led to a burst in the building of Chinese-inspired statues and buildings in Thai temple compounds across the Malay state. Kelantan's Thai temples abound with examples of gigantic Chinese religious art. Wat Ban Phai, for instance, has two larger-than-life statues of the Chinese folk divinities Tua Pek Kong and Kwan Im. The figures sit on thrones next to statues of the Thai-Brahmanic deities Phra Phrom (Brahma) and Phra Phikanet (Ganesh).⁵ When I asked him why he had had the Chinese images built, the late abbot of the temple—a Thai man originally from Ban Klang who had spent some time in Singapore—grinned. "It's just for fun," he answered candidly. But the practice of constructing Chinese or at least Chinese-derived images is more than "just for fun." Their visual preeminence on temple grounds raises interesting questions about inter-ethnic encounters along the Malaysian hinterland. The Chinese images draw ethnic Chinese to the Thai village and form social nuclei for new circuits of movement. Each year Wat Khok Phrao and its large Kwan Im statue—the workmanship of Ban Phan Jao's Na Chao Phi—attract a large number of Chinese worshippers from across Kelantan, who come to the temple to celebrate the bodhisattva's birthday with offerings of tall dragon-laced incense sticks and copious food. The ceremony itself is Theravadin in practice, with the temple's monks chanting Pali texts at the base of the statue, but Chinese in its ritual content. Further away, in the temple of Wat Krai in Tanah Merah's tiny Thai settlement of Ban Tha Jang, a colossal statue of Tua Pek Kong gazes down at Thai and Chinese temple-goers from atop his massive red throne. Large statues of Chinese Mahayanist bodhisattvas have also been built in Wat Phra Non. The statues are housed in a brightly painted Chinese pavilion located at one end of the temple's Reclining Buddha. Next to Wat Nai, Wat Nok's pair of cement-molded folk Taoist deities stare silently down upon the mangy dogs and members of Ban Bor On's local soccer league, who work out on the temple's rusty gym equipment stored in a shed near the images. A red roof decorated with sinuous gold dragons protects them from the elements. The painted statues of the bearded Lao Tze and the ever-popular Tua Pek Kong can be seen from both Ban Bor On's main road and the smaller side road winding through Ban Phan Jao. The statues have become synonymous with the temple and their images adorn each side of the temple's Thai-styled gateway.

The story of Wat Nok's statues points to the way Thais manipulate the surge in Chinese interest in their religion in Kelantan to their personal advantage. In Wat Nok's case, the desire for ethnic assertion emerged from moments of social discord in the community. Wat Nok's statues were commissioned some fifteen years ago by a group of Ban Bor On residents who had become enraged at Wat Nai's abbot for having smashed a large cement phallus (*eh khlik*) that they had built in a shady corner of the temple. Earlier the villagers, led by Tok Mo Dam, had asked Na Chao Phi to erect a pair of male and female genitalia in Wat Nai's cemetery. Sacred phalluses in the form of the erect penis are supposed to have magical properties and to bring luck to their worshippers. But Tok Nai Suk was opposed to having sexually explicit images in the temple despite their associations with popular Brahmanism in Thailand. Over coffee one morning, the headman boomed angrily as he recalled what had transpired:

> Some villagers had seen phalluses [he used the crude term *koedo* rather than the more polite *eh khlik* to refer to these sacred genitalia] in Thailand. They believed that these *koedo* had the property to grant winning lottery numbers. This was a craze that was sweeping through the different temples in Kelantan, with many of them constructing their own phallus statues. But when you make a *koedo*, you also have to make a vagina [*hee*]! So they made both! Chao Phi was the person who made them. They did not ask the temple's permission but instead built them in the cemetery. When Pho Than Di found out about this, he was very angry and smashed them to bits. This irked the villagers, who went on to build the Tua Pek Kong statue at Wat Nok.

Hence the building of Chinese statues was a reaction asserting the views of certain individuals in the village of what temple space meant according to ethnic trajectories. The phallus was a Thai form but its erotic public visuality meant that the community could be seen as marginalizing itself even more from mainstream Malaysian society. It was sacred, but embarrassing and disturbing to many—Thais and visitors alike. Angered by the destruction of the phalluses, Tok Mo Dam had Na Chao Phi build the Chinese images in Wat Nok, stirring even greater controversy in the village.

Writing at a time before the spate of monumental constructions began in the late seventies and early eighties, neither Kershaw (1969) nor Golomb (1978) emphasized the agentive role Thais played in a national environment marked by policies of Malay privilege. Subsequent works by Mohamed (1993a, 1993b) similarly failed to acknowledge the presence of large Thai and Chinese structures within the confines of national and indigenous landscapes. This seeming lack of scholarly discussion on the poetics of mega projects has proven to be a conundrum in Kelantanese Thai studies. Statues as public displays of an indigenous material creativity make visible Kelantan's Thai Buddhist community by placing the once socially invisible group in full public view. Building big legitimizes the community's claims to locatedness on a grand scale. But the new patterns and practices of mobility that emerge around the statues force Thais to think through what local histories and ethnic identities mean in modern times.

Per capita incomes have risen across Malaysia since the fifties, so that Kelantan's Thai temples now receive larger financial contributions from well-wishers. Mohamed's (2000) observations on the capitalist management of ethnicity in Kelantan's Thai temples reflected a general complaint I heard from some of my Thai friends in Ban Bor On and other villages. Simply put, temple abbots embark on projects to build Chinese sculptures so as to attract Chinese tourists and pilgrims to their temples. Ethnic Chinese in general—but especially those from large urban centers—are believed by many Thais to be financially better off than they, often donating substantial amounts of money to the temples during their visits. Temples also secure "Chinese money" from other ethnicity-based sources, including community and religious organizations and Chinese political associations. In particular, the Malaysian Chinese Association has been an important contributor to big and small construction projects in Thai temples. The association poured in large amounts of money to help finance the building of Wat Kao's gateway and the Chinese-style Wat Klang Buddha.[6] MCA funds also supported the creation of the tarred driveway that slices through Wat Nok's otherwise sandy courtyard and links it with Ban Bor On's trunk road. Excess money from these donations is channeled into social welfare projects for the Thai community such as the maintenance of temple schools, or deposited into the temple's bank account for subsequent building activities.

Khun Di told me that he was opposed to the idea of spending thousands (and in the case of the Wat Klang and Wat Nak statues, millions) of Malaysian ringgit on building statues. His opinion represented a general discontent I had heard expressed by many Kelantanese villagers, who viewed the impressive projects as a waste of a precious financial resource. "Instead of building large statues, abbots should use the money to build people (*sang khon*)," voiced Pho Than Num, Wat Bang Rim Nam's abbot. In 2002, at the age of forty-nine, Pho Than Num was one of the youngest and most vocal abbots in Kelantan. Born into a family of farmers in the adjacent village of Thung Kha, he had been educated in Buddhist philosophy in India and Sri Lanka and was conversant in Thai, English, Malay, and Hokkien, which helped him interact with the many Chinese devotees who visited his temple. Unlike other abbots, Pho Than Num was fervently opposed to large construction projects. To him, money was put to better use when it was used for the social enhancement of the Thai community. He suggested to me that abbots should use the money for purchasing textbooks for their villages' Thai students, providing educational bursaries for needy students, or building soccer fields for the village youths so that they would not spend their time idling

3.3 Chinese guests of honor at a Thai Buddhist ceremony

in coffeeshops and rest pavilions. Idleness, the abbot reminded me, besides being frowned upon in Buddhist standards of behavior, could lead to the social ills of alcoholism, smoking, and drug abuse in what was already a small community. At the same time, Pho Than Num feared that Kelantanese Thai youths who were unfamiliar with Buddhist doctrinal teachings would be easy targets for conversions to Islam. Education was the key to the betterment of Thai society, he reiterated time and again. From his personal coffers, he presented prize money to Kelantanese Thai students who had performed well in Malaysia's national exams, always encouraging them to go further in their studies and never give up. Pho Than Num often complained about how his radical idea of not building did not go down well with more senior members of the clergy. Pointing to Wat Bang Rim Nam's gateway, which had cost the temple RM140,000 (US$39,716), Lung Nit, an elderly man from Bang Rim Nam, said to me, "people respect a monk who can build." But respect (*nab thue*) was often mixed in with stinging criticisms.

Khun Di provided an interesting observation on why some abbots are preoccupied with building enormous structures in their temples. Many abbots, he argued, embark on these large and expensive projects out of a desire to publicly and visually exhibit their superior store of merit (*bun*). In so doing, they prove to themselves and the community around them that they are legitimate monastic heads. In theory, Khun Di noted, Buddhism does not require followers to show off their material wealth as a sign of merit. But many of these men, despite their religious positions as temple abbots, have only a rudimentary knowledge of Buddhist teachings (*thamma*), and for them building is a way to justify and perform their social and ritual role. Monks who do not build are often gossiped about by villagers for being stingy and hoarding the large financial donations they receive. What is more, promotions within the national Thai ecclesiastical hierarchy, of which Kelantan's Buddhist establishment is a part, are also based on the impressiveness of one's construction records. Senior *pho than* create material legacies of themselves through the large structures they build. The statues show that monks are actively working toward the development of their temples and not merely siphoning off donations. The more spectacular the statue or monument, the more legitimate the monk's position as a member of the Thai monastic elite.

Even after his death, the abbot's life would be celebrated in the glossy colored photographs of his architectural achievements printed in the pages of magazine-like funeral volumes (*nangsue anuson*). These souvenir booklets, composed in Thai and Malay, contain the monk's biography, condolence messages from his senior monastic acquaintances, and often a collection of short Buddhist ritual verses or discourses. They are distributed free of charge to everyone who attended the monk's cremation rites. In short, statues and buildings are a testimony to not only the abbot's illustrious life and his superior store of merit but also to ethnic economics and its associations with Malaysian national politics. Nowhere was this more evident than in the recent funeral volume of Pho Than Dam, the late abbot of Wat Din Sung.

Pho Than Dam passed away in 2003 at the age of seventy-six after having spent fifty-five years in the monkhood. During his lifetime, the heavy-set man amassed many friends, a large number of whom were wealthy ethnic Chinese from Kuala Lumpur and other urban centers in Malaysia. Many were attracted to the monk's reputed skills in magical Buddhism. Pho Than Dam was a virtuoso in the arts of herbal medicine, astrology, and meditation. Unlike those of most monks, Pho Than Dam's body was not cremated. Instead, it was carefully preserved and ceremoniously laid to rest in a glass coffin in one of the many beautiful buildings he had constructed. The funeral volumes that were distributed at his funerary internment in 2008 celebrated Pho Than Dam's illustrious life through building as well as his close association with his family and a certain Tauke Teck, the Chinese philanthropist and devotee whose financial contributions to the temple helped the abbot build many of Wat Din Sung's monuments. Pho Than Dam's building projects were listed with accompanying black-and-white photographs in five pages of the fifty-six-page volume. The volume's cover bears a black-and-white photograph of the elderly monk sitting in meditation, staring silently at the camera. Behind the gray image looms one of the abbot's most beautiful creations—the *mondop*, an open-walled pavilion crowned with an elaborate spire of gold mosaics and intricate Thai stucco patterns. The building set against the light blue Kelantanese sky frames the monk's portrait as if linking the abbot with his building projects. The book ends with a series of photographs of the Thai and Chinese members of Wat Din Sung's temple committee.

The abbot's life is memorialized through his material accomplishments. The funeral volume's unnamed author carefully lists the various buildings that form evidence of the late abbot's active involvement in the development (*kan phathana*) of Wat Din Sung. A Malay translation of the abbot's biography, including the list of buildings he constructed during his tenure as abbot, is provided in the booklet, possibly directed at Chinese readers who do not comprehend Thai. The Malay text carries with it a list of both material and non-material accomplishments the monk was credited with. These include establishing a Thai language school in Din Sung and initiating Thailand's national celebrations of Songkran (Thai New Year) and Loy Krathong in the village. The biographer also writes about how Pho Than Dam had organized many religious tours across Malaysia and Thailand for his devotees. He set up a shelter in his temple for the mentally and physically infirm. And for those in need of sauna therapy, whereby traditional herbs were used in generating healing fumes, the monk built steam rooms. His accomplishments also included the construction of a special bath area for devotees who wished to have the monk administer magical baths by pouring sacral water over their heads while reciting Pali incantations.

Massive structures such as Pho Than Dam's famed "Dragon Boat" (officially inaugurated in 1984, according to the cremation volume) and Wat Phra Non's Reclining Buddha drew abbots, their temples, and the community into the direct gaze of the state. Statues of immense Chinese divinities and Thai-style Buddhas were conduits through which the Malaysian nation-state, with its varied discourses of patriotism and ethnic classification, filtered into the everyday lives of Thai villagers. Since the violent events of 11 September 2001, the statues have again taken on new meanings. Their immensity has not only brought fame and renown to Kelantan's Thai population but also forced many Kelantanese Thais to reflect on the narratives of fear, ethnic distrust, and religious uncertainty that circulate when a Buddhist statue looms large in a village surrounded by Muslim neighbors. In Kelantan, the Buddha has his feet firmly on Mecca's Verandah, which could prove frightening to a people used to watching scenes of global destruction on television and associating it with a new discourse of Islamophobia. Nevertheless, Kelantan, like Mecca, has traditionally been culturally cosmopolitan. Its population has historically been ethnically diverse. The small border town of Bandar Tumpat, for instance, was once home to Tamils, Chinese, Thais, Malays, Sikhs, Sinhalese, Javanese, and many more. Religious meaning in this plural landscape structured mobile processes and forged real and ideological links among the different groups. It was within this intimate space of cross-cultural encounter between Thai Buddhists and non-Thais that Thainess powerfully asserted itself.

Tok Nai Suk was opposed to the construction of Chinese religious figures in Thai temples. To him, Thai temples were sacred spaces of Thainess where Thai Theravada Buddhism flourished. Therefore, the statues that abbots construct within the perimeters of their temple walls should be Buddhist and not derived from a non-Buddhist Chinese pantheon. "If the Chinese wanted to worship their gods, they would not come to a Thai temple. They have their own shrines [bio] in Kota Bharu," he laughed, adding with a hint of sarcasm, "[The Chinese] come here to worship the Buddha. Some people just don't seem to understand this," in obvious reference to the many abbots who had Chinese-type statues built on their temple grounds. Although Tok Nai Suk was against the idea of building Chinese icons in Thai temples, he was more tolerant of the construction of Mahayanist figures such as those of the Bodhisattva Maitreya and the white-robed Kwan Im. These, he said, were actually Buddhist images regardless of their artistic trappings.

Speaking of the history behind Wat Nok's pair of gigantic Chinese statues that had led to factionalism within the Ban Bor On community between the supporters of Tok Mo Dam and himself, Tok Nai Suk reflected matter-of-factly:

> [Tok Mo Dam and his friends] said they wanted to attract the Chinese into the temple [by building the statues]. But the temple [Wat Nok] is a Thai temple. The architecture and statues in here should be Thai and Buddhist. I suggested that if

they wanted to construct a Chinese statue, they should make one of Phra Si Ariya Metrai [Maitreya], the future Buddha. Khok Phrao's temple has already constructed a Kwan Im statue. But they went ahead and made the Tua Pek Kong figure!

Mohamed (1995: 6) pointed out that although many Thai temples in Kelantan had large Chinese statues built on their premises, they were more often than not confined to the less sacred precincts in the temple. These included the areas around the periphery of the ordination chapel and its far and less-visited corners. Thus, the statues do not contest the sacred topography of the Thai-centered ritual universe (such as the ordination chapel, preaching halls, and abbot's quarters) where the most important Buddhist ceremonies are held. These Thai-style buildings with their gabled roofs and traditional Thai material accents of wood and stucco ensure an exclusive Thai cultural preeminence in the temple space. This makes certain that the temple continues to be a Thai Buddhist social and ritual arena while capitalizing on Chinese monetary support through the outward displays of aesthetic Sinicization.

But not all Chinese statues are positioned in the nooks and crannies outside of sacred Thai space. What Mohamed failed to realize was that large statues often create new sacred geographies. This is especially the case with large Buddha statues that have become ritual centers for ceremonies and public events. The statues are now prominent markers of temple identity to such an extent that Wat Klang has commissioned T-shirts with the Buddha image printed on the front and Wat Nai has incorporated its famed Standing Buddha on all temple seals. Large statues such as these have expanded the generalized domain of sacred space, providing increased opportunities for interethnic encountering between local Thai and Chinese temple-goers through a novel geography of sacred gigantism. These images mark out the perimeters of an alternate ritual space that is patterned upon ethnic management.

On 16 September 2001, the Sitting Buddha at Wat Klang, one of Ban Klang's three temples, was officially inaugurated by senior monks from Bangkok and honored guests from the Royal Thai Consulate in Kota Bharu. The abbot who ordered the construction of the 98-feet-high by 154-feet-wide Sitting Buddha at a cost of some RM 4 million (US $1.1 million) had come under heavy criticism from certain segments of Kelantan's Thai population. The Buddha was built under the supervision of the talented Chao Jim, but it adhered to a prototypical Chinese style; some argue it was a Japanese artistic model that had been syncretized with Thai design accents. The image was sheeted with thousands of brown mosaics, except for the statue's lips, which were plated with bright yellow gold. The week-long festivities at the Ban Klang temple culminated in the placing of a Buddha relic, obtained by the temple's abbot from Sri Lanka, into the statue's massive chest. Thousands of people attended the event and Ban Bor On villagers continued to talk about it for many months afterward.

What was especially disturbing to some of the Thais I spoke with—and something not mentioned in earlier works on Thai-Chinese ritual association in Kelantan (e.g., Kershaw 1973, 1981; Golomb 1978; Mohamed 1993a, 1993b)— was how people talked about this inter-ethnic relationship. Ban Klang does not support a large Chinese population, unlike some other Thai villages. The temple at Ban Jin, richly described by Loo Heng Ann (2003) in his academic exercise, was built in a village comprising a mixed population of both Thai and Chinese residents. Thus, villagers were more accepting of the fact that Wat Nak's Thai-citizen abbot had surrounded his temple with a wall in the shape of two Chinese dragons and had built numerous Chinese-style buildings and statues on the premises. In Wat Klang, the central figure and the surrounding pavilions, statues, fountains, and dragon-laced pillars resemble icons pulled straight out of Chinese mythology. I had heard some Thais refer to Wat Klang as *wat jin* (Chinese temple), a tongue-in-cheek jab at the lack of Thai visual forms on display in the temple. To them, Wat Klang is what a Thai temple should not be; its monumentality and preoccupation with securing Chinese capital had overstepped cultural bounds and the village's Thai space had been compromised. Instead of being a privileged arena where Thainess was celebrated through the temple's visual monumentality and its associations with national Thai Buddhist art, Wat Klang's distinct Chinese-inspired religious landscape has led to popular discontent. The statue was built in the middle of the temple grounds and its sheer size overpowers the visual form of much older Thai-style buildings such as the ordination hall. Many villagers were of the opinion that Thais were now being treated as second-class temple-goers in a temple that was situated in the heart of a large and ethnically homogenous Thai community.

Mae Iam was disheartened about the transformations in ethnic space in Thai temples that had constructed enormous Chinese statues and buildings. Speaking of the reorganization of space that attended the construction of Wat Klang's Sitting Buddha, she grumbled, "The Thais [now] only work in the [temple] kitchen. Even beneath the large Buddha, Thai statues [*phra thai*] have been placed behind the Chinese ones. Take a look for yourself." The statue both called attention to Ban Klang as an ethnic Thai enclave and placed the temple on the national tourist map. But the process of publicly highlighting the community had made the very people who lived there feel increasingly invisible.

In the hushed tones typically reserved for gossip, Ban Bor On villagers revealed to me that urban Chinese had monopolized the running of Wat Klang's internal affairs by entering into its administrative body (*kammakan*) and slyly removing social power from the old Thai abbot and his monks.[7] Even the keys to the temple's coffers were believed by some to be in the hands of the Chinese. "Nowadays if Ban Klang residents want to borrow dishes and utensils for their celebrations, they have to ask for the keys to the temple's storeroom from the Chinese caretaker. Everything has to be done through him," complained one angry Ban Bor On resident, referring to the common practice of Thai households obtaining dishes, chairs, tents, glasses, and stoves from their local temples for communal celebrations.

Thais marginalized themselves through materializing spectacular non-Thai worlds in their temples. They redrew the symbolic boundaries of their community in their attempts to assert a sense of public Thainess through expressions of creative agency. The thing that bothered many of my friends the most was that the statues were not built by Chinese architects or paid for entirely with Chinese money. They were constructed by local Thai abbots in collaboration with Thai village artisans like Chao Jim and Na Chao Phi, who worked for a fee. The high financial outlay of building statues is paid for with money obtained through donations from Thai and Chinese alike. Even though they are against the idea of Chinese statues in their villages, many Thais continue to support their temples with generous monetary contributions as part of merit-making practices. Money donated to a temple brings one merit. How the money is to be spent is up to the abbot. In order to tap into the popular myth of a burgeoning Malaysian Chinese economy, some Kelantanese Thai abbots had, in effect, compromised on their villages' ethnic and cultural identities. With bitter disdain in their voices, my Ban Bor On friends complained that during the September celebrations, Ban Klang's Thai population was nowhere to be seen, having been relegated to hard kitchen work while Mandarin- and Cantonese-speaking Chinese appeared to have taken over the actual running of the event. The loud public announcements that defined Wat Klang's aural environment and feature prominently in all temple festivals in Kelantan and Thailand were delivered in a combination of Thai and Chinese dialects. Many Thais were dismayed that they could not read any of the articles in the temple's free commemorative booklet, which had been compiled in Chinese. Even the glossy pictures of members of the temple's steering committee were of unfamiliar Chinese faces. "Where are the Thais?" they asked rhetorically. The plywood signboards placed around the temple were also written only in Chinese, making the experience of attending a Thai temple festival a confusing and frustrating one for many non-Chinese villagers.[8]

Monuments and Ethnic History

Kelantanese Thai social actors constantly poked fun at their community's greed at soliciting temple donations from Chinese sponsors and political organizations by producing Chinese or Chinese-style statues in their temples. This, according to them, has resulted in the forced compromise of their moral universe. Although building big has been a traditional practice in much of Theravadin Southeast Asia, what was new in Kelantan was the Sinic aesthetics these mega creations now took. Villagers often referred to the past as a time before the politics of ethnic capitalism affected the community. "In the past, the Chinese did not really enter temples. It is only now that they have started coming," Pa Wit, a sixty-seven-year-old Thai woman who lived in a small shack in Bandar Tumpat, told me. This indigenous periodization of history based on materiality, morality, and ethnic movement was not associated with a particular chronological period. With its multiple and crisscrossing historical referents, the past remained embedded in the popular imagination as something to ruminate over. People spoke about it constantly; they compared the past with the present and moralized its temporality. Sometimes the past was seen as a time of criminality and violence, at other times it was one of ethnic harmony and trust.[9] The imagined past was an element of the village's "structural nostalgia," in which an Edenic order legitimized present-day insecurities, sadness, and happiness (Herzfeld 1997).

One version of the past constructs it as a time of "balanced" social relations among Kelantan's various ethnic groups. Chinese, Thais, Malays, and others worked together in what seemed like Edenic harmony. In Kae Chi's earlier tale, the primordial Thai were siblings with Malays and Chinese. Each individual worked within a distinct occupational niche. Chinese lived and worked in the towns and markets, Malays in fishing, and Thais in the rice fields. This structurally nostalgic feeling has been replaced by the newfound ethnic greed that seems to influence the way temples create their visual appearance. Greed, like modernity's henchmen, the AIDS virus, narcotics, terrorists, racism, and immoral monks, is seen as originating from beyond the village's borders. It is something alien to the everyday lives of villagers that has filtered into the space of the village through the newfound religious materiality. Greed brings about the social degeneracy that some villagers believe characterizes many aspects of contemporary Kelantanese Thai life. But this new desire for securing Chinese capital has symbolically expanded the boundaries of the village. Statues, despite being visual sites of locatedness, are nodes in a moving landscape of men and women, pilgrims and tourists, monks and laypeople. They tie the community to much larger categories of cultural and political identification. No longer is the village a self-contained ethnic unit as it was in the stories people told of the past. It is now part of a perplexing array of local and global flows of people, ideologies, histories, and economies that move beyond simple, clear-cut markers of ethnic distinctiveness.

In spite of the negative reaction from some social actors to the Sinicization of village and temple space and corresponding feelings of self-marginalization, the building of Chinese structures display Thai agency and creative genius at their finest. Even though they complained about social invisibility in their own temples, many Thai villagers were quick to point out that Thais continue to have the upper hand in the inter-ethnic game. Thais are not the defenseless pawns of the Chinese, as it may have seemed from first observations, but they have cleverly manipulated the situation to their advantage. They derive large sums of money from the Chinese. As Khun Rien mentioned in jest and with a sly twinkle in his eye, "the more statues one builds in the temple, the greater the flow of Chinese money into Thai coffers."

Notwithstanding their contested meanings — sometimes positive, sometimes negative — monumental projects such as Wat Phra Nok's and Wat Klang's statues are often spoken of by Kelantanese Thais as new visual reminders of their rooted presence in a non-Thai cultural landscape. They proudly point them out to tourists as "must-see" places on the Kelantanese visitor's map but criticize the statues when out of earshot of their guests. Statues and buildings force local actors to engage with a wider society beyond the Thai village. Aesthetic forms may be based on models derived from Thai art manuals bought in Thailand by people like Chao Jim, or based on Chinese images. Wat Nok's Tua Pek Kong figure, for example, was modeled upon a much smaller Chinese porcelain figure of the same deity. Some structures, such as the pavilions in Wat Din Sung, were built by hired artisans from across the border. These artisans were popular with some temple abbots, as Thai citizens often charged lower fees than their

Malaysian counterparts. The intricate stucco and cement reliefs that adorn large monuments also require villagers to make regular trips to Thailand to purchase paint, gold leaf, mirror mosaics, and other materials needed in the production of contemporary temple art, even if it was built according to a Chinese design. Thailand has developed temple construction into a lucrative industry and specific varieties of bright emulsion paints, tiles, and colored glass used in temple work are easily available at hardware stores in Thailand's larger towns. Na Chao Phi only used paints produced in Thailand for his projects. He pointed out that these paints were cheaper and less of an economic burden on already tight temple budgets when bulk quantities were required. Emulsion paints manufactured in Thailand for the purposes of religious architecture are also much brighter than Malaysian-made paints, which were developed for secular use. The statues, situated images of Thai Buddhist cultural status, force movement to occur beyond the borders of the state. Thailand has become a site not only for artistic inspiration but for materializing a cultural inspiration.

Contemporary Kelantanese Thai-type built structures, such as Wat Nai's Walking Buddha, Wat Bot Ngam's ordination hall, and Wat Ban Kao's three-entrance doorway, derive their artistic inspiration from the tenets of classical central Thai art, adhering to a national Thai aesthetic of traditional architecture that is found throughout the kingdom. By building impressive structures that look like they might have come straight out of a Thai art manual bought in Bangkok, Kelantan's Thai population bridges itself with Thailand's national Buddhist culture. As part of this larger "imagined community" (Anderson 1983) of Thai Buddhists—manifest in the standardization of aesthetic principles supplied by Bangkok's Fine Arts Department—Ban Bor On's inhabitants manipulate feelings of cultural marginality in a Malay state and they reassert their cultural affinity to Thailand. Through sharing a common aesthetic tradition, albeit one that was "invented" (Hobsbawm 1983) based on central Thailand's standardized "high" art, Kelantanese Thais place themselves on par with their Thai citizen cousins. They are no longer Thailand's diasporic "lost sheep," living on the furthest peripheries of a geopolitical nation that Thai bureaucrats find so fascinating. Rather, the community is very much at the heart of things. Civilization in this instance is no longer restricted to centers of national power where reified readings of culture are produced via elite narratives, but instead includes the silent and invisible hinterlands that ape them. But this attempt at mimicry remains largely on the level of material representation. And even this is not without its detractors. Not everyone agrees with the form that statues and buildings take, even if the latter are built according to classical Thai artistic tenets. There is always contestation. The meanings these statues and monuments carry for their builders and observers are cloaked within Kelantanese Thai experiences of particular moments in Malaysian history.

Historical Legacies

The Malaysian government's desire to invent an overarching national identity for its citizens emerged from the ashes of communal riots that left a seething scar on the country's fragile ethnic dynamics. The bloody clashes in Kuala Lumpur on 13 May 1969 between the city's Chinese and Malay inhabitants were a consequence of general elections that had been fraught with accusations of racial politics and unequal privilege. The riots were the apex of what had been a post-independence political climate of Malay chauvinism and class and socio-economic tensions. Earlier socio-demographic policies of British colonialism had compartmentalized Malaya's population along biologically defined racial lines, each with its own residential, economic, and cultural spaces. According to this logic of imperialism, Malays were imagined by the state's administrators as simple agriculturalists and fisherfolk and hence as the primary food providers for the colony. The Chinese were primarily coolies and town-dwellers, and the Tamil largely urban laborers and plantation workers. Religion was intimately associated with ethnicity, and Islam became the rallying cry around which Malay nationalism was bred and continued to develop after the Second World War (Lee and Ackerman 1988). The 1969 riots pointed to the tensions that lay beneath the seeming calm of ethnic and religious pluralism. The immediate aftermath of the riots was a period in Malaysian political history in which the country's Malay bureaucratic elite worked to forge a common culture that would unite all ethnic groups while maintaining Malay constitutional privilege.

In line with this attempt to manufacture culture, the Malaysian Ministry of Culture, Youth, and Sports in 1971 organized a congress on national culture for some 1,000 delegates, the majority of whom were Malay intellectuals and politicians (Gomes 1999; Carstens 2005; Kua 2005). Held at Malaysia's prestigious Universiti Malaya and officially opened by the then Prime Minister Tun Abdul Razak, congress participants presented some sixty papers relating to the issue of what constituted national culture. The outcome of the debates was the advocation of a common "Malaysian culture" called the National Culture Policy (NCP) that aimed to override ethnic particularism and feelings of disgruntlement by non-Malay, non-Muslim communities — indirectly targeting Chinese complaints about Malay privilege while ensuring Malay class and ethnic centrality in the new nation-state. But despite its grand agenda, the NCP remained highly Malay Muslim–centric and was structured upon an assimilationist discourse of indigenism (*bumiputera*-ism) that continued to disregard the cultural agency of Chinese, Indian, and other so-called "non-indigenous" Malaysian groups and to be the source of non-Malay frustrations (Goh 2002). Still suffering from the poignant memory of the 1969 riots, elite Malay proponents of the NCP were apprehensive about creating too large a space for overt non-Malay and, in particular, Chinese, assertions of identity. To these government bureaucrats, the Chinese — by virtue of their large numbers, recent immigrant history, economic clout, and presumed nostalgic sentiments for China and Mao's communist legacy — were still looked upon with a certain degree of suspicion and their true patriotism to the fledgling Malay-run Malaysia was called into question. Hence, aspects of Chinese culture were not taken to be a part of the NCP's definition of "Malaysian culture." Anti-Chinese sentiments in the National Culture Policy included a restriction on the use of Chinese characters on public billboards and signs and even an attempt to "modify" the Chinese Lion Dance so as to incorporate Malay and Indian aesthetic elements into the otherwise distinctively Chinese dramatic form (Gomes 1999: 91; Carstens 2005: 167–69). Its close affiliations with Malayness meant that the NCP could not divorce itself from the rhetoric of Islam, since to be Malay was to be Muslim according to the nation's colonial-inspired constitution. Thus the privileging of Malay culture and ethnicity meant a similar bias toward Islam. Writing about the NCP's pro-Islamic policies, Alberto Gomes noted that

> non-Muslims have complained of the difficulty and frustration in obtaining building permits for their temples and churches, the harassment of foreign non-Muslim priests by the bureaucracy especially the Immigration Department, the removal of crosses in mission schools, and the distorted write-ups of religion other than Islam in school textbooks. (Gomes 1999: 92)

Although never explicitly documented, it is plausible that because the pro-Malay, pro-Islam flavor of the NCP discouraged many a Chinese cultural form, Kelantanese and other Malaysian Chinese had to look to other non-national spaces to freely express their cultural and religious agency. In Kelantan, this was to be found in the sandy precincts of Thai temples. Thais, unlike the urban Mandarin- and English-educated Kuala Lumpur Chinese, had not been participants in the 1969 clashes, and their rural and non-partisan lifestyles, social invisibility, and smallness of numbers did not constitute a threat to Malaysia's ethnic discourse of *bumiputera*-ism. For the most part, Kelantan's Thai community was of no overt risk to Kuala Lumpur's Malay political elite. They lived in villages far from urban centers, pursuing agricultural lifeways in Malaysia's most distant hinterlands. Thais and Malays, despite the occasional ethnic flare-ups, had been historically involved in each other's communities. Even the communist menace which had plagued the postwar government in the late 1940s and 1950s was not strongly felt in the Malay state. Communist activities and rural banditry did occur, albeit on a small scale, and they were largely confined to the Hakka-speaking Chinese centers in the Ulu (Ho 2007). In addition, the Kelantanese sultan had historically cemented the strong social bond between the Thai and the Malay. He has traditionally been the ritual patron of all Thai monks in the state and a personal friend of the most senior abbots. Kelantanese Thai villagers are well aware of their clergy's close affiliations with the Malay court and speak with pride of their close associations with the powerhouse of Malay culture in Kelantan. Kelantan's Thai temples therefore proved to be safe havens for Chinese articulations of cultural identity. Even less politically threatening was the fact that the statues were being built by Thai village artisans rather than by Chinese labor. Symbolically, then, the Chinese were not the ones producing visual displays of *Chineseness* and therefore their statues and buildings did not challenge the NCP's rulings.

Historically, all of Kelantan's Thai temples were built on state-recognized "temple land" (*tanah ketik*), although most temples do not have land grants (*gerang*) of formal titleship.[10] Temple lands were traditionally bequeathed (*diwakafkan*) by a ruler or some other member of local Malay nobility for public or religious use before British surveying in the 1930s made mapped land grants a necessary symbol of land ownership. Not all the lands owned by a temple, or, as was more often the case, donated to an abbot, were sites of monastic construction. Many temples owned plots in what are today Malay settlements. Sometimes these plots were used for the cultivation of crops like coconut and palms to be used for food and building needs. Land, given to abbots as gifts, could subsequently be leased out for cultivation to Thai and Malay villagers, who then paid a small sum in rent to the temple's abbot.

The traditional system of presenting Thai abbots with tracts of land for religious use has, however, resulted in the unexpected fear that without grants to demarcate temple space, the lands could eventually be absorbed by the state government as part of future development schemes. Presently, temple lands are free from state interference. Temple abbots exercise the freedom to build whatever they desire without having to seek formal approval from governmental bodies as long as the structures are built on stipulated "temple land." All that is required is that, in the case of large buildings, their architectural blueprints are sent to the state's building authorities so as to ensure that a standard of engineering safety is adhered to. In many cases, even this is overlooked through a generalized neglect of what are believed to be less important government regulations. Thai temples with their Chinese construction projects were thus spared the Islamic/Malay flavor that blanketed the NCP in the seventies and that proved to be a major source of discontent for many non-Muslims living in the country's west coast states.

The Kelantan government's historical non-interference in Thai temple affairs has won Thai votes for the current Islamic administration. During the period prior to the national elections of March 2008, many Kelantanese Thai supporters of the opposition Islamic party (PAS) pointed to the freedom to build as a sign of the party's benign rule. Barisan Nasional, Malaysia's federal party, despite its secular platform, was believed to be more particular about displays of non-Muslim religiosity, as it attempted to gather Malay popular support for its policies by using the opposition's language of Islam. To win Malay votes in Kelantan, the party had to construct itself as staunchly Islamic, perhaps even more so than PAS's theologian politicians. Some Thais cited the 2006 and 2007 destruction of Hindu shrines in the state of Selangor by Malaysian government forces as an example of the national government's religious intolerance of the country's non-Muslim minority. The fact that the shrines were supposedly built illegally on government and private lands was inconsequential. The destruction was evidence of a Muslim state forcing itself on its non-Muslim subjects. Khun Rien, a keen supporter of the Islamic opposition who had once dreamt of becoming a politician, showed me an online video of a Thai monk's residence being razed by government bulldozers in the west coast state of Malacca.[11] The monks who had set up the residence had supposedly broken state law by constructing the place of worship without seeking official approval. The six-minute clip included powerful scenes of the destruction of the building, including the smashing of its cement reclining Buddha with power drills and the wrecking of the residence's two large bronze Buddha statues with bulldozers. Set to the accompaniment of haunting music, the video showed the extent of a non-Buddhist state's hegemony over its minority citizens.

Members of the Islamic front, PAS, helmed by local Kelantanese, are believed by many Thais to be less "arrogant" (*kong*) than representatives of Barisan Nasional, and such severe acts of religious intolerance are unimaginable in Kelantan. The state's respected Islamic scholar and chief minister, Datuk Nik Aziz Nik Mat, himself a Kelantanese, is viewed by PAS supporters to be a friend of the Thai community. He is often seen officiating at important temple functions, mingling with the Thai community, and speaking in the Kelantanese Malay dialect, an act that won him local votes based on the shared cultural and linguistic intimacy of being fellow marginals in Malaysia. White-turbaned and sporting a grayed goatee, Nik Aziz is both respected and feared by his Thai supporters. He is admired for his simple lifestyle and the unassuming demeanor with which he freely interacts with members of the Kelantanese public. He is friendly and gracious to the monks and villagers. In his speeches and political rallies he promises the Thais that they can build whatever they want in their temples. Yet he is feared in the light of an increasing Islamic fundamentalist presence in Kelantan. Some of my friends remarked on the uncertainty of the future; PAS was, at the end of the day, an Islamic party with a strong Malay support base and it was probable that Islam and Malayness would be brought to the fore in governmental policy making should the party come into increasing national prominence. How this would affect the Thais remains to be seen. My friends spoke of how there was uncertainty in Kelantan. Temples without official documents of land occupancy could succumb to the state's forceful eviction anytime—as the Malaccan video and stories of Hindu shrine demolition so poignantly demonstrate. But this risk is impossible to assess. In the meantime many Thais continue to vote PAS into power, all the while smiling at Nik Aziz's assertions of ethnic camaraderie.

The failure of the NCP to create a modern Malaysian culture that overrode ethnic particularisms gave way to a more generic sense of patriotism and national willpower. Within the last ten years, Malaysians have embarked on a number of local and international record-setting feats. Prime Minister Mahathir Mohamad's 1991 project of Wawasan 2020 (Vision 2020) was a political and economic vision that set out to make Malaysia a fully industrialized nation-state by the year 2020, with a citizenry sharing belief in a common Malaysian "nation/race" (*bangsa Malaysia*). This was associated with the national slogan of *Malaysia Boleh*—Malaysia(ns) Can Do It. *Malaysia Boleh* was a political imagery that attempted to foster patriotism and national identity among the country's ethnically and economically diverse citizens, not through the forced and arti-ficial construction of a common culture but through the glorification of large and small achievements. By boasting international and national records, both manmade and natural, Malaysia's political elites hoped to convince the world, as well as their own citizens, that despite the country's third-world status, Malaysia was special. Malaysians were a determined lot and when they put their hearts and minds to it, they placed their country on a par with, if not over and beyond, more developed countries (Goh 2002: 53).

The slogan of *Malaysia Boleh* visualized the country on a global map of spectacular achievements. This was a narrative focused around the celebration of bests and a culture of firsts. But it was not restricted to merely material record-breaking feats. Malaysia proudly reinforced the perimeters of its natural biodi-versity by claiming to have the world's smallest shrew, the largest flower, and the largest cave chamber. On the material level, Malaysians built the longest bridge in Asia and constructed what was then the world's tallest building, the Petronas Twin Towers. These record-setting mega-projects displayed a new materialist and developmentalist orientation in the Malaysian economy.

On the social level, Malaysians of different ethnicities set their own records. They scaled Mount Everest, pulled trains with their teeth, lived in boxes filled with poisonous snakes, and became astronauts. In July 2001, a Kelantanese woman set a world record by staying in a scorpion-filled glass cage for thirty days. Other records Malaysians set included having the world's tallest pencil, hosting the longest variety show in the country, planting the most trees in a minute, and shampooing the most heads in a shopping mall. These achievements were lauded by the state even though some Malaysians laughed at what seemed like a ridiculous celebration of "anything goes." All records and achievements were meticulously listed in the *Malaysia Book of Records*, a local version of the *Guinness Book of World Records* first published in 1995. The record-setting social environment that was *Malaysia Boleh* spurred a television series, also named the *Malaysia Book of Records*, that debuted two years before the book's first edition was published. Two Kelantanese Thai temples have made it into the most recent edition of the book (2008). Wat Klang's Sitting Buddha is featured as the coun-try's "Biggest Sitting Buddha Statue" and Wat Phra Non's reclining statue as the "Largest Reclining Buddha" (*Malaysia Book of Records* 2008: 134).[12]

Even though a large number of Kelantan's monumental Buddhist works were built some years before the Vision 2020 plan, the trickle-down effects of the rhetoric on the way Kelantanese Thai villagers perceive their creations cannot be denied. National jingles and political speeches highlighting Malaysia's determined outlook flash across television screens in Ban Bor On living rooms. In his introduction to the 2008 edition of the book of records, Datuk Seri Abdullah Badawi, who succeeded Mahathir Mohammad as Malaysia's prime minister in 2003, wrote, "while some of the pursuits chronicled in this publication may not seem to have any broader impact on society, it is the singular drive that has been displayed which is vital" (7). This national "drive" cannot be removed from the call for patriotism that saturates press reports and governmental speeches, crafting the way Kelantanese Thais think about the monuments they have built. Having the largest, tallest, and longest Buddha statues, kitchen complexes, and temple gateways, even if they are mere state records, can be seen as a local response to national notions of a modernity that stresses grandeur and success. Monumental art and architecture not only circumscribe the ethnic and cultural identity of the community, making visible what were otherwise silent and marginal peoples and spaces, but they also locate the Thais in relation to larger national and international concerns. These are narratives that circumscribe the boundaries of the nation-state. The statues, regardless of their Chinese or Thai accents, are proud symbols of a Malaysianness not seen anywhere else.

Statues and monuments are expensive investments in ethnic and national visuality. The process of building is marked by a series of festivities through which financial donations pour into temple coffers. These include inauguration festivities (*ngan chalong*) that mark the successful completion of a project, and fundraising events (*ngan ha bia*), through which funds are garnered for building budgets. These events entail the circulation of people and finances from various sources. Like the vacation tours many Thais enthusiastically participate in, temple fetes are public occasions of ethnic and cultural interaction. Fetes bring local villagers into contact with non-residents, Thais with Chinese, villagers with politicians, and Kelantanese with non-Kelantanese. In other words, festivals that fill temple treasuries with thousands of ringgit are also sites for the diverse interactive moments that span Kelantan's historical and social landscapes.

Large celebratory events have significant political undercurrents. Temple committees organizing the festivities usually invite well-known Malaysian political figures to their celebrations as honored guests. Who they invite usually depends on the political camps their members come from. This not only generates a greater attendance by curious participants seeking to see for themselves who these politicians are and to hear their speeches of development, promise, and ethnic comingling, but it is also a financially prudent move on the part of the temple's organizing body. In return for their attendance, political representatives often provide the temple with substantial financial contributions in order to show their support for the Thai population. At the same time, political leaders of Malaysia's Chinese- and Malay-dominated parties use the events as a stage on which to garner Thai voter support, or at least interest, for their parties through their speeches and philanthropic gestures. The politicians, by virtue of their associations with either the state or federal government, are representatives of a distinctive Malaysian identity. Their attendance at these Thai events, like the statues and monuments they come to celebrate and admire, symbolically draws borders around the Kelantanese Thai community, designating it as Malaysian and, hence, "one of us." The community is no longer marginalized by its location in a hinterland Malay state. Rather, small villages become integral parts of the political peripheries of the nation-state. The state enters the village through the form of the political guests and the donations they make, symbolically decreasing the long-standing social and cultural invisibility of Thai villagers.

Well-respected monks from Thailand, many of whom hold high-ranking positions within the Thai Buddhist ecclesiastical council (*mahatherasamakhom*) centered in Bangkok's large royal temples, preside over the ritual and religious aspects of many of these celebrations. They often sit alongside smartly dressed officers from the Royal Thai Consulate in Kota Bharu, Malaysian politicians, and members of the Kelantanese Thai Association, a local ethnic lobby with close affiliations with Malaysia's federal party. When the Buddha relic was to be enshrined in the chest of the Wat Klang Sitting Buddha in September 2001, chief among the invited monk guests was supposed to be Thai Buddhism's supreme patriarch, the *sangkharat*. The old monk, however, was unwell, and his deputy, the *somdet phuttajarn*, came in his place. The participation of these senior urban-based monks in Kelantanese Thai ritual celebrations is an interesting practice that carries a powerful sense of sentimentality to the Malaysian participants. Whereas Malaysian political figureheads draw the boundaries of citizenship around Kelantan's Thai community, senior Thai monks reinforce a sense of Thai Buddhist cultural and ethnic communitas across the borders of international sovereignty that the Malaysian politicians frame. In so doing, they symbolically proclaim Bangkok's religious hegemony over its distant border communities. The Bangkok-based monks associate an otherwise autonomous Kelantanese Thai monkhood with Thailand's official monastic establishment. The frontier is drawn into the ethnic and religious metropole through the movement of its monks. Temple festivals celebrating monumental building reaffirm Kelantanese

Thai understandings of what it means to be the cultural citizen of a larger Thai Buddhist universe. At the same time cultural citizenship does not contest the relevance of the national border and of the Malaysian nation-state.

In her work on transnational Mouride Muslim traders, Victoria Ebin (1996) observed how social distinctions among the itinerant Mouride were activated during the annual visits they had from various Senegalese *cheikhs*. These distinctions were otherwise not stressed by the migrants in their daily life but were important arenas for the performance of a ritualized Mouride identity. Notions of hierarchy and its corresponding relation to ethnic, cultural, and gendered meanings were represented through the temporal reconfigurations of spatial categories that emerged during the cycle of religious visitations by the *cheikh*. Similarly, the large cement statues and monuments that monopolize the Kelantanese Thai religious landscape today construct a sacred topography in Kelantan and function as centers for the social production and experience of Thainess by drawing in various powerful social actors. Like that of the traveling Senegalese *cheikh*, the movement of Malaysian political figures and senior monks from Thailand into Kelantanese villages during important ritual events temporally reasserts Kelantanese Thai definitions of themselves as a marginal people whose cultural identity lay in the hazy interstitial and frontier zones where competing national ideologies and sentiments meet and mingle. Thais for the most part see no contradiction in this.

A new Buddhist monumentality has brought with it a more sinister association that has forced Kelantanese Thais to reflect on what Thainess means in a Muslim political and global environment. As temples build ever bigger statues and edifices, the threat of triggering the ire of local Muslims becomes more imminent. Islam prohibits the fashioning of the human form, not to mention those of non-Muslim religious personas. Nevertheless, these most un-Islamic of creations are being built on Mecca's Verandah. Especially after the terrifying events of 11 September 2001, Kelantanese Thais have been wary of Muslim reactions to their abbots' building sprees. The unsubstantiated fear of possible terrorist attacks seems to blanket the community. This has been especially pressing in the past few years, as ethnic violence regularly flares up in Thailand's southernmost provinces between the Thai state and shadowy groups of supposed Malay Muslim separatists. Although the discourses of international Islamic militancy and terrorism and of Thailand's internal civil unrest have yet to directly manifest themselves in Kelantan, the impact of such occurrences cannot be denied.

The bigger the monument, the more dramatic the spectacle of its destruction. Nevertheless this knowledge has not prevented abbots from building even bigger statues. It generates a fear that has remained very much at the level of hearsay for now. In practice, Kelantanese Thai Buddhist and Malay Muslim communities remain on friendly terms, a fact that has had historical precedents in the ideals of Islamic rulership and Malay-Thai patronage in the state. In the following chapter we move away from contemporary preoccupations with materiality and ethnic politics, returning once again to the past to trace out the role of power-filled encounters between kings and villagers in forging Thainess in Ban Bor On.

CHAPTER 4

Circuits

ONE KNEW OF SULTAN ISMAIL PETRA YAHYA PETRA'S UPCOMING visit to Bandar Tumpat from observing the road in front of Wat Nai. Miraculously the plastic bags, soda cans, drinking straws, bits of paper, and cigarette butts that littered Kelantan's thoroughfares seemed to disappear overnight. Colorful flags decked street lamps. Banners written in Jawi and Romanized Malay proclaiming the Kelantanese's love for their ruler and exhorting that Allah bless and protect him and his wife with long and illustrious lives stretched across the elaborate gantries that bridge the route from Kota Bharu to the Tumpat district. The sultan owned a handsome British villa known as the Istana Bukit Tanah (Palace on the Earth Hill) in a shady corner of Bandar Tumpat and visited it a few times a year.[1] Sultan Ismail's travels to Bandar Tumpat echoed earlier sojourns that his father and grandfather had taken. Both rulers were known to have been close to wealthy Tumpat Chinese and Malays, some of whom were presented with the royal Malay honorific of *datuk* (connoting an officially recognized rank of magnanimity) by the ruler himself. These earlier visits were grand events in Bandar Tumpat's calendar and the sultan was entertained with the much-loved bullfights of old, traditional Malay and Thai theatrical performances, and martial arts demonstrations. Today the royal tours are much quieter affairs. The bullfights are gone—gambling is now illegal in the state—and there are no longer any performances. The sultan now travels to Bandar Tumpat only to attend small-scale civic events.

The monks and I had been working hard on renovating Wat Nai's enormous kitchen. Preparing the mortar floor was especially backbreaking, as the cement had to be smoothed over before it dried in the hot sun. Khun Nyai took a break from shoveling granite pebbles into two wheelbarrows which were to be poured into a noisy cement mixer. Looking out at the flags that now decorated the road in front of the temple, the bespectacled monk remembered an incident some years back when the sultan had visited Bandar Tumpat. That day, Ban Bor On's residents had gathered along the road in eager anticipation of catching a glimpse of their ruler. Some had even brought with them little red flags decorated with the state's crest to wave at the royal entourage. But the sultan's motorcade zipped past the assembled crowd without pomp or ceremony. The moment was over in no time. The downhearted villagers put away their flags and returned to their day-to-day lives. "I guess he must have had diarrhea that day," grinned Khun Nyai cynically. Then he said something that reminded me of the interstitiality of hinterland spaces in Kelantan. He compared the level of interest shown by the sultan in his Thai subjects' welfare with that of Thailand's monarch, King Bhumipol Adulyadej. To the affirmative nods of Khun Sung and his brother Khun Tam, who had by now joined in our little conversation next to the cement mixer, Khun Nyai spoke of how Thailand's king was a people's king. He initiated and oversaw the implementation of social welfare projects throughout Thailand so as to improve his subjects' standards of living, regardless of their ethnicity or religious affiliations. "He would even plant rice in the fields with the farmers," announced Khun Nyai proudly. This popular impression of the hardworking Chakri monarch laboring tirelessly for the happiness of all Thai citizens is a scene that flashes over Thai television channels every night during the fifteen-minute palace news (*khao nai phra ratchawang*) broadcast. A brief rundown of the daily affairs of members of Thailand's monarchy, the news segment features highlights from royal tours, speeches, visits to temples, attendance at cremations, and the meetings the royal family had with important and unimportant people. These images enter the private world of Ban Bor On's living rooms and monks' quarters and shape their viewers' perceptions of the Thai royal family and, with that, of the country that lies just across the Tak Bai river. This positive media image of Thailand's ruling house is juxtaposed against the privacy that seems to cloak the affairs of the current Malay sultan.

No one really knows of the sultan's private life, except when such occasions are reported in the press or when the ruler visits schools, mosques, and government offices in the state. Even his occasional visits to Bandar Tumpat are brief and somewhat mysterious. In a recent article outlining the work of celebrification in the construction of a power-filled image of Yogyakarta's present sultan, Hamengkubuwono X, Felicia Hughes-Freeland (2007) argued that it was the media-saturated frenzy of high modernity that created a charismatic sultan out of an otherwise publicly uninteresting man in the central Javanese city. This king-making process reached its zenith during the Javanese sultan's accession to the throne. In the few weeks leading up the investiture ceremony in 1988, Central Java's Indonesian and Javanese language media had a field day reporting on the soon-to-be sultan's traditional associations with indigenous Javanese belief in regal power and sacredness. Through newspaper columns, gossip magazines, tabloids, televised images, Google write-ups, and videos, the Javanese ruler was ascribed a Weberian-like charisma otherwise unattainable in secular life or in his political capacity as Yogyakarta's governor.

In Thailand, the king's celebrity status and his corresponding charismatic persona is constructed through a history of media images that have emerged since black-and-white photography first framed images of the Chakri monarchs in the nineteenth century (Morris 2009). Coupled with the circulation of the royal image in print form is the simple fact that King Bhumipol is ethnically Thai and religiously Buddhist and therefore shares two of the most basic and exclusive of "primordial attachments" with Kelantan's Thai villagers (Geertz 1973: 259). This is a powerful and symbolic association that was celebrated in a magnificent array of media representations that was denied the Malay Muslim ruler regardless of his how close his affiliations were with the state's Thai populace.

Living along the hinterlands of two nation-states, each with their own hereditary rulers, made it inevitable that Kelantanese Thais would compare and contrast the two kingly images — one public and the other private and secretive. Although King Bhumipol and his immediate family members have yet to make a visit to Kelantan, villagers through their exposure to the Thai monarchy's media cult seem more aware of what is going on in Bangkok's royal household than of happenings in their local palace less than an hour away. They decorate their homes with pictures of the Chakri monarch and his family — images they brought home from trips to Thailand, bought from itinerant vendors at temple fairs, or carefully cut from used calendars.[2] Rarely does one find photographs of the sultan in Thai houses. Unlike in Thailand, images of Malaysian royalty are restricted to the stock portraits of the stern-faced ruler one finds hanging on the wall of all government offices. One cannot purchase these images from fairs or cut them out from old calendars and magazines. The images remain the prerogative of the state and can only be acquired from official government bodies.

Thais felt socially neglected by their sultan, whom they knew from only the windows of a passing motorcade or the pictures hanging in police stations, post offices, hospitals, and schools. But despite their grumbles about him, the sultan is after all, Kelantanese, a fact that my friends in Ban Bor On happily acknowledged. He speaks the Kelantanese dialect of Malay, lives in a palace in the state, and (sometimes) visits their temples. The sultan's illustrious predecessors had already cemented a strong bond with the Thai community and its monks that carried over into the way villagers thought about and asserted feelings of marginality and cultural personhood. So intimate was the sultan-Thai relationship at the popular level of a shared Kelantaneseness that some Kelantanese Thais referred to him simply by a nickname, Mat Ea, as they did their friends and fellow Kelantanese. They talked about Mat Ea as one would speak of a close friend, rarely resorting to the distanced formality they used when talking of the Thai king, whom they called Phra Chao Phean Din—the lord of the land—or of the Yang di-Pertuan Agong, Malaysia's king. This close relationship, which Kelantanese Thais were proud of but also uncertain about, has its origins in an older system of social and ritual patronage between Kelantan's Thai monastics and the Malay and Siamese courts that ruled through and over them.

The earliest account of the Kelantanese monkhood written in English is found in Graham's 1908 "handbook of information." In describing the "Siamese" of Kelantan, Graham pays particular attention to the monastic community:

> There are forty "Wats" or Buddhist monasteries in the State, the yellow-robed inmates of which minister to the spiritual needs of the Siamese portion of the population. The affairs of the "Wats" are managed by the ecclesiastical head of the province of Lakon (Chao Ka Na Nakon Sri Tammarat). The chief Buddhist monk of the State, an old man of eighty-four years, who had lived in Kelantan all his life, and whose memory was stored with highly interesting information regarding the history of the State, died a short while ago, much regretted by everybody, his superior sanctity having long been fully recognized alike by Mohammedans and Buddhists.[3]

Of particular interest to us is Graham's point on the "sanctity" of the old monk and what must have been his close associations with Muslims and Buddhists in a state popularly known for its staunch Islamic administration. Unfortunately, Graham does not provide us with the name of the monk or on which bank of the Tak Bai he lived. Given that Graham's *Kelantan: A State of the Malay Peninsula* was published in 1908, a year before the official signing of the Anglo-Siamese Treaty between the British and Siamese territorial forces, it is likely that the monk he mentions was the final ecclesiastical head of a Siamese-ruled Kelantan that encompassed Thailand's present-day Narathiwat province along with Malaysian Kelantan. The monk referred to in the text was likely the predecessor of Wat Ban Kao's Than Khru Kio (1848?–1931), who was appointed the chief monk of the British-ruled Kelantan in the early colonial period.[4] Graham's "old monk" was probably a man by the name of Phut, who was the chief monk (*chao khana nyai*) of Siamese Kelantan from 1900 to 1903. Pho Than Phut, whose royally derived monastic title was Phra Khru Ophat Phutthakun, was the abbot of Wat Chehe (Wat Choltarasinghe) in Tak Bai and was instrumental in establishing a number of smaller temples in the vicinity (Wanipha 1992: 68).[5] Wanipha Na Songkhla noted that before being promoted to the rank of Phra Khru (Than Khru in the Kelantanese Thai dialect) by Bangkok's monastic administration, Pho Than Phut had already been conferred the ritual status of preceptor (*phra upatcha*) (ibid.: 67), and thus he had the state's official mandate to ordain men into the monkhood.[6] This change in status from that of the lower-ranking preceptor to the higher Phra Khru was formally performed by a Kelantanese monk of the high monastic rank of Somdet Chao Thep under the directives of the supreme patriarch himself.

Herein lies an enigma in the history of monasticism in Kelantan. Wanipha does not provide us with much information on the monk who performed the honors. Villagers I spoke to in Kelantan and Narathiwat did not recall hearing of such a Somdet Chao Thep. Even his name escapes the reader. Searches in Thailand's National Archives and in the ecclesiastical records kept by the Buddhist Council in Bangkok also failed to reveal the identity of the monk. According to Bishop Pallegoix (1854), in his two-volume *Description du Royaume Thai ou Siam*, the ecclesiastical title of *somdet chao* (Pallegoix's *somdet-chao*) was reserved for "the princes of the monks" (Pallegoix, cited in Tambiah 1976: 231). These were the abbots of royal monasteries (*wat luang*), who were directly beneath the supreme patriarch in the monastic hierarchy. Pallegoix noted that senior monks of the rank of *somdet chao* were placed in office by the king himself. If the monk from the Kelantanese village of Bang Rim Nam was indeed a *somdet chao* with the monastic grade of Thep as Wanipha (1992) claimed in her study of Wat Chehe's history, then it is a clear example of the direct historical link Kelantan's Thai community had with the powerful Bangkok court.[7]

To add to the mystery, Wanipha does not provide us with the given name of the Somdet Chao Thep. According to her, the Somdet Chao Thep was supposedly born in the Kelantanese village of Bang Rim Nam in present-day Pasir Mas and spent some time in Bangkok during his monastic career. Wanipha writes that before being ordained as a monk the Somdet Chao Thep had been a dance dramatist (*nura*) in Kelantan, but after a failed performance during a *nura* competition, the man who was soon to be the Somdet Chao Thep traveled up north to the provinces of Songkhla and Nakhon Sri Thammarat, where he studied esoteric arts (Wanipha 1992: 63). Kelantanese Thais have historically had a close affiliation with the temples of Songkhla and Nakhon Sri Thammarat. These are centers of pilgrimage and learning. "For us to go to Nakhon was like for a Muslim to go to Mecca," I was told many times by Kae Chi and Ban Bor On's older residents. Toward the end of the nineteenth century, the Somdet Chao Thep was requested by Bangkok's ecclesiastical council to return to the southern provinces so as to reform Buddhist practice in the area and bring it in line with the orthodoxy emanating from Siam's royal temples, a practice well documented in the history of religious standardization in nineteenth- and early twentieth-century Siam (e.g., Wyatt 1969; Reynolds 1972; Tambiah 1976; Keyes 1989; Jory 2002; Tiyavanich 1997; Hansen 2007). This included standardizing monastic discipline and ordination procedures according to a core structure developed in Bangkok. The Somdet Chao Thep journeyed back to Tak Bai, where he held a meeting at a temple in the district of Phron for the abbots of all the temples in the Tak Bai region (Wanipha 1992). The meeting discussed the comprehensive ossification of Buddhist discipline, which had taken on one too many local permutations and proved uncontrollable to a Siamese polity bent on cultural uniformity. The Somdet Chao Thep conducted reordination ceremonies for the abbots present at the meeting according to a standard ordination procedure set forth by the Siamese state.

Wanipha's mysterious figure joins up with the remembered past when the author noted how at the time of the Somdet Chao Thep's visit to Tak Bai, Pho Than Phut was living in the now defunct temple of Wat Bang Toei. He, too, had attended the meeting (again evidence is lacking) and by the end of the event had been made a preceptor. In 1860, Pho Than Phut established Wat Chehe after spending six years at Wat Bang Toei. The land on which the temple was built officially belonged to the Kelantanese Sultan in Kota Bharu and was granted to the monk after the latter requested it from the palace. Pho Than Phut was conferred with the title of *chao khana nyai*, bearing the new monastic name of Phra Khru Ophat Phutthakun (similar to that of Than Khru Kio after him), by King Chulalongkorn (r. 1868–1910) in 1900, two years after the king's visit to the Malay provinces. Pho Than Phut passed away at the age of 90 in 1906 (Wanipha 1992: 13).[8]

On the evening of 23 November 1908, Wat Ban Kao's Than Khru Kio was promoted by King Chulalongkorn in a ceremony held at Bangkok's Dusit palace

4.1 Than Khru Kio

to the position of formal head of the Thai monkhood in Siamese Kelantan.[9] Popular oral histories surrounding Than Khru Kio often refer to his physical and emotional attributes and his close associations with the Malay and Thai courts. In one story, Than Khru Kio was said to have jumped into a pond to cool off after having to deal with the irritating squabbles between contending *nura* performers during celebrations marking the inauguration of Wat Khok Phrao's ordination hall. The actor-dancers were arguing over where to set up their stage. Each troupe wanted the best spot on the temple's premises and this irked the monk. On another occasion, Than Khru Kio, frustrated at watching his villagers' futile attempts to pull up an *on* tree that they had felled, grabbed the tree's heavy, thorn-covered trunk, tucked it under his arm, and hoisted it up by himself. His superior strength was the result of the magical incantations he memorized. He was an exponent in the recitation of the *khatha maha muen*, a sacred Thai-Pali ritual text he had supposedly picked up during a visit to Siam and from which he derived magical powers. His amazing strength was further featured in stories of his using heavy temple foundation stones as weights during his daily exercises.

Ordained in 1871, Than Khru Kio took over the abbotship of Wat Ban Kao from his elder brother Thit Sa, who had left the monkhood and returned to lay life after falling in love with a Malay Muslim woman.[10] As with many Kelantanese monks, Than Khru Kio spent a number of years in Siam. He resided in Bangkok for some time before returning to Ban Kao to take up abbotship. Than Khru Kio was on close terms with the sultan, who gave him land in and around Tumpat's Malay villages.[11] Some sites, including the uninhabited islet plot at Cik Tahir, served the Ban Kao temple as sources of the much-needed palm leaves for roofing and coconuts for cooking. The fact that these sites were awarded to the abbot for the upkeep of his temple showed the sultan's concern for the monastic institution and its inhabitants. Thais continue to be proud of this fact, even to this day.

The actual procedure by which Than Khru Kio received his royal appointment in 1908 is uncertain. As with the procurement of monastic titles in Thailand today, royally derived honors, including that of Phra Khru, were supported by the Thai monarchy, whose seal of approval was stamped on certificates issued to appointed monks. Nevertheless, the actual conferment ceremony did not require the direct participation of the king or his immediate family and could be graced by a representative of the court, usually the supreme patriarch or his deputy. In Than Khru Kio's appointment the honors—in the form of a certificate of office, an elaborate ceremonial fan (*phat jot*), and a new set of robes (*pha trai*)—were believed by villagers to have been presented to the monk in Bangkok by the king himself, thereby drawing an inseparable connection between the marginality of Thainess in present-day Kelantan with the concerned Bangkok court of the past. Than Khru Kio's official appointment certificate was printed in Thai and cased in a small dark wood frame inlaid with mother-of-pearl. It is currently kept under lock and key in a glass showcase by the abbot of Wat Ban Kao. The certificate reads:

May Master [chao] Athikarn Kio (of) Wat Ban Kao become Phra Khru Ophat

Phuttakhun over the major monastic administrative district of the patriarch of the *mueang* of Kelantan.[12] May this monk please accept the work of the Buddhist religion, the duties of which are to instruct, prevent allegations (of misdemeanor) and to watch over and assist the monks and novices in his administrative area as deemed fit so as to be happy and prosperous in the Buddhist religion forever.

This (appointment) begins on the 23rd of November in the 127th year of the Rattanakosin Era, Buddhist Era 2451 and which coincides with the 14,622 day of the present king.[13]

The certificate concludes with three stanzas of Pali verses in old Khmer (*khom*) and the faded signature of the issuing officer.

In line with King Chulalongkorn's Sangha Act (*kot phra song*) issued on 16 June 1902, the certificate formally invested Than Khru Kio as the patriarch of the *mueang* of Kelantan. The 1902 act, which incidentally also coincided with the year in which Siam reasserted its sovereignty over Patani and Kelantan, placed the Buddhist king (Chulalongkorn) as the de facto head of the Thai monkhood (Keyes 1971). This meant that all ecclesiastical honors and promotions in the Siamese state had to pass through senior monk officials in Bangkok. This helped standardize religion according to Bangkok's dictates across the country—a move that was part and parcel of the Thai monarch's policies of provincial reorganization in 1892. The second of the eight-chapter act divides the boundaries of monastic administration in Siam into four major sections known in standard Thai as *khana yai* (Kelantanese: *khana nyai*).[14] Each division was administered by two senior monks (*mahathera*): a chief monk or patriarch and his deputy. The eight heads of the *khana yai* formed part of the Council of Elders (*mahatherasamakhom*), which was the governing body of Siam's new national Ecclesia (Tambiah 1976; Ishii 1986).[15]

Than Khru Kio's official incorporation into Siam's monastic hierarchy placed the Ban Kao abbot and his monks under the direct jurisdiction of Bangkok. Kelantan's tiny Thai villages, once socially invisible to many British colonialists, were now part of a larger and more powerful sphere of political administration based on religion. It is likely that Than Khru Kio continued his close ties with Siam's religious elites even after the drawing of the state's British Malayan borders in 1910. In a royal correspondence detailing the 1915 coastal visit of King Chulalongkorn's son and successor, Vajiravudh, to the southern Thai administrative groupings (*monthon pak tai*), it was stated that Than Khru Kio had been among a delegation of fifty monks that included the then chief abbot of Wat Chehe, Pho Than Chan, and a large number of lay men and women who welcomed the king at the Tak Bai temple.

King Chulalongkorn's attempts at bureaucratization and cultural reforms in Siam's provinces took power away from native elites and forced a standard interpretation of Thai culture (language, religion, art, decorum, education, health) on once-independent principalities and vassals. In his annual reports (1902–1907) to Bangkok's Ministry of Education, the monk Phra Sirithammamuni, the director of Nakhon Sri Thammarat's bureau of education, of which Kelantan was a part, lamented the fact that Kelantanese Thais did not show much enthusiasm toward formal Thai education. They preferred a traditional curriculum based on memorizing Pali chants and learning to read old Khmer. The northeastern Khorat plateau, parts of northern Thailand, and the Muslim principalities of the south occasionally resisted Bangkok's attempts at cultural colonization through brazen attacks on representatives of the central government. Couched in indigenous terms and shaded with millenarian ideologies, these revolts, although unsuccessful politically, shook the foundation upon which the modernizing Chakri court stood (Bunnag 1962; Gesick 1983; Chatthip 1984; Tanabe 1984; Turton 1991; Wilson 1997).[16] In response, Bangkok felt that it needed to pay more attention to the "problematic" frontiers and began sending its representatives to the region more frequently, a practice that has continued to this day.

To many of these traveling officials, places like Kelantan are strange locales. They are politically imagined as Siam's ex-colonies, and, hence, the Thai nation-state feels a moral obligation to ensure the continued welfare of its Buddhist residents. As political assistance is illogical in an age of sovereign borders and divergent citizenship ideologies, this has been done through Buddhism. During my stay in Ban Bor On and on subsequent return visits I met with a number of representatives of the Thai state who had traveled to meet with Kelantanese Thai villagers. They ranged from Thailand's foreign ministry officers and military men interested in finding out about ethnic coexistence between Buddhists and Muslims in strife-free Kelantan to teachers, university students, academics, and missionary monks. Many had not heard of Thai communities inhabiting the Malaysian frontier prior to their visit and were amazed at the large number of Buddhist temples in the Tumpat plains, with their mega-creations, and at the cultural practices of villagers that hinted at their close associations with Thailand. Many of these practices have been deemed museum pieces of an archaic form of a Thai cultural essence no longer seen in the modern nation-state. The Kelantanese Thais have somehow been left out of the developmental discourses and trends of modernizing Thailand.

The direct involvement of Siam and, since 1939, Thailand in managing the affairs of the Kelantanese Thai monkhood points to the way a frontier community is entangled in circuits of power. It is this engagement across space and time that forms the base for expressions of an ambiguous Thainess. Kershaw (1969: 147) pointed out that Kelantanese Thais have never existed in a "political and social vacuum." Notwithstanding his affiliations with Thailand's national monastic establishment, Kelantan's chief monk receives his official appointments to office from the Kelantanese sultan. The dual nature of religio-political management is unique to the Kelantanese case. The appointment of the chief Thai monk of the west coast states of Kedah and Perlis, for instance, bypasses the authority of the states' Malay rulers and relies entirely on Thailand and the local council of monks. The difference between monastic organization and administration in Kelantan and the rest of Malaysia's northern hinterland states is due to the different historical moments that have molded Thai-Malay cultural and political encounters on the peninsula since the nineteenth century. These processes of cross-cultural clientelism had much to do with the political machinations of a nervous Siamese polity in the wake of the encroachment of British colonization in northern Malaya and Burma.

Overlapping Sovereignties

It is uncertain when and why Kelantan's sultan became the chief patron of Theravada Buddhism in the state. In a 2002 article titled "Special Thai-Malaysian Relations," Kobkua Suwannathat-Pian did not mention the role of the Buddhist clergy as a mediating factor in the political associations between Siam and the northern Malay states. She did, however, acknowledge Kedah's cordial relations with Bangkok in the nineteenth century, which amounted to "near ideal tributary relations in the region" (11). Kedah's ruling house, unlike Kelantan's, had enjoyed the favor of Bangkok since at least 1841, and its Malay elites had forged even stronger links with the powerful Siamese state by marrying Thai women. It is possible that this cordiality and political intimacy forged the Kedah Thai monkhood's reliance on Bangkok for its overt management.

Among the Kelantanese Thais, arguably the most revered and talked about

Kelantanese sultan is Sultan Muhammad II, who ruled from 1837 until his death in 1886. He was the adopted son of Sultan Muhammad I (also known as Long Muhammad I, r. 1800–1838). Thais commonly refer to him as Phja Pak Daeng (the Red-Mouthed King) after his rosy, or perhaps betel-stained, lips.[17] The latter part of his reign was marked by a period of stability, peace, and prosperity, in part due to his heavy-handedness. Phja Pak Daeng's early years on the throne were marred by secessionist disputes between himself and Long Jenal, the disgraced younger brother of Sultan Muhammad I, whom Phja Pak Daeng succeeded. By 1839, a full-scale civil war had erupted in the state. Known to local Thais as the "*suek phi nong*" (Malay: *perang saudara*) or the "battle of the kinsmen," the war pitched Long Jenal, who had proclaimed himself the legitimate raja (ruler) of Kelantan, against Phja Pak Daeng's forces.[18]

The civil war had political and historical antecedents that stretched beyond the bickering of Malay royals over the Kelantanese throne. In 1818, Sultan Muhammad I had initiated closer ties between Kelantan and Bangkok by establishing the tradition of Kelantan's triennial tribute of gold and silver trees to the Siamese court.[19] These elaborate presents were used as a means to court Siam's favor in matters pertaining to local politics, in particular to discourage the southern state of Terengganu's increasingly hostile stance toward Kelantan. Vassalage proved beneficial to the weak Kelantanese court, as it allowed Kelantan's rulers to seek Siam's assistance whenever political unrest plagued the state. Kelantan thus continued to remain on affable terms with Bangkok even after Sultan Muhammad I's death. During the war between Long Jenal and Phja Pak Daeng, the latter's troops were assisted by Siamese military personnel and gunboats, forcing Long Jenal to eventually concede defeat. Siam seized this opportunity to make its political influence felt even more in the governance of the Malay state.

Phja Pak Daeng also maintained a strong affiliation with the state's local Thai community, possibly as a means to win the favor of Siam's Buddhist administrators, who had supported his rise to power. He offered land to Pho Than Phut for the construction of Wat Chehe in Tak Bai and to Than Khru Kio for the upkeep of Wat Ban Kao.[20] Yet no material evidence remains of this relationship—only the stories older villagers tell. The relationship between the Thai Buddhist establishment and the Malay court was based on mutual cordiality and respect. Than Khru Kio was no stranger to the Kota Bharu palace and had the privilege of entering it anytime he wished. R. J. Farrer (1933) described witnessing a forty-day purification ceremony (*cha roen*) conducted by a delegation of Kelantanese Thai monks at the palace of Sultan Muhammad IV in 1918.[21] The ritual was sponsored by the *raja muda* (deputy ruler) after a flagpole at the residency had been inauspiciously struck by lightning.[22] It was likely that the chief monk engaged in the ceremony was none other than Than Khru Kio. Farrer (262) observed that, "[at] 7 p.m. the Head of all the Siamese priests in Kelantan, 'To Raja (who is treated as of royal blood and addressed as 'Ku'), arrived and was introduced." "Ku" is likely a Malay mispronunciation or misspelling of Kio or Khru.

Than Khru Kio's successor to the rank of state patriarch was Than Chao Khun Khron (1876–1962), chief abbot of Wat Bang Rim Nam. The monk Khron was appointed by Bangkok's *mahatherasamakhom* to take on the ecclesiastical title of Phra Khru Wijaranayanmuni in 1941 and was subsequently promoted to the high rank of Than Chao Khun and became patriarch of the state of Kelantan four years later. He passed away on 19 November 1962, just fifteen days before he was to have received yet another royal promotion, this time to the rank of Than Chao Khun Chan Rat.

Like Than Khru Kio before him, Than Chao Khun Khron was a close friend of the Kelantanese royal family. He was believed by some to have used his sacred powers to heal Sultan Ibrahim IV's (r. 1944–1960) wife from a curse she suffered as a result of malignant magic. The latter's successor, Sultan Yahya Petra (r. 1960–1979) even visited the old monk while he was unwell in his final months. Photographs of the monk talking to the ruler decorate the pages of the funeral volumes of Wat Bang Rim Nam's two subsequent abbots—Than Chao Khun Chan and Than Chao Khun Mit—both of whom were also the chief monks of Kelantan and held the Phra Wijaranayanmuni title. By the time of Phra Maha Chan's royal promotion to the rank of Than Chao Khun in 1963, a Jawi-inscribed certificate detailing the monastic promotion in Malay and the obligations of the new head of the Kelantanese monkhood had been developed and issued by the Kota Bharu palace. The framed certificate carried with it the official seal of the sultan's house as well as a translation of the Jawi document in Thai. The certificate was presented to the monk by a representative of the Malay court during the formal investiture of the monk. Since then, all subsequent state patriarchs have received similar regal proclamations, prepared by the Malay palace at the request of the office of the Kelantanese monkhood. In the formal Jawi statement-of-appointment (Malay: *perlantikan*) the Chao Khun's role is to be the "head of all temples" (Malay: *ketua agong bagi sekelian ketik*).[23] An English translation of the accompanying Thai text reads as follows:

Contract for the Appointment of the Head of the Thai Monkhood
(Chao Khun)

Yahya Petra, the Raja and ruler of the State of Kelantan and all her jurisdictional borders to Phra Maha Chan Kesaro. This contract assures us, the people, that: It has been established as tradition that the Head of the Thai Monkhood (Chao Khun) in Kelantan is put into office by the ruler's appointment and his seal of office. Phra Wijaranayanmuni who was elected into office by our father, the former Sultan Ibrahim who passed away on the 15 November 1962. Because of this, the position of the Head of the Monkhood has been vacant. Hence, we who are empowered as the representatives of the Sultan and ruler of the State of Kelantan, request that this contract allows for the appointment of Phra Maha Chan Kesaro as the Head of the Monkhood (Chao Khun) for the state of Kelantan. This contract comes into effect on 8 June 1963 which coincides with 8 June 2506 of the Buddhist Era.

With this appointment, the abovementioned Phra Maha Chan Kesaro will gain power and monopoly over performing his duties according to the responsibilities and commitments as the Head of the Monkhood as stated in this contract. We request that all relevant parties take note of this.

We at the Istana Balai Besar present our signatures and royal seal [of approval] on 8 June 1963 coinciding with 8 June 2506 of the Buddhist Era and the Fourth year of the Present Reign.

In return for the intimacy afforded by the Kelantanese sultan to the *sangha*, monks would present the Malay ruler not only with the sacred power of Pali chants during ritual and healing events but also with token Buddhist amulets (*lok phra*) and cabalistic cloths (*pha jan*). Likewise when Pho Than Di and Khun Di were granted a brief audience with Thailand's Queen Sirikit at the Narathiwat airport in 2003, they presented the Queen and her son, the Crown Prince, with replicas of Pho Than Sao and Pho Than Daeng, two of Wat Nai's former abbots. Pho Than Num, the abbot of Wat Bang Rim Nam, who accompanied the Wat Nai monks at the royal audience at the airport, gave her a rare amulet and an image of Than Chao Khun Khron. In a more recent example of interfaith encountering, Datuk Nik Aziz Nik Mat hosted Kelantan's Thai monks at a lunch reception at the Kota Bharu stadium in 2010 as part of his celebration of the Islamic holiday of Hari Raya Aidil Fitri. PAS invited forty monks to attend the feast. On 17 July 2010, the elderly Malay statesman invited the monks to his residence to celebrate the wedding of his daughter. In appreciation for his invitation and to reassert Buddhist affinity with Kelantan's Islamic state apparatus, Pho Than Di handed the soft-spoken Islamic scholar and spiritual leader a sacred wood baton (*mai thao*). Such batons are much prized among the Thai community and revered for their magical associations. The baton was wrapped in a green cloth when presented to Nik Aziz—the color of Islam and of his party.[24]

Like batons, *phra pit ta* amulets are common throughout southern Thailand. They carry an effigy of a monk (*phra*) with his hands covering his eyes (*pit ta*) and face. Original *phra pit ta* amulets made by Than Chao Khun Khron are rare and can fetch thousands of dollars among collectors in Singapore, Malaysia, and Thailand. The amulets and the magical stories surrounding their makers' efficacy have placed Wat Bang Rim Nam on the pilgrimage circuit for people seeking out amulets in Kelantan. Articles and stories about Wat Bang Rim Nam's famed *phra pit ta* amulets abound in the glossy amulet magazines published in Thailand, such as the Bangkok-based *Phra Khrueang Pak Tai* (Amulets from the South) (volume 3, undated). Numerous websites devoted to the collection of these Kelantanese amulets have been set up and maintained by Malaysian Chinese amulet aficionados. Sellers can be found hawking Kelantanese and, in particular, famed Wat Bang Rim Nam amulets in Internet chatrooms and online auction houses.

Amulets carry particular social and ritual significance for both the Thai and the non-Thai-non-Buddhist Kelantanese community. This interethnic amity was vividly spelled out to me by Pho Than Di one afternoon as we waited outside the Kota Bharu post office for Khun Di and Khun Nyai to return from paying their telephone bills. Pho Than Di noted that monks used to present sultans with Buddhist amulets as gifts for the latter's support of the monastic institution. The conversation came up as we talked about the Muslim ruler's relationship with Buddhist monks in historical Kelantan. We had just come out of a meeting with the sultan's representatives at Sultan Ismail's Kubang Kerian palace on the outskirts of Kota Bharu, where we had discussed the formal presentation of royal honors for Pho Than Di on his appointment as the state's chief monk. Pho Than Di explained that in the days of *tang raek*, gifts of Buddhist potency had been kept by one of the sultan's courtiers. Soccer player Phi Thong, who had accompanied us to the meeting and who had worked in the palace until his resignation some five years earlier, agreed:

> This man had even traveled to Bangkok to collect amulets. He was a Malay man who wore amulets around his neck. He enjoyed collecting amulets and they say that in his house are all the old amulets and *pha jan* that had once been donated to the Sultan by respected monks.

As with all rumors, Phi Thong could not confirm the stories he had heard. What is important, however, is that these discourses of Muslim-Buddhist camaraderie circulated as a nostalgic device upon which local understandings of the past were based. This is juxtaposed against a plethora of everyday narratives that revolved around the increasing religious and cultural tension felt between both groups, especially in the wake of 11 September 2001. In an age marked by global threats of extreme violence, the sultan's historic relationship with the Buddhist monastic community symbolically prevented spectacular outbursts of ethnic and religious animosity in Kelantan. This ideal ruler-ruled relationship, however, remained at the level of indigenous theorizing. In practice, the climate of fear spared no one.

Mohamed stated that "the Sultan of Kelantan, who is the titular head of Islam, plays a role similar to that of the Thai monarch, as a protector of the Buddhist religion (*phutthasasanupathampok*)" (1993a: 38). Yoneo Ishii (1986: 39) noted that the earliest textual declaration of the Thai king as the *akkhara sasanupathamphok* (protector of the religion) is found in the Sangha regulations of 1782. Religion (*sasana*) during the early Bangkok period was synonymous with Buddhism. After the 1932 revolution that saw an end to absolute monarchy in Siam and the drafting of the country's first constitution, the definition of religion was expanded to include non-Buddhist belief systems. Henceforth, *sasana* as religion was differentiated in official discourses from *phra phuttasasana* (Buddhism), thereby effectively incorporating all of Siam's faiths under the protection of its Buddhist kings. As the *akkhara sasanupathamphok*, the Thai Theravadin monarch was dutifully responsible for ensuring the order and purity of the Buddhist religion in his domain so as to maintain his own political legitimacy in the eyes of the populace. An increasingly immoral, corrupt, and unpoliced monastic community indicated that the ruler was not observing his own ritual duties, which seriously undermined the legitimacy of his office.

So strong was this relationship between senior Thai monks and members of the Muslim court that the funeral pyres of Kelantan's chief monks since at least the time of Than Khru Kio were ritually lit by the sultan himself. The act was a public declaration of the sultan's role as Buddhism's chief patron in a Muslim domain and, on a more intimate and emotional scale, as a dear friend to the monks and the Thai community. The tradition took a back seat, during the recent cremation ceremony of Than Chao Khun Mit in 2005. It is debatable why Sultan Ismail did not attend the ceremony, since his father and grandfather had been close friends with Than Chao Khun Mit's famed predecessors. Uncle Tan, a bespectacled Singaporean Chinese in his eighties and a longtime devotee of Wat Bang Rim Nam, speculated that the ruler's strange absence was a politically sound move and did not reflect a distancing of court-temple relations. Uncle Tan linked the absence of direct Malay courtly participation in the funeral with the current turmoil in south Thailand. The ruler's highly visible support for Buddhism could be interpreted by southern Thai Muslim extremists as the sultan giving in to the whims of what they view as an unjust and diabolical Thai nation-state. If not carefully managed, this could lead to a possible spillover of the ethnic tension that continues to rock Thailand, as unhappy fundamentalists attempt to reassert their vision of Islamic dominance in Malay Kelantan.

The monk's elaborate funeral pyre was in the shape of a spired pavilion set atop the peak of a stylized Mount Meru, the center of the Thai Buddhist cosmos and abode to the Hindu god Indra. The pyre was made of wood and carefully decorated with intricate trimmings in gold paper. It was lit by a representative of the Bangkok court. This was, after all, a royal cremation (*phra ratchathan phlo-eng sop*). It was attended by members of the Kota Bharu's Royal Thai Consulate and representatives from the office of the supreme patriarch in Bangkok. The royal office contributed five sets of monks' robes to be used in the cremation ceremony under the sponsorship of Princess Maha Chakri Sirindhorn, daughter of King Bhumipol. The office of the Sangkharat—Thailand's highest monastic body—contributed an additional five robes. Two lay representatives from the royal office traveled to Bang Rim Nam to ensure that the ceremony adhered to the strict protocol demanded for royally sponsored cremations. On the day of the cremation proper, the Thai government officers arrived in the formal uni-form of Thailand's grim-faced civil servants—a pressed long-sleeved white shirt and matching slacks, heavy with shining medals of honor and decorated with a black arm band signifying mourning. The presentation of the robes from the princess and the Sangkharat and the flame (in the form of a lit lantern) from the Bangkok palace formed the highlight of the cremation, which despite the light afternoon drizzle attracted a crowd of thousands.

Kelantan's monkhood negotiates the "gaps" between the encounters of two powerful figures—one Thai and Buddhist, the other Malay and Muslim. Both courts are symbolically responsible for the formal management of what is otherwise an autonomous monastic community. This intimate bond of interfaith and interstate support continues in the contemporary appointment procedures of the chief monk of Kelantan.

4.2 Thailand's royal representatives at the cremation of Than Chao Khun Mit

Ambiguous Patrons

After the unexpected death of Than Chao Khun Mit from a massive heart attack
in May 2001, the Kelantanese order of monks was without a formal head. In
order to fill this void the Kelantanese council of monks, comprising the abbots
of all its twenty temples, put forth a number of possible candidates. All were
senior monks (*pho than*) within the state's monastic establishment. Seniority
depended on the number of three-month Lenten seasons (*phansa*) one had
spent in the monkhood as well as on the various honors and titles (*samanasak*)
each monk had received from Thailand's administrative monastic body. After
months of deliberation, it was decided that Than Khru Di (Pho Than Di) of Ban
Bor On's Wat Nai was the most suitable person for the position of *chao khana
rat*. A complete biography of the abbot was compiled by his secretary, specifying
his accomplishments within the Buddhist order, his religious (*nak tham*) and
secular educational qualifications, and the social and construction projects he

had undertaken. The computer printout was then submitted to Malay palace officials in Kota Bharu for final approval by the sultan. "The sultan really doesn't know anything," laughed Khun Di. "All we need to do is submit to him a monk's name and he will approve it. We are the ones who select the candidate, not the sultan." The sultan's formal approval of the candidate is marked by the presentation of the Jawi-scripted letter of entitlement described above.

The Royal Thai Consulate acts as a bridge between the bureaucratic machinery of Thailand's many governmental departments and the local worlds of the Kelantanese Thai villages. Once the sultan has given his approval to the candidate, the consulate informs Bangkok's Department of Religious Affairs (*krom sasana*). Henceforth all correspondence on the ecclesiastical appointment—a constant circulation of letters and telephone calls—travels through the consulate's officers. The Department of Religious Affairs, like the Kelantanese sultan, is a mere actor in the religious play staged by Kelantan's governing order of monks. The department arranges for the formal presentation of the insignias of office to the newly appointed *chao khana rat*. These include a diamond-shaped embroidered fan (*phat jot*), the framed letter of appointment, and a new set of robes.[25]

In contrast to the formal presentation of the Jawi-scripted endorsement letter by the sultan or his representative, which takes place on a day convenient to both parties, Thailand's presentation ceremony for high ecclesiastical honors takes place on the fifth of December, King Bhumipol's birthday and Thailand's National Day. Having the ceremony coincide with these events is significant. It provides a striking legitimating force for the Thai monarch's traditional duty as the nation's foremost protector of Buddhism and reinforces the idea of the nation as a moral Buddhist universe that extends its influence from the king across international domains. Instinctively Kelantan's Thai community is drawn into an imagined space of cultural Thainess that overrides political and territorial affiliations.

In the past, Kelantan's saffron-robed candidates accepted their honors directly from the Thai king in Bangkok—or so the stories go—but today the process has been decentralized and palace and monastic council representatives now distribute the insignias on behalf of the ageing king at ceremonies held throughout the kingdom. Although the royal symbols of office are presented in Thailand, the newly appointed *chao khana rat* undergoes a formal consecration ceremony (*chalong*) in Kelantan upon his return. The *chalong* event, like all grand temple affairs, usually involves the participation of all of the state's monks. The Thai consul and members of the consulate's secretariat are also often in attendance as guests of honor, thereby reinforcing Thailand's powerful cultural presence in the Malaysian countryside.

Aside from its political and historical significance in cementing Thai-Malay relationships, the ritual support the Kota Bharu court affords its minority Thai Buddhist subjects can be seen in the performance of an idealized Malay rulership. Islamic Malay kingship has much in common with the Asokan-inspired model of the *dhammaraja* (Righteous Monarch) celebrated in Thai Buddhist ideals of statecraft and with which Kelantanese Thais are familiar (Tambiah 1970, 1976; Kobkua 1988).[26] In both Theravadin and Islamic models of statecraft, the king represents the chief patron of the religion and it is through the visible displays of this patronage that the ruler maintains the support of his subjects. Islamic Malay rulership derives a substantial part of its political culture from earlier Akbarian Sufic and caliphate jurisdiction, which positioned the sultan as the Shadow of God on Earth (Milner 1983). In his analysis of early Islamic kingship, Aziz Al-Azmeh (1997: 39) described how Sanskrit and Pali ideals of rulership probably influenced Islamic philosophical considerations of the microcosm and macrocosm relationship in leadership. In Southeast Asia these Sufic-inspired principles that entered into early Malay political philosophy may have syncretized with earlier Indian and Buddhist ideas.

As with the idealized Theravadin *dhammaraja*, who as a ruler merely ensures the proper functioning of religion while leaving its day-to-day management in the hands of the monks, the sultan remains the symbolic protector of Islam, although the actual affairs of religion are in the hands of Islamic scholars and theologians (*ulama*). Although Islam was the main religion of the classical caliphate polity, this did not mean that other religions were disallowed or oppressed by rule of law. Writing on Buyid social history, Roy Mottahedeh (2001) demonstrated that practices of sultanic patronage known as *istina* and the distribution and conferment of royal titles were political strategies developed in early Muslim polities to ensure the loyalty of culturally diverse subjects and prevent partisan interests from taking hold.

Sharia scholar Mohammad Hashim Kamali (1997) suggested that the ideology of religious freedom (*al-hurriyah al-diniyyah*) was a manifestation of personal liberty emphasized in Quranic texts and subsequently translated by Islamic lawmakers into sharia codes. This can be put to good political use, as when Kelantan's chief minister attended Thai temple functions as a guest of honor. The Islamic spiritual leader walked alongside the monks, talked freely with them on their temple grounds, and posed for photographs with them. It was precisely the chief minister's visually strong support for the Buddhist establishment that gained his party Thai votes during election years. Nevertheless, despite theoretical Islam's ideal of religious freedom within the borders of Islamic jurisdiction, religious zealotry is still common among certain segments of the Malay Muslim population. Throughout my fieldwork in Ban Bor On, I heard many young Thai students complain about how they could not eat lunch during the Muslim fasting month of Ramadan for fear of being chastised by Muslim peers and teachers. Some students complained about being subjected to Islamic sermonizing and encouraged to convert to the faith by their Muslim teachers. Most students did not pay much attention to these attempts at proselytization, although it did bother them and their parents to some degree. They were aware of the fact that Kelantan is Serambi Mekah — Mecca's Verandah — and located in a country where Islam is the primary religion. What made them most uncomfortable was the fact that religious diversity and a long-standing social harmony were being challenged by some, and that this increased their community's marginalization. At the same time as these private grumblings were made, the sultan continued to do his duties as Buddhism's main patron.

The Muslim leader's allocation of religious honors upon non-Muslim figure-heads is not unique to the Kelantanese Thai situation. Such practices of inter-faith patronage were already being practiced in Ottoman Jerusalem during the sixteenth century. As long as officially legitimated non-Muslim religious chiefs were present in the Muslim ruler's realm of control, religious diversity was respected and the authority of the Ottoman-ruled state was anchored (Cohen 1982). The position of the Malay sultan as the chief protector of all religions within his jurisdiction was exemplified during a meeting between the leaders of Kelantan's Thai community and Sultan Ismail Petra at the Kubang Kerian palace in 2003. The sultan regularly holds meetings with his Thai subjects, often select members of the Kelantanese Thai Association who represent the intellectual elite of the community. The Thais had alerted the sultan to the supposed threat that Wat Klang's abbot had received in an anonymously crafted letter detailing the possibility of terrorist violence to the temple's colossal Buddha statue during the statue's inauguration festivities in September 2001. The construction of the monumental image was believed by some Thais to have offended Muslim religious sensibilities not only by virtue of its sheer immensity but also because statues — representations of the human form — are considered taboo (Malay: *haram*) and popularly associated with the practice of idol worship (Malay: *sembah tok kong*). This threat was exacerbated by earlier news reports detailing the

Taliban's destruction of a pair of Buddhas in Bamiyan, Afghanistan, in March 2001.[27] Images of the hollowed-out cliff face haunted many Thais. The question on everyone's mind was, if the Taliban could destroy the monuments despite protests from powerful world leaders and international heritage watchdogs, what then of Kelantan's mega statues, which were unknown to many? Who would defend them? Compounding this fear was the fact that a number of Kelantanese Thai temples were built at a time before 1888, when residence grants began to be issued by the state's land office. Only Wat Khao in Kota Bharu and Bachok's Wat Nak have land grants in their name, having been built on designated plots of "temple land" (*tanah ketik*). Temple lands as religious zones are safe from the state's drive toward development. The lack of land grants could prove a problem should court orders and summonses revoke the temple's claim to its land. Most villagers, of course, agreed that this was a highly unlikely scenario, but the fact that it was a possibility, especially in the wake of Kelantan's drive toward rural development projects—housing, industries, and infrastructure—disturbed some. In bringing up the issue of possible threats to Wat Klang's Buddha with the sultan, the Thai leaders performed their role as loyal clients, thereby reaffirming the sultan's symbolic position as the chief protector of all faiths in his kingdom. The sultan listened patiently to the Thai insecurities and reassured them of their safety and of the state's responsibility toward and support of its minority populations.

It is undeniable that the sheer visibility of Wat Klang's statue created stirs among some members of Kelantan's Islamic community, in part as grounds for critiquing the state's Islamic administration and the Kuala Lumpur government. In a strongly worded article in the weekend edition (27 January 2002) of *Berita Harian* (Daily News), a leading Malay-language newspaper, journalist Dusuki Ahmad criticized Datuk Nik Aziz's earlier comment that "the Prophet Muhammad . . . would definitely enjoy living in Kelantan and not in any other state because PAS practiced Islamization." Dusuki argued that had the Prophet visited Kelantan, he would probably have been shocked at the crime, drug addiction, unemployment, and the large number of mammoth "idols" (Malay: *berhala*) in the state. "Have the PAS supporters forgotten the Prophet's reaction during the siege of Mecca when he realized that the Kabah was surrounded by hundreds of idols?" Dusuki (2002: 10) rhetorically asked his readers. The journalist was referring in particular to Wat Klang's Buddha, whose large black-and-white photograph was printed in the center of the editorial column.

In his historical analysis of Christian holy sites in Ottoman Jerusalem, Oded

Peri (2001) observed that the degree of religious privilege granted by the Muslim polity to its Christian subjects revolved around a political ideal of sharia legislature. Peri (57) remarked that within the "Abode of Islam (*dar al-Islam*), areas in which Muslims rule and Islam prevails . . . the lives, property and liberties of non-Muslims are protected, and their religions tolerated, provided they live according to the rules of the 'Covenant of Umar.'" Yet this did not prevent religious discrimination from occurring. In Jerusalem, this amounted to the implementation of sumptuary laws for both Jews and Christians (*dhimmis*) and the destruction of churches during a spate of anti-Christian sentiment between A.D. 894 and 896, and again from 1488 through 1490 (Cohen 1982: 49). To date, Kelantan has been spared acts of anti-Buddhist (or anti-Muslim) terrorism, although discourses of ethnic discord regularly surface and circulate within Thai village communities (Kershaw 1969). Expressions of unhappiness are often triggered by practices of supposed discrimination (*hino*) against Thais by certain policies of the Malaysian government and segments of the local Malay population. For the most part, however, Thai and Malay relations have been and continue to remain amicable in the Malaysian state, with instances of ethnic animosity restricted to grumbles and the occasional gang fight involving drunk and embittered youths over social turfs, taunts, and girlfriends.

In addition to monks, Thai village heads (*nai ban*) were often royally appointed individuals and were presented with the regalia of Malay office, such as ceremonial daggers and spears, by the Kota Bharu court. These symbols of status and loyalty were displayed on the body during formal state ceremonies involving meetings with palace representatives. One well-known *nai ban* was a man by the name of Pho Kae Bo who lived in Din Sung in the early years of the twentieth century. He was friends with the sultan, who would sometimes visit him at his home.[28] Today, most Thai villages have their own *nai ban*, who receives an allowance from Malaysia's federal government in Kuala Lumpur. Of late, some villages such as Ban Bor On have two *nai ban*—the other being a supporter of PAS and drawing a salary from the state government. The latter *nai ban* is often in charge of dealing with matters at the state level, such as land transactions, whereas the federal government's *nai ban* handles affairs at the national and intra-state level. Before World War Two, skilled Thai *nura* artistes also received royal patronage from the Malay court. Troupes were selected from Kelantan's many *nura* groups during competitions staged in the palace. As winners these royal entertainers (*nura phja*) were exempt from court-imposed corvée obligations (Malay: *kerah*). Lay temple representatives, called *sangkhari* in

Thai, were also given annual gifts of white cloth by the state through the office of local Malay district administrators (*tok gawo*). In return for the state's support of the Thai community, Thai villagers were obliged to pay an annual tribute of rice to the district officer. Known as *khao yakat* after the Muslim system of mandatory tithes (*zakat*), the practice was abandoned soon after the Second World War. At least one Thai was elected to the office of the *tok kweng*, the head of a cluster of villages that comprised Kelantan's subdistricts (*daerah*).[29] Under British administration, the *tok kweng*, a Siamese administrative designation, was replaced by the Malay *tok gawo* (*penggawa*), who was answerable to the British-appointed district officer (Azizah 2006: 19).

The historical practice of Malay-Thai patron clientelism has had political implications on voting behavior as well. Political parties in Kelantan are aware of Thai loyalty to the royal regimes within which they are subjects and they manipulate the discourse to their advantage in securing votes. At the Barisan Nasional's rally held at Tok Nai Suk's house in September 2001, its Tumpat branch representative, a Malay man in his early fifties whom Ban Bor On residents affectionately called Cikgu Mat (Teacher Mat) spoke of the social bonds that tie Kelantan's Thai community to their sultan. From the window of Tok Nai Suk's large wooden house, Cikgu Mat spoke to the assembled crowd of Ban Bor On villagers sitting below. A feast of rice, curried eels, and other Thai and Malay delicacies were laid on a buffet table in the garden, courtesy of the Barisan Nasional officials who were desperately attempting to win the favor of their Thai brethren. Cikgu Mat spoke of how PAS was trying hard to Islamicize Kelantan, a popular point of concern I heard articulated by Thai party sympathizers. The so-called fundamentalist move, argued Cikgu Mat in crisp Kelantanese Malay, was the result of a displacement of royal power by the opposition's Islamic party officials. Cikgu Mat appealed to the sense of sentimentality and loyalty Thais feel toward their sultan, an association that was undoubtedly drawn in part from Thailand's televised images of the king as a people's monarch. To Cikgu Mat and his party representatives, loyalty to the ruler is a powerful marker of Thainess.

Using this model derived from Thailand's popular media representations and traditional Kelantanese social history, Cikgu Mat pointed out how "of all the peoples in the world, the Thai [*kaum thai*] are the most loyal to their king." Speaking with the emotions typical of an up-and-coming Malaysian politician, his voice booming and confident, Cikgu Mat painted a picture of Kelantanese royal power for his Thai audience. He emphasized that the sultan had held meetings with representatives from the Thai community on three separate occasions to discuss the social issues affecting them. "If the sultan did not love the Thais, he would not have scheduled these meetings," raved the schoolteacher, his voice shattering the stillness of the night. Unfortunately, PAS was attempting to divest power from the sultan, as when the Islamic party suggested that all matters dealing with religion be placed in its own hands. This shook the very foundations of the Malaysian constitution, which guarantees the position of the sultan as protector of Malay customs and religion.[30] Indirectly, Cikgu Mat appealed to an emotive Thai nostalgia for a past before the complexities of party politicking had taken hold in the state and when patron-client relationships between the sultan and his Thai subjects were at their zenith. In his speech to the villagers, Cikgu Mat portrayed the sultan as a threatened child who needed to be supported by his subjects in the trying times of election years. Thais had to help their sultan, and the only way to do so was to vote for Barisan Nasional.

"Take your campaigning to the Malay villages," blurted Na Dam. "You know we will vote for you. Those are the guys you need to convince," he yelled at the teacher, to the amusement of the audience. But voting is a complex matter in Ban Bor On and other Thai villages. Not everyone supports the ideals of the Barisan Nasional Party and no amount of free buffet meals, cigarettes, T-shirts, or emotive calls for sultanic assistance would influence them otherwise. In fact, PAS won more Thai political converts as it stepped up its campaigning, using a language of religious tolerance that made many Thais smile and nod. After all, Thainess to the villagers was intricately tied to Buddhism and the freedom to practice it.

The Kelantanese political playing field is complex and confusing and involves a tussle over Islamic moralism and Malaysian federalism (Kershaw 2001). To Ban Bor On residents, the sultan is a stable political and public figurehead. Like Kelantan's chief minister and Malaysia's supreme ruler, he is Muslim and, thus does not carry with him the element of sacredness that accompanies the cult of the royal image in Thailand. Thainess means more than simply being patriotic clients of a Muslim ruler. It has to do with the successful management of cultural and political clientelism by royalty on both sides of the border.

Kelantan's Thais consider themselves the subjects of two kings—one Buddhist and the other Muslim—whose overlapping spheres of power engulf their tiny communities and shape the way they produce and negotiate their sense of Thainess. Their unique position—as ethnically Thai yet politically Malaysian and inhabiting a historical Kelantanese state—allows them to benefit from the interactions afforded by both regal figureheads. The close relationship the Kelantanese Thai monkhood maintains between the Thai Buddhist monarch, his ecclesiastical officers, and the Malay Muslim sultan is appreciated through social memories of inter-ethnic interactions that permeate indigenous histories. Kelantanese Thais proudly speak of visits to their temples by members from both courts and of the travels of senior Kelantanese monks to distant royal centers. Photographs of royal visits and the presentation of honors and insignias of rank are visibly displayed in temple buildings and as printed images in the cremation volumes distributed to well-wishers at monk funerals. The late abbot of Wat Nai, Than Khru Daeng, who passed away in 1992 at the age of eighty-one, was formally conferred with his symbols of office to the position of Phra Khru by King Bhumipol himself. A large black-and-white photograph of the presentation ceremony held on the occasion of the king's birthday on 5 December 1970 at Bangkok's Amarin Palace shows the Thai king offering the insignorial fan to the monk. One of the two framed photographs hangs on the wall of Wat Nai's preaching hall (*rong tham*) and another one hangs between the life-sized statues of Than Khru Daeng and his predecessor Pho Than Sao in the abbot's quarters. The episode was a key one in Kelantanese Thai monastic and political history, as the king usually only hands out ecclesiastical honors to the highest-ranking monks in the kingdom, those of the rank of Somdet and Chao Khun. Than Khru Daeng is believed by Ban Bor On residents to be one of only nine monks to have been given such honors by the king himself. The photograph has been reproduced many times and copies were distributed to visitors as souvenirs during Than Khru Daeng's cremation festivities in 1997. Many Ban Bor On and Ban Phan Jao households display this snapshot of village-court association on their altars. The photograph, including close-ups of the abbot's royal fan and his certificate of office, was reproduced in color in the funeral volume. Likewise, the funeral volumes of the two former Chao Khun of Bang Rim Nam, Than Chao Khun Chan and Than Chao Khun Mit, both contain pictures of visits by Sultan Yahya Petra to the Pasir Mas temple.

The exhibition of symbols of Thai royalism in Kelantanese Thai homes and temples is not an attempt to negotiate contesting political loyalties. Indeed, despite what seem to be outward displays of royal patriotism for a neighboring nation-state, most Kelantanese Thais I spoke to were clear as to where their political loyalties stood. Kershaw's contention that the Thai kingly image was "no more than an expression of ethnic, not political identification" (Kershaw 2001: 158n) is helpful in understanding the symbolic relevance of these popular images in Kelantan. Like many other Kelantanese Thais, Phi Sung, who incidentally is also the current PAS-appointed *nai ban* for Ban Bor On, referred to the Thai king as *phra chao phean din* (lit., lord of the land) in direct emulation of formal standard Thai parlance. The Kelantanese sultan is the *phja*, a local Tumpat Tak Bai epithet referring to a generic monarch. Unlike the distant formality reserved for the Thai king, the Malay *phja* is to the Kelantanese Thais more than just a political figure. He is the symbolic head of the state and a friend—someone who is referred to by a simple nickname. There are no royal titles or formal terms of address here. He is, like everyone else, a Kelantanese through and through. Like it or not, he is one of them and they are his subjects.

The deep respect that Kelantanese Thais exhibit toward Thailand's formal kingly image goes beyond the ethnic expression of solidarity that Kershaw (1969) identified in his doctoral thesis. Ethnic affiliation, Kershaw wrote, is built upon a shared mythic geography centered on a locally conceived Thai political universe: the *myang* (*mueang*), with the king of Thailand as its ruler. Kershaw's *myang thaj* (his spelling, 194) reminds us of Anderson's oft-cited notion of the imagined community (Anderson 1983). It is a borderless space that incorporates Buddhist Thais from both within and beyond the nation-state; it is held together by their members' collective feelings of Theravadin identification. Kershaw argued that Kelantanese Thais "conceive of themselves to be members of the *myang* by virtue of their race and religion."

Conversations with Ban Bor On residents revealed a very different concept of the *mueang* as a distinct and mobile Thai space. To them, *mueang thai* was a specifically demarcated place marked by the circuits that entangled it. It encompassed the international border, customs and immigration checkpoints, duty free shops, army patrols, bandits, passports, a Buddhist king, sex workers, and tremendously spicy food. These vivid perceptions of place were associated with an unquestioned mapped location that developed after 1909. It was an expansive geopolitical entity that began where territorial Kelantan ended, on the opposite bank of the Tak Bai and Golok rivers. Ethnically *mueang thai* was made up of Malays, Thais, Chinese, and people from other groups. Although older men and women I spoke to recalled experiencing a time when the Tak Bai river was a mere hindrance to travel rather than a distinct political space ("we did not need passports and border passes back then," they told me many times), any movement across the river today is clearly an encounter with a different polity.

Passports, identity cards, and border passes, symbols of stasis and national affiliation in a moving world, are what define international travel for Kelantanese visitors to Thailand today. These papers allow for mobility to manifest itself, but they also restrict movement. The multiple-journey Malaysian border pass—a simple sheet of white paper affixed with the photograph of its holder—is one of the most common travel documents held by Kelantanese Thais. Costing only RM10 (US$2.79), the pass is an affordable alternative to the more expensive RM300 (US$83.50) to RM600 (US$167) international passport. Border passes are issued by Malaysian Immigration to Malaysian citizens and permanent residents "of Thai origin" who have lived in the border provinces of Kelantan, Kedah, Perlis, and Perak for more than three years. Valid for half a year, the pass allows its holder to travel anywhere within a restricted twenty-five-kilometer radius of the border. For most Thais I spoke with, this was more than sufficient, as their short visits to Thailand often took them no further than Narathiwat or Hatyai anyway. Border passes encourage movement across the frontier and increase the cultural exposure of Kelantanese Thais to Thailand.

Yet it is the idea of circulating between polities across an aquatic frontier, despite shared cultural and historical experiences, that is most powerfully engrained in the way Kelantanese Thais experience their adventures in *mueang thai*. Even before the border was as stringently policed as it is today, with increasing cross-border traffic and the fears of international terrorism, villagers were well aware of their entering a different *mueang*. The border at the Tak Bai river was what Tim Ingold (2007: 49–50) aptly defined a "ghostly line." Like the invisible connections we make between stars in the night sky to form constellations of big and little dippers, lions, oxen, dogs, and bears, the border is imagined as a very real line even though it is in effect, invisible. Ingold gives a very good example of the invisible frontier in an episode from his fieldwork among the Lapps along the Finnish-Russian border. "The border," Ingold put it, "was marked by a clear cut strip of forest down the mid-line of which the actual frontier was supposed to run. It was marked in no other way save by occasional posts. Had I attempted to cross it, however, I would have been shot at from one of the many observation towers on the Soviet side" (ibid.).

Ban Bor On residents remain clear as to where they stand. They live not in *mueang thai* but in *mueang lantan* or *mueang Malaysia*, depending on the context of the conversation. One does not need observation towers or customs checkpoints to define the border. All that is required is the belief that the river separates two independent polities, each with its own ruler. There is no real emotional attachment to the polity on the opposite bank; in fact, the Kelantanese Thais I know much prefer living in Malaysia. When faced with the question of contesting loyalties during Thailand versus Malaysia soccer matches, for instance, my friends were quick to emphasize their support for the Malaysian team. "When I hear Malaysia's national anthem, Negara Ku, being played, my hair stands on end," admitted Phorn, as she drove through the Tanah Merah rubber plantations. Phorn, like many others I knew, was proud of her Thai cultural identity but unquestionably patriotic to her birth country, Malaysia. The circuits that move people and ideas between Thailand and Malaysia forge emotional connections between people and the place they called home. Being in Malaysia was comforting for my Ban Bor On interlocutors. Its long history of inter-ethnic accommodation coupled with a belief in the doctrine of "having always lived here" made Kelantanese Thais feel proud of their political identity. In Thailand, a place they looked to for so much of their cultural inspiration, they were like strangers—confused and somewhat out of place yet at times longing to fit in.

In chapter 5, I turn the ethnographic gaze away from Malay centers of regal and social power and toward what is happening across the Tak Bai tributary. Kelantanese Thais creatively generate a sense of personhood and meaning for themselves out of the ambiguity that engulfs their lives and experiences in the hinterlands. Although there is no serious attempt to associate themselves with *mueang thai* beyond the knowledge that the polity is peopled with men and women who are culturally akin to them, Kelantanese Thai villagers constantly negotiate their identity as Malaysians with practices of cultural nationalism emanating from Thailand. Thailand provides a rich and exciting array of tropes through which Thainess in Kelantan can be experienced. It manifests itself in the new and strange encounters people stumble upon, bringing its subjects out of an undefined past and into an uncertain future.

CHAPTER 5

Dreams

THE SPREAD OF A NATIONAL THAI ETHNO-CULTURAL CONSCIOUSNESS via an officially standardized Buddhism purged of its local variations is nothing new in the modern history of the Thai polity. Writing about northern Thailand's Yuan and Shan sects of Theravadism, Charles Keyes (1971) remarked that it was not until Chulalongkorn's program of monastic centralization into a "single national church" through the promulgation of the 1902 Sangha Administration Act that Siam's outlying principalities were incorporated into a unified and state-centric Buddhist fold. Prior to this, local monasteries had been largely autonomous. Abbots were appointed internally by local monk chapters without the formality of a national Buddhist organization. Buddhism and Thai national identity thus engulfed one another, with each being inseparable from the other.

Thai political leaders have been concerned with the production of a common Thai identity since at least the time of King Vajiravudh (r. 1910–1925), if not earlier. Vajiravudh intimately associated being Thai with being Buddhist, and for him Buddhism was what held the nation together (Barme 1993: 30). As with Chulalongkorn before him, Vajiravudh made tours to the territorial extremities of the kingdom. During these trips he would spread his militaristic doctrine of Thai nationalism, one that was based upon the seminal holy trinity of king (*phra mahakasat*), religion (*sasana* [as equated with Buddhism]), and nation (*chat*). This doctrine was subsequently taken up by Field Marshall Sarit Thanarat in the latter's post–World War II vision of a national political creed (Vella 1978: 198). According to Walter Vella, Vajiravudh made two royal visits to the deep south, one in 1915 and the other two years later, largely to strengthen the relationship between the region's Malay Muslim majority and the Bangkok court.

On 8 June 1915, Vajiravudh paid a short visit to Wat Chehe in Tak Bai. Than Khru Kio, along with many other Kelantanese Thai monks, was at the temple to greet the king (Wanipha 1992: 9). It is likely that such an occasion included a mixed audience of both Kelantanese and Tak Bai villagers, as do large festivals on both sides of the river today. Na Chao Nuat remembered hearing from his grandfather that a delegation of Ban Kao villagers had accompanied Than Khru Kio for the royal visit. As the monk's boat approached the temple, the Ban Kao villagers fired two canons (*puen nyai*) they had brought with them from the temple, announcing the arrival of the respected senior monk to the Chehe villagers. Than Khru Kio was believed to have spent some time in Bangkok and was therefore familiar with the Chakri house. He had gone to Chehe to see for himself which of Chulalongkorn's seventy-seven children was Siam's new ruler. In a lighthearted episode, Na Cao Nuat recalled hearing from older Ban Kao villagers (most of whom have passed away) that Than Khru Kio had been unimpressed by King Vajiravudh's pet canines. "He was a man who did not like dogs but the Thai king had brought his pets with him on his tour," reflected Na Chao Nuat. He laughed at the monk's anger toward the dogs. "They said that Than Khru Kio fumed at the dogs playing at his feet. Than Khru Kio said, 'If these were not the king's dogs, I would have kicked them,'" the mustached Na Chao Nuat laughed.

Than Khru Kio's wanderings back and forth across the border were part of a wider system of monastic circulation that involved monks from both Siam (Thailand) and Kelantan entering into each other's ecclesiastical domains. Many such monk journeys after the Second World War can be seen as part of a national exercise of Buddhist missionization that emanated from Bangkok but was felt as far south as Kelantan. Initiated by Thailand's Religious Affairs Department (*krom sasana*) under the auspices of the Ministry of Education in 1965, the *thammathut* program of missionary monk activism aimed at propagating a standardized Buddhism within and beyond the borders of the kingdom.[1] This version of Theravadin activism emerged out of Bangkok's two main Buddhist universities, the Mahamakut and Mahachulalongkorn, with their underlying royal and political roots.

Thammathut projects in the 1960s attempted to purge the Thai Buddhist practice of syncretic localisms, thereby generating a common Buddhist culture that could symbolically link all Thai Buddhists as one homogenous people regardless of their geographical location. The program, although formally initiated two years after Sarit's death in 1963, contained many of the field marshall's dreams of national development (Keyes 1971: 560; Thak 2007: 232). Monk volunteers who participated in the program were dispatched in pairs to the farthest reaches of the country, beginning first with the northeast and subsequently extending their movements south and then across the border into Malaysia. Monks were also sent to places farther away, including London and Los Angeles. The young and highly motivated university-educated monks were representatives of urban Buddhist centrality and modernism, which had begun during the reign of King Chulalongkorn. Since then, Bangkok's Buddhist universities and temple schools have been attracting students from across Thai-influenced Theravadin Southeast Asia (Hansen 2007). Like the soldiers, policemen, provincial officials, border-patrol guards, teachers, doctors, and others who were dispatched to the frontier provinces as symbols of national development in the early twentieth century, the orange-robed *thammathut* monks crafted new perceptions of space and power (Thongchai 1994). They were conduits through which Prime Minister Thanom Kittikachorn's (1963–1973) propaganda of a unified Thai Buddhist cultural citizenship flowed. As Stanley Tambiah (1976: 439) poignantly observed, the *thammathut* movement had strong political undercurrents of "decreasing regional grievances (particularly of the northeast), of stemming communism, and of mobilizing loyalty to the king and nation and by extension to the government through the agency of religion." Thus the *thammathut* movement was more than simply about the standardization of doctrine and its practice; it was about the consolidation of a Thai state, purged of its internal opposition, that was on the path to moral and social advancement (Mulder 1969).[2]

In Ban Bor On, *thammathut* monks established a Pali school at Wat Nai sometime between 1973 and 1974. The school—the only center for Pali education in Kelantan—was administered by Thailand's Department of Religious Affairs and staffed by *thammathut* monks from Bangkok. Wat Nai's Pali school held classes in the two most basic levels of Pali education (*prayok* 1 and 2). In total, a graduate needed to pass nine *prayok* to complete a full course in Pali studies. Upon completion of the first two grades of elementary Pali, Kelantanese monks could choose to continue their Pali education at Songkhla's Wat Liab. The phenomena of Kelantanese Thai monks pursuing Buddhist studies at temples in south Thailand harked back to a much earlier practice when Kelantanese monks traveled north to receive formal education in *nak tham* (Buddhist doctrine), Pali, and, for some, magical practices (*akhom*). After successfully completing three *prayok*, the monk is awarded the title of Maha by the educational establishment, which he retains throughout his monastic career and adopts as a personal honorific should he decide to leave the monkhood. Seventeen Kelantanese monks attended Pali classes at the Wat Nai school. Most however, did not continue with their training. Wat Nai's Pali school closed after some five years, as *tham-*

mathut fervor in Bangkok declined and monks were no longer dispatched to teach abroad.

During the height of the *thammathut* frenzy, Wat Nai experienced a regular circulation of Bangkok-trained monks amongst its monastic staff. Most came as Pali teachers but also taught Thai at the temple school that Tok Nai Suk and Chao Ruai had set up. By the end of the five years of active teaching at the school, Wat Nai had hosted a total of six *thammathut* monks.[3] Besides teaching Pali and elementary Buddhist doctrine at the school, these monastic activists were also instrumental in propagating their version of a common performance of Thai cultural personhood that extended beyond the borders of the Ban Bor On community (Kershaw 1969).

Mae Doh remembered the *thammathut* monks fondly. She lived across the road from Wat Nai in a large compound with her sister and their extended family. The land on which her house stood once belonged to the Datuk Kaya Budi of Bandar Tumpat and Mae Doh paid his family rent for occupying it. Na Bong, her late husband, was a famous artisan and sculptor who had been instrumental in starting the tradition of the *loy krathong* parade in Kelantan, now Ban Bor On's biggest annual festival. He designed and built numerous structures in temples across the state, including Wat Nai's elephant gate and the abbot's quarters in Bang Rim Nam's temple. Mae Doh contrasted the ritual piety and discipline of the *thammathut* monks with what she considered the laxity of the Kelantanese clergy. *Thammathut* monks, she argued, were even particular about the way villagers used their bodies during services. She remembered how Maha Phrom would be upset about the way some villagers clasped their palms during the recitation of Pali verses or when listening to monks chanting. "Your fingers should point up and not down," laughed Mae Doh as she mimicked the Bangkok monk's words. "Maha Phrom would always correct us. He would remind us that we were worshipping the Buddha and not the ground. Our monks never teach us these things." She sighed with a hint of nostalgia. To Mae Doh and many other Ban Bor On villagers, these standard Thai–speaking monks were held in high regard. Villagers admired their discipline and teaching abilities. Their constant attempts to impart a fixed definition of Thai Buddhist culture and tradition were in line with contemporary middle-class cultural practices of Buddhist modernism in the Thai metropolis. This connection allowed Ban Bor On villagers to feel that they were a part of a larger Thai Buddhist moral polity, reducing feelings of social and ethnic marginalization as a cultural minority in a Muslim state. The village was suddenly part of a dynamic Thai global universe that expanded across small spatial locales through the silent movement of the *thammathut* monks and their Kelantanese admirers.

The admiration Ban Bor On residents had for the *thammathut* monks of the sixties, a fact also noted by Kershaw (1969), is reflected in the way some of my friends spoke about a new breed of missionary monks in their midst. The Dhammakaya Foundation is an active Buddhist society that began as a school of meditation based on the teachings of the monk Phra Mongkholthepmuni (1885–1959). Originating in Thailand's Wat Phra Dhammakaya in the 1970s, the Buddhist group is now an international organization with meditation centers across Thailand and in major cities worldwide. The organization also runs its own 24-hour satellite cable channel called the Dhamma Media Channel (DMC), broadcasting a variety of programs related to Buddhism and education, and even operates an open university. Dhammakaya's bright orange–robed clergy aim to foster a uniform Buddhism based on a unique form of meditation known as the Dhammakaya Method that overrides clerical divides in Thai Buddhism. Much has been written about the Dhammakaya movement in the scholarly literature on new Buddhist movements in Thailand, especially in relation to the urban and middle-class flavor that the group has assumed and recent controversies and allegations of fraud, embezzlement, and corruption involving the mega-foundation.[4] What is pertinent to our discussion here is the fact that Dhammakaya Foundation monks began appearing in Kelantan's Thai temples in the 1990s and their presence brought about internal friction in the community and raised questions about what constituted Thainess. Dhammakaya monks, like the *thammathut* monks before them, were young, articulate, and well-versed in Buddhist philosophy and meditation techniques. Their academic credentials and gentle demeanor soon won them a loyal following of villagers, many of whom were somewhat disheartened by what they felt was the shabby state of Buddhism in Kelantan. These villagers admired all things Dhammakaya and the movement reframed the way some villagers looked at local religion. Dhammakaya monks and their intellectualizing discourse of "proper" religion indirectly hinted at Ban Bor On's encounters with a new Buddhist internationalism and rationalism that has brought middle-class urban Thailand right into the village. Villagers spoke in a language of zealotry one finds when talking to new converts. By 2004 many had bought DMC cable boxes and had them installed in their Ban Bor On homes for RM800 (US$229), the installation done by a lay Dhammakaya member from the center's Penang headquarters. Besides watching

Dhammakaya channels on cable television, Ban Bor On's Dhammakaya support-ers made frequent trips to the sprawling eighty-acre Dhammakaya Center in Pathum Thani, Thailand. Their obsession with the new form of Buddhism irked more traditionally minded villagers, including abbots and monks. Although most temples, including Wat Nai, played host to visiting Dhammakaya monks out of politeness, abbots such as Pho Than Di and his deputy did not see eye to eye with them. With the exception of one or two visits to see for themselves what the fuss was all about, Pho Than Di and Khun Di refused to have anything to do with the foundation.

In 2001, Dhammakaya fervor had reached fever pitch in the village. It had spread itself through the community and was a regular topic for conversations. I was constantly reminded by Dhammakaya supporters like the late Mae Daeng how large and wonderful the Dhammakaya temple was, how well-organized their celebrations were, and how knowledgeable, learned, and charismatic their monks. Inadvertently, these comments revealed a general unhappiness people like Mae Daeng had with local Buddhist practice. To them, to be Thai was also to practice Buddhism "correctly," and this, with all its historical and nationalist trappings, was to be found in the technical competency of the Dhammakaya movement. The Dhammakaya monks brought urban Thailand's class-oriented reflections on Thainess and Buddhism into the village, and with it a new experi-ence of religious modernity (Lee and Ackerman 1997).

Both Dhammakaya and the *thammathut* monks exposed Kelantanese Thais to cultural and symbolic landscapes far away from their tiny villages. Reflecting earlier associations of the Thai capital with Buddhist learning, they brought Kelantanese Thai monks to study in Bangkok and beyond, as well as organized tours to visit temples in Thailand. Other Buddhist reformist doctrines, such as the largely middle-class-centric work of the late Buddhadasa Bhikkhu (1906–1993), did not have much influence in shaping Kelantanese Thai definitions of religiosity. Buddhadasa's numerous books and poems espousing a less materially oriented Buddhism that was politically and socially engaged remained nothing more than works of religious literature. Villagers rarely made the journey to the late monk's famed temple and meditation center in southern Thailand's Surat Thani province. Although some of the monks at Wat Nai did read his work, most villagers seemed uncertain as to his vision. Buddhadasa's teachings, unlike the media-savvy Dhammakaya, remained largely confined to books and the urban-educated, middle-class Thais across the border.

Communes

Although the missionization of Thailand's cultural citizens in Kelantan occurred under the flag of the *thammathut* movement, *thammathut* ideology did not attempt to create new political citizens. The *thammathut*'s primary objective was to use standard Buddhist practice to generate a firm sense of cultural identification with Thailand among Thais everywhere. It was this politically non-threatening stance that allowed for the establishment of Thai temples in the United States, Europe, Australia, and Malaysia. Both *thammathut* and the later Dhammakaya monks entered Malaysia legally, and their low-key activities in small and (to the government) socially invisible communities were not deemed a threat to the Malaysian state. Had there been the possibility of patriotic realignment for the Kelantanese as a result of the arrival of Thai monks in the country, it is likely that an anxious Malaysian government in the throes of post-independence nervousness would have curtailed their influx. Unlike monastic projects of religious evangelism that did not politically challenge Kelantanese Thai citizenship, Thai government land settlement schemes in Narathiwat, called *nikhom*, were indirectly aimed at creating Thai citizens out of Malaysian settlers. The schemes were devised, in part, as a means to control and domesticate Thailand's communist-rife southern peripheries by toying with ethnic demographics and enhanced rural development.

The pro-U.S. front of Thai premier Sarit Thannarat (1958–1963) meant that he viewed communism as Enemy Number One. The red threat posed by the Communist Party of Thailand (CPT) in the deep south, coupled with a generalized U.S.-inspired phobia of burgeoning communist activism in mainland Southeast Asia's hinterlands, meant that the "messy" south was a political challenge for the Sarit politburo, a fact that had precedents in the earlier anti-communist rhetoric of Field Marshall Phibul Songkhram (1948–1957). Based on my conversations with older *nikhom* residents, it is probable that an idea for the scheme was already in the works during the Second World War, although its development did not really happen until the beginning of the U.S.'s anti-communist purge. *Nikhom* communes, like British Malaya's New Villages, continued for many years and led to the clearing of vast tracks of jungle in and around Narathiwat's market districts of Waeng, Sukhirin, and Sungai Golok. Similar communes were also established in northeast Thailand, another hotbed of restive communist activity and regionalism.

By the 1950s and 1960s, *nikhom* lands had introduced into Narathiwat's frontier zones a population of supposedly patriotic Thai citizens from northeast Malaysia and the more impoverished regions of Thailand. Developing the south subsequently played into Sarit's obsessive association between a good citizenry with the ideals of orderliness (*riab roi*) and social and economic development. Development was about maximizing the potential of a place and the people living within it, which could only come about once things were in order. For this to happen, the messiness that was the forested interior had to be domesticated and the cultural heterogeneity of national peripheral gaps brought under Bangkok's domination. Sarit ensured that government funding for the building of roads and infrastructure was channeled into the nation's trouble spots, including the southern provinces. In 1961, the political strongman made a trip to the Malay provinces and was appalled by the cultural ambiguity of the region's population, many of whom did not speak Thai. Thak (2007: 132) cites a remark made by Sarit to southerners during the tour, pointing out the need for development in the region so that villagers could participate in the patriotic fervor that had engulfed Sarit's version of despotic paternalism. In a highly emotional moment, Sarit called for migrations into the furthest peripheries of the kingdom:

> You must persevere, you must work. *I want my Thai brothers from Isan, the North, and South to pour to the South to settle and work there. . . . Bring down Thai blood and the love of the nation to spread there.* (Emphasis mine)

And pour in they did. Land settlement schemes were set up throughout southern Narathiwat with mixed populations of Thais from poorer parts of the country, especially the northeast (*isan*). Sarit does not mention in his stirring speech that the schemes would also be open to Thai Buddhists from Kelantan, so much so that some of the earliest immigrant communes in the Thirty Hills district of Waeng known as *nikhom kao* (old *nikhom*) comprised almost entirely Kelantanese Thai settlers. To these Malaysians the Thai government offered token citizenship, and soon the once dangerous and communist-infested frontier was populated with Thailand's new citizens. The migration of Thais from Kelantan into the *nikhom* communes of Waeng bears similarities with a more recent movement of Thai settlers into Narathiwat. Na Rong, who lived in the Tumpat village of Ban Iak, with its interesting mix of Thai and Malay residential sectors, told me that his village had experienced a slow outmigration of inhabitants in search of employment opportunities.

In the past, up until about twenty years ago, Ban Iak residents went to Narathiwat and the surrounding areas to buy land and to work. This was because living in Malaysia was hard. There were no jobs here. The only job they could do was to harvest rice in Kedah and construction in Kuala Lumpur. At that time, Thailand was more prosperous [than Malaysia]. Construction was booming there so many people went to Thailand to work. They took Thai citizenship. It was easy to get citizenship because all you had to do was declare that you had lost your [Malaysian] identity card and your birth certificate. Then you registered yourself as a Thai citizen.

What the Thai government did not know, or did not care to know, was that many of these Malaysian settlers continued to hold on to their Malaysian identity cards and passports, effectively benefiting from being dual political citizens. Possessing dual nationality facilitated movement across the international divide and symbolically maintained the migrants' sense of historical identity and cultural continuity with Kelantan. Settlers used their Malaysian citizenship as a means to enter Kelantan without the hassle of applying for immigration papers from Thai and Malaysian border officials. When in Thailand, they made use of their Thai citizenship documents. For many a Kelantanese migrant, *nikhom* lands were seen as economic cash cows with which to improve harvest incomes. Many continued to live in Kelantan but returned to their *nikhom* plots regularly to check on the growth of seedlings or to harvest fruit (the small, sweet, brown-skinned *longkong* being especially popular) and latex. Participating in *nikhom* projects allowed people to experience two nation-states as an enlarged space of cultural continuity. Kelantanese settlers in the early *nikhom* projects saw their movement as practical sojourns into virgin territory rich in land resources that could augment their farm holdings back home. Before *nikhom* schemes were introduced in Narathiwat, enterprising Kelantanese Thais were already buying up tracks of land in the province on which to set up fruit orchards. These early migrants moved regularly between Thailand and Kelantan, tending to fruit and rubber trees in the former and rice and vegetables in the latter.

Nikhom's first settlers did not have it easy. They had to clear their own eighteen-acre jungle plots and construct their own houses from the wood and cement provided at a subsidized rate by Thai government cooperatives. Villagers often worked together in groups of five or more during the initial settlement phase. Each person was provided an allowance of no more than 100,000 Thai baht to purchase the materials and equipment needed to set up home in the forest. Key materials for constructing houses were provided to the settlers free of charge. These included wood, zinc roofing, and nails. To make a difficult situation even more challenging, the settlers' backbreaking work was often interrupted by the threat of wild animals and marauding ex–Communist Party of Thailand bandits. To protect themselves, some villagers were issued shotguns by the local police, indirectly spawning an illegal system of personal self-defense in the lawless hinterlands. Despite these dangers, a large number of Kelantanese Thais took to the *nikhom* projects with gusto. Although never stated, Sarit and subsequent governments' active encouragement of Kelantanese Thais to participate in its *nikhom* projects can be seen as a possible sideline attempt to populate the predominantly Malay Muslim reaches of southern Narathiwat with a larger Thai-speaking Buddhist population, thereby decreasing the support base for Islamic militant networks working out of Narathiwat's rural landscape.

Thai Buddhists were the only Kelantanese who were able to participate in *nikhom* schemes, although Malay Muslims from southern Thailand were also beneficiaries of the land resettlement projects. Kelantanese Malays were denied all *nikhom* opportunities by the Thai government. Peopling the hinterlands of the state with economic migrants seen as docile Thai citizens allowed for the extension of nationalism into the farthest reaches of the geopolity—roads were built to reach *nikhom* communes, police posts set up, schools constructed, and temples founded. The Thai government saw development as necessary to decrease the threat to national security felt along the borderlands. So popular were the early *nikhom* projects with Kelantanese Thais that some Malaysian settlements became almost deserted, as eager Thai villagers rushed across the border. For instance, about half of the population of Khok Din in Pasir Mas took up *nikhom* lands in Sukhirin. Although the *nikhom* areas were vast and spread across much of southern Narathiwat, Kelantanese migrants preferred living close to one another in the new settlements, thereby replicating their familiar lifeworlds across the Golok river. Thus *nikhom* communes such as *Soi Lantan* (Kelantan Avenue) emerged, comprising primarily villagers from different Thai communities in Kelantan.

Growing up, I heard my mother talk about *nikhom* lands a lot. Her father, Pho Chan, had planned on moving the family to a *nikhom* settlement but my mother refused to go, claiming that life was hard there and that she had not heard anything positive about living in the middle of a communist-rife jungle. Some of her relatives, including Pho Chan's sister, had taken up lands in *nikhom kao*, but my mother never visited them. Until the early 1990s, the one and only road that cut through *nikhom kao* in Soi Lantan was a narrow dirt track that was impassable during the rains. Banditry was common in the area and stories of robbers forcefully closing off rubber smallholdings and demanding a fee from their terrified cultivators are still heard. A cultivator who refused to pay the ransom risked death. My mother's fears were not unfounded: her step-uncle, Eh Toh, a man in his twenties, had gone missing in a *nikhom* settlement many years earlier. No one knew what had happened to him, but rumors circulated both in the commune and in Kelantan that he had been murdered by communist fighters who were unhappy that they had not received the RM30,000 (US$8,364) ransom they demanded from his parents. Years later, a settler stumbled across a skeleton in a forested part of the commune. Eh Toh's parents concluded that the bones must be those of their lost son, bringing closure to their life and terror to the commune's repute.

Pho Chan's younger sister Tok Joi married Lung Lin. When I last visited her in October 2010 — a few months prior her death — Tok Joi could no longer walk. She was in her nineties and lived with her granddaughter in a small house near a rundown kindergarten. Her husband had passed away a few years earlier. Lung Lin was already eighty years old when I met him in 2002. Both Tok Joi and her late husband were born in the Tumpat village of Ban Jai. Lung Lin was one of the first Kelantanese pioneers to take up *nikhom* lands. Some say that his move was motivated by a crime he had committed in Kelantan and that he was on the run from the Malaysian authorities. He was known to be a man of many vices, one who enjoyed gambling and betting on bull- and cock-fighting tournaments. His social persona as a ruffian (*khon chua*) made him unpopular with many villagers, including his father-in-law — my great-grandfather. Although he moved to Narathiwat, Lung Lin continued to maintain close ties with his family and friends in Kelantan. His younger sister, Na Tip, still lives in Ban Jai and used to visit him frequently. Her visits were triggered by his failing health and by the easy accessibility of the settlement via a new tarred highway that now links the *nikhom* communes with bustling Sungai Golok and Waeng. No longer does one have to travel through muddy paths on the back of hired motorcycle taxis or fear attacks by bandits when entering *nikhom* settlements, a memory that Na Tip resurrected each time I asked her about life in a *nikhom* commune. *Tang raek* for *nikhom*ers was about hardship and fear as villagers attempted to carve out a space for economic prosperity and a new sense of cultural belonging in an unruly landscape beyond the safety of the Malaysian border.

Lung Lin spoke to me in a soft, almost inaudible voice that belied the fact

5.1 Tok Joi (*left*) with Lung Lin in 2002

that in his youth he had been a feared village leader. "Malays were afraid of me," he laughed, his eyes brightening as he recalled the early years of his life in Narathiwat. "I would shoot them. Some died," Lung Lin announced matter-of-factly.

> These were Malays who had joined PULO [Patani United Liberation Organization, which had been fighting the Thai state in the Muslim-dominated south]. A number of them died after I shot them. They were bandits (*jon*). We were afraid that they would kidnap us. They were a mismatch of locals as well as people from the other side [Kelantan].

With the cool mountain breeze wafting through house windows that bore the emblem of the Thai Ministry of Public Welfare and Social Services (*krom prachasongkhrok*) on their metal grilles, Lung Lin brought me on a narrative adventure through the *nikhom* of yore. He had taken up *nikhom* lands just before the Sarit era. His first visit to the area was in 1947 when he was twenty-five, after having learned of the possibility of Kelantanese Thais being granted jungle plots in Narathiwat after visiting his brother, who was, at the time, a monk in Sungai Golok. Lung Lin remembered hearing an announcement about the land schemes from representatives of Thailand's Ministry of Public Welfare and Social Services. Nai Duang Athit, who was Lung Lin's friend and a petty district official in Narathiwat, had asked him if he wanted to participate in the pilot project. As with most *nikhom* settlers, Lung Lin did not sell off his rice lands in Ban Jai even though he spent most of his time working on the new commune. He spent one year clearing the assigned plot in the jungle of trees and undergrowth with money loaned out by the Ministry of Public Welfare and Social Services. At the time, each settler was granted a loan of 50,000 baht (US$1,465) and given seven years to cultivate his rubber crop before debt repayment need begin. The money could be used to purchase daily necessities, wood, rubber seeds, and so on. Loans could also be repaid in kind through selling the collected latex to government-run collection centers.

Lung Lin lived in an area known as the Thirty Hills (*khao sam sib*). The single tarred road that runs through the settlement ends abruptly at the foothills of Narathiwat's mountainous core. Houses cling to the sides of the road, many of them no more than simple wooden shacks built on heavily eroded red clay soil. *Nikhom kao*'s settlers comprise both Kelantanese Thais and southern Thai Malay Muslims. Lung Lin often spoke fondly of the friendly relations both groups enjoyed with one another. There was no ethnic animosity here, he reminded me.

The success of the communes in *nikhom kao* encouraged the Thai state to continue with its land resettlement projects. As with the earliest communes, only Kelantanese Thais were officially given the opportunity to accept these lands. However, unlike the initial pioneers of *nikhom kao*, the later group of Kelantanese Thai immigrants arrived under the auspices of Kota Bharu's Royal Thai Consulate. The consulate aimed to tackle border security issues as well as provide assistance for Thai citizens living and working in Kelantan (Kershaw 1969: 208).[5] Moreover, the consulate then (as now) provided Kelantanese Thais with an avenue for experiencing a nationally defined Thai identity through its regular interaction with villagers and support of Kelantan's monastic culture.

Kelantanese Thais had now to approach the consulate in order to gain access to new *nikhom* plots. Villagers were introduced to *nikhom* schemes and encouraged to participate in them during meetings held between officers from the consulate and Kelantanese Thai villagers. With the establishment of the consulate in 1966 and the ritual agency of the *thammathut* monks, Kelantan's Thai population was being slowly transformed into Thailand's cultural and political citizens through rural development and religious standardization. In what seemed to be a political move to protect the Thai nation-state against the threat of communist and Muslim insurgents, its cultural citizens were being mobilized along the frontier zones, expanding the very notion of the borderland beyond the Tak Bai waterfront. Their relocation in *nikhom* villages populated the hostile no-man's land of the nation-state with Buddhists who, by practicing rubber and fruit tree cultivation, also helped contribute to the development of the impoverished southern Thai economy. This inadvertently fed into Sarit's early dream of a strong and internally unified Thailand grounded on the concepts of modernity, economic progress, and national development.

But patriotism to the Thai nation-state by the Kelantanese Thai social actors who took up *nikhom* settlements was balanced with the practical reality of their historical rootedness in Kelantan. Living in isolated *nikhom* villages was unlike living in the rice-growing Tak Bai settlements or farther afield in Narathiwat, which had historically been part of a Kelantanese Thai world. *Nikhom* settlements attempted to imitate Kelantanese Thai communities in miniature rather than form Thai political communities. Primary loyalties among the migrants were still to villages and the nation-state across the border, despite the political symbols of Thai citizenship in the form of identity papers and window grilles, which the settlers received as tokens of appreciation from the Thai state.

By the late 1960s, the demographic and economic success of the earlier *nikhom* projects had led to a burst of newer but smaller communes, each divided into a number of residential sub-units called *kilo* (kilometers). The *kilo*s ranged from zero to seven. Upon a migrant's request for *nikhom* lands, the Thai Consulate in Kota Bharu would assign the settlers to their particular *kilo* based on a first-come, first-served system. Migrants from the same village in Kelantan were usually settled in the same *kilo*, forming distinct pockets of village social and spatial organization that resembled their parent communities in Malaysia. But these settlements, like the earlier communities in *nikhom kao*, were constantly plagued by thugs and a corrupt and inefficient Thai police force, and a large number of migrants returned to Kelantan in disgust. Pho Di had tried his hand at living in a *nikhom* commune but soon returned to Malaysia after two northeastern Thai migrants were murdered near his commune. Reminiscing on life in the settlement, Pho Di recollected that "even the police told us that if we went into the jungle, we had to be flexible like the jungle. We cannot be harder than it." Hence, settlers needed to know what they were getting into — *nikhom* was a dangerous place, and one should be well prepared for this.

Today, Kelantanese Thai *nikhom* settlers continue to maintain intimate and regular relationships with their kin and friends living across the Golok river. Temple festivals and ritual and social celebrations provide a space for interaction between both groups. Some Kelantanese villagers visit their *nikhom*-dwelling friends and family as part of weekend shopping excursions to Sungai Golok town or spend lazy evenings drinking Thai beer in the settlement's little sundry shops. A few *nikhom* settlers have found jobs in Kelantan through their Malaysian contacts. Although illegal, these Thai citizen laborers blend right in with their Kelantanese cousins, living among friends and family while earning wages in the much sought-after Malaysian ringgit. Often the only distinguishing feature between the two citizens is the Thai license plate on the *nikhom* resident's motorcycle.

To date, the circulation of monks and migrants into and out of Kelantan has slowed down. The violent face of international terrorism since 9/11 and the ongoing bombings and vicious attacks in southern Thailand have altered the way men and women conceptualize what travel, belonging, and movement mean. Since 2004, southern Thailand has experienced a slew of terrifying moments—public shootings, gruesome beheadings, and sporadic bombings and burnings in markets, bars, schools, hotels, and at ATM machines. *Nikhom* residents who visit Kelantan now tell of how unsafe the region has become. "You do not want to go there now," they warned me. The roads leading to Waeng are dotted with military roadblocks and cell phone signals by unregistered Thai service providers are automatically cut off as terrorists have been known to detonate bombs via cell phones. The social orderliness that had been the initial aim of the *nikhom* projects has been replaced with chaos and disarray. Villagers live in fear of when the next attack will occur and who its target will be. Images of slaughter—bloodied bodies and decapitated corpses—fan across the Thai and international media. Horrific scenes of mutilation and death in YouTube videos shape the way people talk about the region and the world they live in. The borderland has ceased to be a space of opportunity and dreams and is now avoided. Temple festivals along Narathiwat's frontier are no longer large affairs attracting people from both sides of the border but are kept low-key. Movement between settlements is restricted largely to the daylight hours.

The escalation in attacks since 2004 has ossified the once fluid and easily crossed border. Both Malaysian and Thai security forces have stepped up their patrols of the border and the people who cross it. As residents on both sides of the Golok and Tak Bai rivers attempt to come to terms with the violence, asking the usual unanswerable question of "who is responsible?" they are forced to think through issues of cultural and political affiliation. Long-standing friendly relations between Thai Buddhists and Malay Muslims have become plagued by insecurities as Thais now fear the local repercussions of angry elements within an international Islamic community with local sympathizers. Yet life goes on in these frontier worlds. Villagers still attend to their fruit and rubber gardens, their shops and market stalls. Children continue to attend school even though threats of school burnings and the horrific execution of teachers are not far off. *Nikhom*ers speak of caution — they must be mindful of the world around them. Increased ethnic and religious social distancing has also led to an increased reflexivity among borderland inhabitants. As images of violence percolate through the lives of Thais and Malays, many now reflect on how they are but unsuspecting victims of a war neither group supports. Older patterns of inter-ethnic and cross-cultural friendships surface in the wake of new terrorist attacks across the southern Thai landscape, fanning shared feelings of victimization, fear, and sadness.

Visions

Ban Bor On's residents enjoy watching television. Even the abbot of Wat Nai watches soccer and boxing matches devotedly on a large flat-screen television placed strategically in front of his faux leather couch. Televised images take viewers on fantastical journeys. The fleeting visions of modernity, history, and the future unfold each time the television is switched on, encapsulating viewers in thought-provoking visual voyages even as they remain safely seated on their rattan settees. Television brought change to Ban Bor On and, of late, it has been instrumental in shaping ethnic interaction in the Kelantanese community. It is with this dynamic that my last story in this book unfurls. "People in the past did not fight as much as they do now. Malays and Thais weren't angry at one another," sighed Pho Di in a tone of nostalgic resignation as we spoke of the changes that television had brought to Ban Bor On. That was in 2007 and Pho Di was seventy-four years old. He, like many other Thais I spoke with, blamed cur-rent Thai feelings of anger and hostility toward the majority Malay community in both Kelantan and southern Thailand on the ongoing insurgency across the border that had claimed close to 4,000 lives since 2004. Images of violence in Thailand's southern border provinces — blamed by Kelantanese Thais on Malay Muslim extremists fighting a Buddhist nation-state — flickered across Thailand's televised news broadcasts almost every night. Scenes of carnage and destruction penetrated the hearts and minds of Ban Bor On's villagers, striking terror and creating uncertainty in the way they viewed Thailand and their own interstitial locatedness so close to the danger zone. Malays had been generalized through the conduit of television reporting into an undifferentiated "Muslim" other—an enemy of global proportions. Television, more than newspapers, the radio, and Internet sites, is the primary mode of national and global news transmission in Kelantan's Thai villages. Writing of the necessity to include news in ethnographic inquiry in an age marked by Appaduraian "mediascapes," Elizabeth Bird concludes that "news may help empower and transform—or to press and obfuscate. Either way, news and journalism play a significant role in the construction and maintenance of culture at the local and global levels, and anthropologists have a place in interpreting that role" (2010: 18).

The ubiquity of television in the day-to-day lives of Thais in Kelantan points to the cultural framing of events in faraway places in locally historicized terms. Recent discussions of media and culture (e.g., Ravi 2005, Postill 2006, Abu-Lughod 2004) have pointed to the way audiences interpret media news events in contextually cognizant ways. Bird (2010: 12) adds that people pay attention to different news events in different ways. Some news features generate greater talk in the community, often leading to a variety of "stories" about a single reported event. Others are simply brushed aside, ignored, and forgotten. Thinking about and reflecting on their encounters with television programs provides men and women with an avenue for commenting about their own lives and the myriad worlds they are entangled in.

Ban Bor On's residents are privy to television broadcasts from both Thailand and Malaysia. Most residents rarely watch Malaysian television, except for the occasional Hollywood blockbuster, preferring Thai programs instead. News reports from Bangkok fill their living rooms with stories and images of violence in a tumultuous border region that has for a long time shared historical and cultural ties with Kelantan. These disturbing scenes of gore are interspersed with powerful images of war and political unrest in the Middle East and elsewhere.

Although many of the Thais I knew felt that inter-ethnic relations between Kelantan's Buddhist Thai and Malay Muslim populations had taken a turn for the worse since the spate of bombings and killings in southern Thailand, they were also quick to point out that spectacles of such violence never crossed the international border. Images were circulated via television broadcasts in a realm of hyper-reality. The border was a powerful moral space and an important zone of demarcation and difference. Some villagers questioned whether Islamic terrorism in the region had anything to do with Kelantan, despite rumors of supposed training camps in Kelantan's thick rainforests. Nothing was proven and, to many of my friends, Malaysian newspapers were the mouthpiece of the federal government and hence were engaged in a campaign to point fingers at the Islamic state. Thus far, there had been no instances of terrorism on the Malaysian side of the border. Many southern Thai Malays had taken up jobs in the state and its Islamic party was looked at favorably by Muslims from across the border. In fact, some of my Thai friends claimed that Kelantan's chief minister occasionally visited southern Thailand, where he delivered rousing sermons to packed mosque halls. The recent success of his party in the 2008 general elections was pointed to as a significant moment in practices of cross-border circulation. My friends reasoned that many Malays from Narathiwat and even Pattani further north had dual citizenship and were in tune with political developments in Malaysia. They crossed the border to vote as Malaysian citizens during election months, thereby increasing the number of opposition supporters in Kelantan. The ease of movement between southern Thailand and Kelantan made my Thai interlocutors wonder if Kelantan could be the next hotbed of ethnic strife. The ease with which the international border could be breached despite increased surveillance scared them. This was a new fear, one that had at its core the terrifying images from the television.

Narratives of violence, like the dreams of Thainess, are never static. They slither along roads, cross international waterways, and play tricks on the mind through cyber channels. Ban Bor On villagers referred to possible terrorist bomb attacks on Thai railway stations and images of southern Thailand's extreme violence by suspected Muslim insurgents that saturate Internet video sites. "They slaughter people like pigs," a distraught-looking Khun Rien exclaimed to me one afternoon in late 2010 after he witnessed the horrific YouTube video of supposed Malay Muslim extremists beheading a man they claimed was a Thai soldier. The murderers also mutilated their victim's genitals. The young monk's initial shock turned to rage as he assured me that the men he had seen in the video spoke Malay.

The roads in Narathiwat have become danger zones not because of historical memories of trauma fused by colonial exploitation as Masquelier noted in the Niger, but because of their future potentiality as a space for violence and death. People have become afraid of the roads. When I began my fieldwork in 2001, Narathiwat's wide highways were seen as symbols of modernity and national development—something that was lacking in northeast Malaysia. Kelantan's roads were rutted and potholed, Thailand's were not. Traveling on them was smooth and comfortable, unlike the bumpy experience of Kelantanese roads (except during election campaigns, when the roads were paved over). But times had changed. The road across the border was now a feared place. Anyone could be a victim of brazen terrorist attacks, especially once the sun goes down. A Malay Muslim taxicab driver who was driving me around southern Narathiwat one afternoon in 2006 reminded me that the journey would have to end by dusk. "It is not safe in the dark," he said. Roads were best avoided, as were crowded markets, banks, and government offices. Ban Bor On residents spoke of felt tensions and fears of the future rather than of actual scenarios of ethnic violence in Kelantan. Thai roads stop at the Tak Bai and Golok rivers, but the many small boats and ferries that ply it link the two nations, as do cyber worlds that need no material artery. Thinking about the future made them reflect on their identity as Malaysian citizens—their Thainess. They were marginals in a country they were fiercely proud of but they also expressed uncertainty for the future.

Television watching forces social actors to engage with powerful narratives of transnational events on a daily basis. Much of the current fear held by Ban Bor On villagers about moving through southern Thailand is produced by the villagers' own engagement with Thailand's news broadcasts. The visual impact of these powerful but fleeting scenes forces Ban Bor On's villagers to ponder the political and cultural implications of living in a borderland and what it means to be Buddhist in a Muslim cultural environment.

Televisions are not only found in houses. They are also in coffee shops, temples (most monks have their own sets in their quarters), and in the communal sheds where men gather to drink palm wine each night. Even Mae Nyai's little rice salad shack had a dusty and cob web–laced television balancing precariously on a high wood shelf. It was switched on in the evenings as the monks gathered at Mae Nyai's for their hot chocolate drinks. The sonic and visual environment of the village was monopolized by Thai television programs throughout the day and night. Televisions were always switched on. Villagers watch a variety of programs—the most popular being the Thai evening news, tear-inducing soap operas, and late-night variety and entertainment shows. Music videos, reality shows, recorded shadow puppet performances, cartoons, Thai-dubbed Hong Kong and Korean serials, sitcoms, talk and game shows, and sporting events prove extremely popular. It is common for the television to be left on for hours at a time as families go about their chores. Children do their homework to the accompaniment of news reports and ads for shampoo and MSG, older men drink palm wine while Bangkok-produced soap operas play in the background, and farmers often spend the hottest hours of the day in their homes watching afternoon music videos and, on some days, shadow puppet performances. As with the calendars and the framed pictures of King Bhumipol and his queen that villagers hang on their walls, Thai television broadcasts symbolically bring Thailand into the lives of Malaysian audiences.

Benedict Anderson (1983) noted how the development of print culture was crucial in the formation of imagined communities and the common nationalist sentiments that hold these groups together. The mass media brings with it an impression of the nation-state as a uniform entity comprised of like-minded citizens. Writing about Indonesian news reports in South Kalimantan, Anna Tsing (2003) questioned the applicability of Anderson's argument in an area that was peripheral to the metropole. She observed how Meratus Dayaks and Banjarese Muslims inhabiting the furthest corners of the Indonesian nation-state interpreted news events as opportunities to assert their identification as homogenously Indonesian while simultaneously reading a nationally forged discourse of cultural heterogeneity, along lines of gender, ethnicity, and social status, into the reports. She wrote of how political imaginations "do not spread evenly; they are lumpy, thin, patchwork, overlaid, unraveling" (Tsing 2003: 194). Nevertheless Tsing's analysis confined itself to the borders of the nation-state. What happens when news reports cross national frontiers, as when Indonesian news coverage reaches Malaysian Borneo or Thai news reach Kelantan?[6] Television programs—like invisible sound waves and cyberscapes—test the supposed cartographic and political reification that people associate with nation-states. Programs easily flow across international borders and seep into the lives of their viewers. How do persons living on the other side of national frontiers then read meaning into the events they watch and how do they then position themselves within its phantasmal and transnational flowing spaces?

News of the terror attacks of 9/11 reached Ban Bor On almost immediately through images on Thai and Malaysian TV news. It started slowly but soon gained momentum as villagers began to grasp the terrifying immensity of what had just happened. By September 12, villagers were talking about the event, although its ethnic and religious implications had yet to emerge. When I told Kae Chi (who did not own a television) about 9/11 she stared at me, her eyes wide open. But she was not surprised. Even before I mentioned the attack to her as we washed the dishes, Kae Chi had already heard of it from someone. Malaysian newspapers were sold out at newsstands in Bandar Tumpat for days, as villagers, both Buddhist and Muslim, tried hard to unravel the riddle of what had actually happened in a place many had only heard about. Television news carried graphic images of the now classic scene of global terror—a United Airlines jet slamming into a burning World Trade Center, the twin towers erupting in a tangle of thick black smoke. News reports on both Thai and Malaysian channels showed similar pictures, sometimes even at the same time. My Thai friends asked me if I had been to New York, if it was close to Boston where I went to school, or if I knew anyone in the buildings. There were more questions than answers, and global terror in Ban Bor On soon began to be reinterpreted according to local particularities and historical sensibilities. Suddenly New York City became part of the Kelantanese Thai landscape, as were the villages of Ban Phan Jao and Ban Kao. Osama bin Laden and George W. Bush became household names, to dread or to be made fun of: Na Dam called the former "Utsa Ma"—an onomatopoeic pun on the Al Qaeda leader's name—which in Kelantanese Thai literally means "to try hard (*utsa*) at being a dog (*ma*)." To call someone a dog is one of the worst insults in the Kelantanese Thai lexicon and to Na Dam and many other Thais, Osama's frightening actions made him no better than a mutt.

The global chaos surrounding the destruction of the World Trade Center led to rampant speculation in Ban Bor On as to who the perpetrators behind the event were. Many Thais believed that Muslims—*khaek*, a word they used interchangeably to refer to Malays—had been instrumental in the attacks, a belief they had derived from news reports on Thai television. The late Na Rod, who proudly claimed to be one of only two ethnic Thai taxicab drivers in Kelantan and who would relax at Wat Nai on hot afternoons, concluded that 9/11 was the work of Islamic terrorists following the directives of a certain Osama bin Laden. He pointed out that the event had sparked religious fervor among many Malay Muslims in Kelantan. He spoke excitedly of how some Malays he knew were supportive of the act. They felt that America had gotten what it deserved, in part for its pro-Israeli policies in the Palestinian question. Through his encounter with 9/11 and the effects it had on Kelantan's Thai and Malay villagers, Na Rot strengthened the borders of his ethnic and cultural community. Thainess was writ large as ethnic difference. To be Thai in the days, weeks, and months following 9/11 meant that one was *not* a *khaek*—a Malay or a Muslim. What had at one time been a closely knit community of Thais and Malays patterned on the movement of sultans and their monk friends and by discourses of cultural complementarity had been shattered by an event in a place many had only dreamed of visiting. "Who else would do such a thing?" Na Rod asked rhetorically. "Can't be a Christian or a Jew. A Buddhist is even less likely to commit such an act. There can be no doubt about it. It has to be a *khaek*."

Na Rod's conclusion about Islamic support for Al-Qaeda's attack on the United States is but one side of a complicated picture of intercultural encountering and the histories of connection along the Malaysian-Thai frontier. Many Malay Muslims I spoke to detested the act and angrily denounced bin Laden and his philosophy as the antithesis of Islam's doctrine of peaceful coexistence. Some pointed to the fact that in Kelantan, Buddhist statues dotted the religious landscape, a clear example of an idealized Islamic state where people of all religions lived in harmony. Terror emanated from the outside—from the United States, Middle East, Afghanistan, Israel, and Thailand. It hid its hideous form in the shadowy gaps of non-encounter when indigenous processes of historical cultural adaptation were being torn apart by forces from beyond the nation-state.

By 2010, Ban Bor On villagers had stopped talking about 9/11, although they remained uncertain of the violence plaguing Thailand's southern provinces. Media attention was now directed at the massive protests that brought downtown Bangkok to a standstill, as thousands of red-shirted activists waged a war of words and, for some, ammunition, against the government of Abhisit Vejjajiva. Thirty-two-year-old Chao Wat of Ban Kao expressed an opinion I had heard many times before in Ban Bor On and elsewhere as I attempted to rationalize the popularity of Thailand's television broadcasts amongst Kelantan's Thai residents. Thai news was, to him and to many other Kelantan Thais I knew, about unbiased reporting coupled with the feel of cultural affinity with their Buddhist cousins across the international border. When the events of 9/11 occurred, Ban Bor On's television sets were tuned in to Thai news reports. Thailand did not have the stringent censorship rules Malaysia imposed on journalistic reporting, some informed me. "Malaysian news, whatever the case, is about BN (Barisan Nasional, Malaysia's federal party). It's brainwashing," complained Chao Wat bitterly, adding: "In Thailand, even though it's controlled by the state, the media has more room for their reporters." One Thai villager told me that Malaysian Malay-language news reporters had even described the 9/11 terrorists as "crusaders" (Malay: *pejuang*), while criticizing their inhumanity. Thai news reports, he pointed out, adhered to less value-laden linguistic categories. To him Malaysia's Malay news, even though of a high international caliber, contained traces of the Islamic favoritism that irked Buddhist Thais in the state, which he considered evidence of biased national reporting. For older Ban Bor On residents, Thai television programs, although broadcast in standard Thai, were easier to understand than standard "book" Malay (*khaek nang sue*), which was to them an almost alien language. This preference for watching Thai television programs has resulted in a community well acquainted with the ongoing political struggles and cultural developments of a nation-state they are not citizens of and have no desire to be.

Tsing (2003: 194) argued that "cultural citizenship within the nation is shaped by transnational identities and resources; transnational news flows similarly influence national political subjectivities." The indirect production of a diasporic Thai cultural citizenry living in Malaysia has been achieved in part through television-watching practices. To many of Ban Bor On's residents, television watching is an avenue to experience a sense of cultural citizenship with a Buddhist state they feel a strange affinity with but to which they do not want to belong. Malaysia's pro-Malay and pro-Muslim policies of *bumiputera*-ism frustrated many Kelantanese Thais who felt that they were being marginalized as second- or even third-class citizens in a country that prided itself on its ethnic plurality. This disgruntlement with the state has found expression in the indirect boycotting of Malaysian news programs for Thai ones. In classical Andersonian fashion, televised images allowed Kelantanese Thais to feel a part of a larger global community of Thai Buddhists. But this was an imagination that went beyond the boundaries of the nation-state, circumscribing shared cultural and ethnic meanings. Terrorist attacks on supposed Thai targets were seen by many Ban Bor On residents as assaults not only on the foreign Thai state but also on their own identity as Buddhists. Although confined to Thailand's southern provinces, shootings and bombings were spoken of by Ban Bor On's men and women as visual indicators of local Muslim menace even though the actual perpetrators of the violence were unknown and victims came from both communities. "It's about *chuea chat* (ethnicity)," Chao Wat put it to me matter-of-factly as we talked about television watching. "If it's about *chuea chat*, our people are shocked. They know all about news happenings in Thailand. For instance, if there is a bomb explosion in [Sungai] Golok everyone will know. If it is about Thailand, they feel it is about their *chuea chat*."

Through associating themselves with the Thai nation-state as victims of a Muslim insurgency, Kelantan's Thai residents expanded their personal marginality into a transnational world. But at the same time, violent images of 9/11 and the southern Thai crisis were confined to nation-states beyond Malaysia's borders—fictive sites of non-encounter. Whereas Chulalongkorn, Vajiravudh, Sarit, *thammathut* monks, and Dhammakaya followers attempted to forge a uniform sense of Thainess that was centered in Bangkok's standardized reading of what constituted Thai ethnicity and Buddhism, Kelantanese visions of Thainess in an age of news flows were cartographically constrained and always hinted at the community's sense of belonging to Malaysia. Although many Thais I knew sympathized with their Buddhist neighbors in Thailand as well as with the international victims of 9/11, they were quick to point out that these events were occurring in distant places. Malaysia, despite its national rhetoric of ethnic asymmetry and cultural plurality, was still the best place to live. In fact, the more Islamic extremism rocked the boat of ethnic pluralism, the more one heard stories of Buddhist-Muslim sociality in the villages of Kelantan. On the one hand, Thais expressed frustration, fear, and unhappiness at what was happening around them. On the other hand, the current state of events made villagers reflect on their own societies and on historical incidences of Muslim-Buddhist neighborliness that marked them as distinctly Kelantanese and Thai. Thais regularly spoke of their close associations with their Malay neighbors and recalled stories of Muslim-Buddhist interaction such as Than Khru Kio's friendship with the palace and the state's chief minister's visits to Thai temples and his promises of support for the Thai.

Phi Lan recalled a story of how his Malay Muslim friend had revealed to him that his pilgrimage to the Islamic citadel of Mecca had not really been an eye opener, as the Muslim pilgrims there were dressed in white robes and had shaven heads "just like Thai monks." Lung Chu, a silver-haired, mustached man from Ban Phan Jao often teased for his eccentric ways, praised Malay Muslims for their religiosity, pointing out that mosques were packed to the brim on Fridays, whereas Buddhist temples were rarely filled even on the weekly Buddhist Sabbath (*wan phra*). "How many men can you find in the Preaching Hall on a *wan phra*?" he asked me sarcastically. Minutes earlier, the elderly man had spoken of how some Muslims refused to drink from their Thai hosts, claiming that the Thai-owned cups and glasses were ritually polluting (*hare*).

"Pinning things down" in a world marked by the entanglements of physical and ideological journeying is not easy (Green 2005: 5). The circulation of travelers, visual images, dreams, and ideologies — along Ban Bor On's roads and through its television cables — points to the ambiguity that has come to be the hallmark of culture in a postmodern world (Harvey 1990). Despite the impossibility of finding stable identities, the Thai villagers of Kelantan ceaselessly reify themselves, their friends, their community, their borders, their encounters, and the society they live in. Ban Bor On's residents spoke of their Thainess in a complex language that moved from cultural citizenship and common religiosity to a bureaucratic obsession with political belonging. In part through their encounters with televised news images, they not only constructed powerful borders of ethnic and cultural identity but also symbolically dismantled national imaginings in the process. Their stories about these events and their agents—missionary monks, communists, Osama bin Laden, and southern Thai extremists—point to the very instability of dreams in borderland spaces. For these communities, translocal histories of movement and encounter become messy allegories for the nations in which they find themselves sandwiched and are symbolic markers of cultural distinction.

CONCLUSION

MUCH HAS CHANGED IN BAN BOR ON. MANY OF THE ACTORS WHOSE lives we encountered and shared in this book have moved on. Some have gotten married and now have children of their own. Others have secured new jobs in new places. Many of my monk friends with whom I spent hours in conversation about identity, politics, cell phones, and ghosts have left the Buddhist order. A number of the older residents have passed away. Village houses and coconut groves have been torn down and converted into profitable private housing development projects. Two-story row houses now rise from where vegetable plots, coffee shops, and fruit trees once stood. Younger Thais are now linking up with one another not just via the common cell phone and Internet chatroom that had been all the rage when I was doing my fieldwork, but through more recent social networking websites like Facebook. Temple ceremonies are filmed and their moving images uploaded onto YouTube. In 2008, Wat Nai became the first Kelantanese Thai temple to host the Royal Kathin Ceremony (*kathin phra ratchathan*) sponsored by the office of the Chakri monarch and the Thai government. Amidst great excitement and fanfare, the annual presentation of robes to the Wat Nai monks was conducted by a representative of the Thai monarch. Also in attendance at the November event were Nik Aziz Nik Mat, local Malaysian political figures, and hundreds of Thais from across the state. Since then, the Royal Kathin Ceremony has taken place in two other temples in Kelantan, cementing ties of cultural citizenship and subjecthood between Malaysian Thais and their counterparts across the border.

As though riding the wave of cultural symbiosis across national spaces, Ban Bor On villagers successfully organized their first ever "Dhammakaya-style" robe-offering ceremony. The festival participants were dressed in the white garb typical of Dhammakaya wear and paraded around the temple in neat, well-coordinated rows. The drunken fanfare that epitomizes so many traditional Buddhist fetes in Kelantan was significantly absent from the occasion. In its place were the formalism, minimalism, and discipline popularly associated with the Dhammakaya sect that had many in the village excited and others worried as to the future of an older Kelantanese Thai distinction.

The social dynamism inherent in these large and small transformations is entangled with an emotional sense of cultural stasis. Enormous statues stand as silent representatives of a history of non-moving, sultans and Buddhist kings are still revered and gossiped about as they have always been, and elderly Tok Nai Suk is still the headman. Thais, Malays, and Chinese continue to interact in line with age-old values of cordiality and friendship, despite global violence having cast a terrifying shadow over the community. Buses 19 and 43 continue to ply the trunk road in front of Wat Nai, although in 2010 they were upgraded to the newer red-and-white, air-conditioned coaches. Express Timuran still chugs into Bandar Tumpat every morning without fail from towns along Malaysia's east coast. But there is talk about the state government moving the train station (no one seems to know exactly when). Ban Bor On is a located place on Wikimapia, an online map that combines the satellite cartography of Google Maps with Wikipedia's user-contributed content. On this cyber map, Ban Bor On is tagged according to its geographical coordinates (although such directions mean noth-ing to villagers). The bird's-eye-view pictorial image allows one to glide over the two arterial roads that distinguish Ban Bor On's mobile landscape, surveying the area's vast green fields and gardens. From the map one notices the gray, brown, and blue roofs of the houses that line the road. With the click of a mouse one can search out temple buildings and list the homes of friends and kin, many of whom we met in this book.

Cartography, however, does not bring us into the lives of the men and women that populate mapped spaces. The Wikimapia image does not show us where the village ends or where it begins, either formally through national and state boundaries or in the minds of its inhabitants. Also omitted are the physical and ideological symbols of social rootedness that villagers point to as indicators of their ancestral presence in the region—ancient spirits, travel stories, particular trees, rest pavilions, and a strange rocky pond surrounded by *on* trees. Maps do not bring one into the living rooms of wood and cement homes, to chat a bit with their residents over cups of steaming chocolate, and to join them in their nightly television watching. One cannot see Thainess on the map, as Thainess is a sensual, ephemeral, and emotive experience. It emerges from the spectacular and banal moments of everyday life as people (including anthropologists) move across the landscape. It is shaped in the shadows of encounters, in chance meetings and wondrous tales. It revels in the dreams and visions of Ban Bor On's inhabitants and in the anthropologist's ethnography.

Space is silent on the map. The cacophony of everyday existence is replaced by the formality of shapes, printed words, and empty roads. Cartography makes visible what are otherwise invisible borders of geography. Maps imprison mobility, pinning it down for ease of observation, management, and control. Thongchai Winichakul's fascinating discussion of the historical role of mapping and the production of Thainess in Thailand (1994), although fresh in its approach, does not seep into the messy and often paradoxical lived experiences of the social actors who populate the changing map of the Thai nation-state. The stories told here push Thongchai's analysis in a different direction. Incorporating geography, history, and anthropology, they bridge the formalities of cartographically bounded spaces (nation-states, villages, districts, roads, temples) and the subjective experiences people have in these spaces (Bird 2002).[1] The protagonists and storytellers we met in the earlier chapters were (and, for those still living, are) entangled in a culture of flows that brought their feelings of marginality and social invisibility in Malaysia to the forefront of their ethnic and cultural identification. Thainess to them was about being different from everyone else, not just demographically, but spatially as well. They inhabited the gaps of the nation-state but traveled regularly to places near and far—sometimes to the market just down the road or to the state capital Kota Bharu—where they worked and ate Kentucky Fried Chicken. Occasionally they explored places further afield, such as Thailand, Indonesia, the United States, India, Sri Lanka, Korea, China, or Singapore. Souvenirs from their exotic adventures dot their homes, photo albums, and Facebook pages. And for those who did not embark on such journeys, there were the many tourists, soldiers, pilgrims, journalists, politicians, students, academics, monks, entertainers, missionaries, smugglers, and surveyors who passed through their villages, bringing with them their own engagements with mobility and history that they shared knowingly or unknowingly with the villagers. People, images, goods, dreams, and fantasies flowed unceasingly through the mapped village. Ban Bor On's residents' voices—sometimes happy, sometimes sad, but always confusing—flowed along with every experience of movement they encountered and confronted and wrapped themselves in.

Kelantanese Thai villagers speak of a located community—one that "has always been here." There are no grand historical narratives here, although national governments and academics often seek them out in their interviews with local leaders and monks. To the villagers of Ban Bor On and elsewhere, myths of migration are unimportant. Local history is expressed through places, persons, and objects. Stories of mysterious cremation grounds and interesting personalities are pointed to as symbols of the Thai community's long and unquestioned presence in a Malay state. These are the temporal boundaries of the village and their associations with fixed locales draw spatial borders around the community. The men and women we meet in this book are actively searching out what identity means to them. They are not passive recipients of cultural models imposed upon them by faceless regimes of power—states, governments, rumors, the media, and so forth, but speak of a personal and at times unconscious rendition of what it means to be Thai. And it is this moral and emotional feeling that makes their lives habitable, and this is what my ethnography explores (de Certeau 1984). They ponder and obsess over it, yet never once use the word Thainess (*khwam pen thai*) to describe their feelings or tactical actions. To some, being Thai is about performing one's identity according to a set of cultural prescriptions carefully laid out by the Thai nation-state. Nevertheless with each attempt at cultural assimilation across the international frontier comes a simultaneous reassertion of Kelantanese primordialism. The more Thailand tries both directly and indirectly to influence its cultural citizens, the more Kelantanese Thais reflect on who they *really* are. Kelantanese Thainess emerges at the interstices of these moments of encounter. It dwells in the flows of ideas, thoughts, and visions. But in so doing, it also plugs these flows, reifying it as an unchanging essence that is unique and distinct to the borderland inhabitants.

Montesano and Jory (2008) have called for a realigning of southern Thai scholarship from its traditional obsession with the artificiality of the modern border to an understanding of social and cultural interactions in the region. In this book, the metaphor of encounter allows us to look at the way people produce powerful but questionable identities for themselves in northern Kelantan. Yet it is undeniable that in the process of consolidating this vision of personhood, national and international concerns with political boundaries come to the fore. In short, encounters work within, through, and across modern political landscapes. Borders continue to matter.

Thainess is the product of encounters. It is what gives Ban Bor On its unique identity as a situated and mapped place. It is also what links the village with other Thai communities across Malaysia. Thinking about how ethnic and cultural personhood are constituted shaped the way people spoke not only about their village but about themselves and one another and the social worlds they were entangled in. Sometimes they viewed Ban Bor On as a *ban*, a historically rooted Thai settlement with a long but uncertain past. At other times, they looked upon their community as an embryonic town, a *banar* awash with the symbols of modernity that characterize urban living. They wondered what effects the federal government's proposed plans for the East Coast Economic Region (ECER), covering the states of Kelantan, Terengganu, Pahang, and Mersing in Johor, would have on their community. The 66,736-square-kilometer ECER was part of a larger project initiated by the national oil conglomerate Petronas to spearhead growth and development across Malaysia, Indonesia, and Thailand. Under the ECER's twelve-year master plan, Pengkalan Kubor would be developed into a major industrial and tourism hub. What this would mean for the Thai and Malay villages in its vicinity is frightening. Some people I spoke to feared that their farm lands would be taken up in the name of regional development. Where were they to live? What would happen? They shuddered as they thought of some of the possibilities.

In this book we have traveled along dirt paths and major thoroughfares. Along the way, we have reflected on the meanings of movement and space and on the many characters that crisscross it. "Historical development," Engseng Ho rightly reminds us, "is not everything. Location too is important" (Ho 2006: 222). To the villagers of Ban Bor On space matters in their imagining of who they are culturally, ethnically, and politically. Villagers regularly engage with the space that is the international border. They travel across its muddy aquatic expanse to shop, eat, receive monastic promotions, attend fairs, worship, find marriage partners, go to the hospital, visit relatives and friends, and so on. Traveling links the past with the present in a series of neverending flows. It makes them mull over the complex meanings of citizenship, both political and cultural, and what it means to be contained by spatially defined national boundaries.

Roads link Mecca's Verandah with the ideal Buddhist king's realm in Bangkok. Roads are also the conduits along which sultans and busloads of Chinese tourists travel hoping to gaze at the mammoth Buddhist statues and Chinese-style monuments that have come to define many Thai villages in Kelantan today. Boisterous ordination parades move along these roads too, performing a colorful rendition of cultural exceptionality for curious Malay onlookers. Along the sides of the road, vivid evidence of the village as a distinctly Thai place appears in the guise of wandering dogs, an occasional pig, and Buddhist temples.

People travel along roads and talk about the personalities—both real and mythic—they meet. Each story they tell is a reflection of their understanding of Thainess. When followed to its end, the nameless thoroughfare that passes in front of Wat Nai eventually reaches the Thai border. Here, the Tak Bai river forces the asphalt highway to come to an abrupt stop. But mobility is not stalled. Colonialism secured the border as a symbol of a new sovereignty. Victorian sovereignty and the rise of the nation-state made travelers aware of new spatial configurations. Boats, large and small, allowed travelers to continue their movements across the border, both legally and illegally. At the border towns of Rantau Panjang in the district of Pasir Mas and Bukit Bunga in Tanah Merah the road took the form of a causeway that spanned the wide Golok River.

Ideologies and historical narratives move too. Like those of people, these invisible movements provided the residents of Ban Bor On with their sense of Thainess. It is futile to attempt to produce an ethnography of the Kelantanese Thai village without paying close attention to these flows. Each movement is a complex process that involves many personalities, ways of thinking, histories, and, of late, global connections (Gupta and Ferguson 1992b). These mobilities, as the anthropologist Tim Ingold (2007) reminds us, occur everywhere. These include the paths traced out by circulations of capital as Chinese pilgrims travel in search of magical amulets, by televised images of 9/11 that emanate from faraway newsrooms, by local predictions of global and national events, and by stories of ancient ghosts and long-deceased sultans that villagers recall with excitement and trepidation.

Ban Bor On's villagers articulate Thainess in various ways. In some contexts, Thainess is expressed as a proud association with the powerful Thai nation-state, while at other times, it emerges in the stinging condemnation Thais have of the country. Their Thainess reveals itself in its ambiguity. It celebrates Thailand but favors Malaysia. It is critical of Malaysian policies of affirmative action and what villagers feel to be Islamization but enjoys the peace and strong governance of the country. The story of Thainess in Ban Bor On and other Thai villages throughout Kelantan is one of contradictions. In attempting to write about this state of social and historical messiness, I have resorted to the classic ethnographic method of "thick description" within a single village. Nevertheless the tales woven in the ethnography showcase fleeting moments of entanglement as communities like Ban Bor On move through and encounter a diversity of spaces, personas, pasts, and futures.

By looking at what goes on in the "gaps" of national spaces, we see how people make sense of taken-for-granted categories like culture, citizenship, and ethnicity. Kelantanese Thais continue (and will probably do so for a long time to come) to grumble about their feelings of marginality, powerlessness, and uncertainty within the nation. They strive to be visible in a myriad of colorful and exciting ways. Thinking about the expansive worlds that mobile people, things, and ideas inhabit resonates with anthropology's traditional practice of single-sited ethnography. Fieldwork today has moved out of the village to envelop a number of shifting "locales." Early functionalist concern for a close scrutiny of culture in one particular location has faded into the shadows of an anthropology that celebrates ambiguities, spatial zones, oceans, fissures, cyber spaces, networks, and connections. A careful analysis of Ban Bor On has shown that there continues to be room in the blurred disciplinary zones among anthropology, history, cultural studies, and Southeast Asian studies for explorations into small spaces. But any endeavor to look at what happens in zones far from the machinations of national powers forces one to think of the wider social and historical circuits that form the bulk of recent postmodern scholarship. Small communities live within expansive and confusing spaces.

Let us now return to where we began this book. Ban Bor On is a space on the map. On the ground, the village is bordered by road signs and rest pavilions that announce the presence of the community along a moving landscape of travelers, stories, and pot-holed roads. Ban Bor On is bounded by derelict rice fields, lush green vegetable plots, Buddhist temples, shops, smelly chicken coops, and houses. Ethnic and cultural spaces are not small, self-contained social units that sway according to the whims and fancies of national governments and their political agendas. Rather so-called marginal communities creatively negotiate these political processes when shaping their own versions of culture. These tactics of identity management are both fixed and fluid at the same time. They are confined within the borders of everyday experiences and cartographic spaces but also spill over them, generating fodder for subsequent cultural entanglements. Thus, the bitterness and sadness, fear and confidence, humor and sobriety, fluidity and fixity that mark the daily lives of the Thai men, women, and children of Mecca's Verandah continue unabated.

NOTES

Preface

1   *The Buddha on Mecca's Verandah* is not a book about "native anthropology" (Kuwayama 2003). Throughout my research and personal reflections I was never a "native" in the fullest sense of the term. Despite occasional attempts at being "just like us," I was still very much the ambiguous outsider. Kirin Narayan (1993) wrote of the futility of attempting to generate a native anthropology. Rather, she argued, it is more prudent to speak of "shifting identifications amid a field of inter-penetrating communities and power relations" (671). Besides being an account of the various "interpenetrating" agents that symbolically comprise and contest the ballast of what it means to be Thai in Kelantan, this book, like Lila Abu-Lughod's earlier work on the Bedouin (1988), is also about the reflexive encounter between the anthropological self and his friends, family, and host society.

Introduction: The Kelantanese World

1   Kelantan is economically peripheral to Malaysia's national narrative of gross domestic product measurement, lagging behind other states in terms of agriculture, manufacturing and mining, and wholesale and retail trade (Rumley 1991).

2   In 1817, greater Patani (today's provinces of Narathiwat, Pattani, and Yala) was divided into seven principalities (*jet hua mueang*) each under its own political ruler. These were Ra-ngae (Leggeh), Raman, Yaring, Yala, Saiburi, Patani, and Nong Chik. Kelantan was an administrative division (*mueang*) under the political jurisdiction of Ra-ngae, but by 1902, Kelantan's Malay rulers were directly answerable to the Bangkok court. In 1906, the seven principalities were reorganized into one main administrative center (*monthon*) with the *mueang* of Kelantan now coming directly under the suzerainty of the *monthon* of Patani (Loos 2006: 77).

3   *Bumiputera*-ism (lit., sons of the soil) is a system of ethnic privileging that attempts to ensure the special rights of so-called indigenous groups in Malaysia.

These national policies include the administration of financial loans, employment quotas based on ethnicity in government departments and university admissions, the distribution of scholarships and bursaries, and so forth. In theory, Thais were not considered *bumiputera*, but in practice, some Thais did receive some of the rights given to *bumiputera* Malaysians while being denied others (Mohamed 2010). This inconsistency was a major headache for many Kelantanese Thais (Kershaw 1984).

4   British censuses listed the number of Thais (Siamese) in the state of Kelantan for the years 1911, 1921, 1931, 1947, and 1957 as 5,355, 6,255, 6,643, 7,092, and 7,727 persons, respectively (Dodge 1980: 470n). In order to tabulate the approximate number of Thais in Kelantan, I noted the number of Kelantanese listed as ethnically *Other* (10,748) with those religiously categorized as Buddhists (11,031). Ethnic Chinese who practiced a syncretic blend of Taoism, Confucianism, and Mahayana Buddhism had their own ethno-religious category (labeled as "Confucianism, Taoism/ other traditional Chinese religions" [*Confucius, Tao/Agama tradisi lain orang Cina*]) in the national census.

5   Early Southeast Asian statecraft has been studied by a number of scholars; for instance, see Tambiah 1976, 1977; Wolters 1982; and Hagesteijn 1989.

6   In this book I use Patani (spelled with one "t") to refer to the older, pre-Thailand Malay sultanate that was both a vassal and later a province of the Bangkok court. The present-day Thai province (*changwat*) of Pattani incorporates only part of this older sultanate.

7   Money for making the *bunga mas dan perak* was derived from a poll tax. During the reign of Kelantan's Tuan Long Senik (r. 1900–1909), the tax was levied at one Straits Settlement dollar for every adult Malay and three dollars for every adult Chinese, paid once every three years (Talib 1995: 26). Talib does not mention the tax being imposed on Kelantan's Thai community.

8   Nakhon Sri Thammarat has, since the eighteenth and nineteenth centuries, played a crucial role in the political affairs of the Kelantanese Malay court, for instance in its official support for Tuan Senik during the Kelantan civil war of 1838–1839 (Skinner 1966: 10). The southern Thai principality has maintained intimate relationships with the Kelantanese Thai as well, albeit on a ritual rather than political plane, with Nakhon Sri Thammarat's Mahathat temple (Wat Phra That) being a major node in the traditional Kelantanese Thai pilgrimage circuit.

9   Rumley (1991: 141) has noted that the actual international division at the mouth of the Golok River is often contested, as small islets and sandbars in the river emerge and disappear seasonally. See also Rachagan and Dorall 1976.

10   In 1915, King Chulalongkorn changed the name of the *mueang* of Bang Nara (once incorporating Saiburi and Ra-ngae) to Narathiwat or "the place where good people live" (Wanipha 1992: 69).

11   For a list of the terms of the treaty, see Mohamed 1974.

12   Building the rail line in Kelantan was not without its share of peasant disgruntle-
      ment. Land was taken away from farmers who were promised cash repayments.
      However, these repayments were slow to materialize and often farmers were paid
      at rates lower than current land prices. In protest, local villagers living along the
      Tumpat–Kampung Laut–Pasir Mas line removed screws and nails from the rail
      in 1912. In response to this form of everyday protest, the British advisor at the
      time, J. E. Bishop, had policemen patrol the lines daily (Mohd. Kamaruzaman
      1990: 61).

13   The older Tumpat Tak Bai–speaking villages include Ban Ta Phruk, Bang Noi,
      Khok Mafueng, Tapang, Khok Sawad, Ban Khlong Lai, Sai Khao, Ban Tor Lang,
      Ban Tha Maprang, Ban Khok Phut, Khok Yang, Khok Chumbok, Khok Phai,
      Khok It, Tasek, Khok Sathorn, Khok Ngu, Ban Ba Wong, Ban Thung Fai, Ban
      Lak Chang, Khok Mamuang, Wat Mai, Ban Phra Phut, Khok Kian, Khok Hawad,
      Thung Kha, Nam Tamlang, and Hua Thanon. Golomb (1978: 12) believed that
      these settlements were possibly the ancestral source for many of Kelantan's Thai
      villages. Other villagers I spoke with pointed out cultural and linguistic similari-
      ties between the communities on both banks of the Tak Bai but were also quick
      to dismiss ideas of common historical origins in lower Narathiwat. They claimed
      that even though they shared kin and cultural links, there was no evidence, either
      real or mythic, of migrations from Tak Bai into the Kelantan plains.

14   Khun Rien was a year younger than I. He was a computer programmer and a
      smuggler who had now devoted his life to Buddhism. Whenever we talked about
      smuggling, his eyes lit up and he recalled excitedly how he used to smuggle
      suckling pigs from Laos and northeastern Thailand into Malaysia. The pigs were
      frozen and brought by boat from Thailand to his village along the banks of the
      Tak Bai river. From there they were packed into refrigerated trucks bound for
      Chinese restaurants in Pasir Mas, Gua Musang, and Kuala Lumpur. Sometimes
      he would also smuggle wild boar meat into Thailand. The boars had been hunted
      in different parts of Malaysia and frozen. They were brought by boat into Tak
      Bai's Thai villages, where the fur was burnt off and the animals chopped up. The
      pork was then transported by truck to Bangkok, where boar meat fetched high
      prices.

15   In her study of Kampung Bendang Kerian, a predominantly Malay village a few
      kilometers from Ban Bor On, Hasimah Mat Kasim (2007) concluded that the
      government's introduction of double cropping in the Tumpat plains had primar-
      ily benefited wealthier farmers who could afford the new farm technologies. The
      so-called revolution devastated already impoverished farmers, who could no
      longer find work as farm laborers or manage the expensive equipment, pesticides
      and fertilizers needed for double cropping.

16   Kelantanese Thais I spoke to did mention how the highways in Tak Bai were
      much larger and in better condition that those in Kelantan. However, they con-

trasted this public development with the poverty they associated with their Tak Bai cousins—some of whom they claimed still lived in thatched bamboo houses. In reality, most Tak Bai communities were very much tied in to the dizzying flows of materialism that structured Thailand's modern economy. For a discussion on material consumption in Tak Bai's Thai villages, see Wattana 2000, 2005.

17   On the reason behind Thai permanent residency in one Malaysian village, see Kershaw 1984.

18   British privateers such as the Duff Development Company Limited, based in London, began gold mining and extractive industries in the Galas and Sungai Lebir region of southern Kelantan as early as 1900, after securing a concession from the raja of Kelantan on 10 October 1900. By 1905, the Duff Development Company's subsidiary in the Ulu, the Kelantan Gold Dredging Company Limited, was extracting gold worth some $72,290 (Mohd. Kamaruzaman 1990: 44). On the history of the Duff Company in Kelantan, see also Robert 1971.

19   See, for example, Kershaw 1969; Golomb 1978; Winzeler 1985; Mohamed 1989, 1990, 1993a, 1993b, 1995, 1996, 2000, 2010; Wavell 1958, 1965; Sharifuddin, undated; Mohd. Naim 1986/87; Leng 1990; Lim 1990/91; Eh Mooi 1997; Mohd. Sofi 1984; Rogayah 1999; Kejiam 2007; Zainuddin 2007; N. Mohamed 2007; Chantas 1993; and Praphon 1982, 1986.

CHAPTER 1 / Places

1   On a number of occasions, I heard Thai villagers lament about how the fire station and the other government administrative compounds nearby had been constructed on land once owned by Ban Bor On's Thai farmers, forcibly bought from them by the state for an inconsequential amount.

2   The institution of women renunciates in Thai Theravada Buddhism has been the subject of many anthropological works. See, for instance, Adiele 1987, Chartsumarn 1991, Kapur-Fic 1998, and Falk 2007.

3   Kelantanese women, both Thai and Malay, are well-known in the historical and anthropological record for their active participation in the commercial economy, and Kae Chi was no exception. See, for instance, Firth 1943, Nash 1974, and Rudie 1989, 1994. Although older women are still dominant in the Kelantanese market economy, the rising cost of living has meant that urban labor with its higher profit margins has resulted in a disparity of income along gendered lines. Men participating in urban employment usually secure higher real wages than their agrarian-based womenfolk. Younger women (most of whom have completed some secondary school or tertiary education) prefer employment in the urban sector either in Kelantan or elsewhere in Malaysia and Singapore.

4   For a discussion on early Kelantanese international trade and relations, see Talib

1981, Nik Hassan 1987, Rahmat 1987, Othman 1987, and Wee 1987.

5   In an early account of Kelantan, the Scottish author-traveler Patrick Balfour describes Tumpat town as "a tranquil spot. In its sandy main street are cafes and Chinese shops, selling a variety of European and Eastern junk, and its side-streets peter out into coconut groves, where the poorer Malays inhabit dwellings of plaited straw, on piles" (Balfour 1935: 219).

6   Also known as Cik Puteh (Mister Fair-skinned) after his light complexion, Datuk Kaya Budi was a wealthy cloth merchant and landowner in Bandar Tumpat during its economic boom in the 1930s. He owned large tracks of land in Ban Bor On as well as in the market town. He was the only ethnic Chinese to hold the royal title of *datuk* in the Tumpat district. Sultan Ismail visited the *datuk* every Thursday during the bullfighting season, often spending the night at the *datuk*'s mansion near the Bandar Tumpat market, a beautiful colonial bungalow built in 1927 that has now been converted into the government's District Office (Majlis Daerah). During these trips the sultan would have afternoon tea at his Bukit Tanah palace near Ban Bor On. So close was his relationship with the Kota Bharu court that the *datuk* personally drove the sultan to Ban Kao's temple for the ceremonial lighting of the revered Than Khru Kio's cremation pyre, probably sometime between 1931 and 1941. The monk had been the head of all Thai monks in the state and a close friend of both the *datuk* and the sultan.

7   I have listed these villages according to their real names and have placed in parentheses the administrative districts in which they are found. These are Tuwa (Tumpat), Jung Kao (Tumpat), Bang Nyang (Tumpat), Nya Rong (Tumpat), Khao Din (Tumpat), Bjai (Tumpat), Ban Nai (Tumpat), Trad (Tumpat), Khao Din (Tumpat), Bormed (Tumpat), Lamcit (Tumpat), Khok Koeya (Tumpat), Jamu (Tumpat), Ban Gong (Pasir Mas), Bang Saet (Pasir Mas), Khok Ko (Pasir Mas), Thung Phrao (Pasir Mas), Arey/Sidang (Kota Bharu), Seligi (Kota Bharu), Tha Song (Tanah Merah), Moering (Tanah Merah), Balai (Bachok), Bukit Jong (Pasir Puteh), Semerak (Pasir Puteh), and Tok Chit (Pasir Puteh). The Thai-Chinese villages of Pok Kiang (Besut) and Batu Bala (Besut) are administratively in Terengganu but close to the Kelantan border. Kershaw listed Ban Thanong (his spelling) as a Thai village but despite its supporting a large Thai-style temple, the Kelantanese Thais I spoke with were quick to point out that it was in effect a Chinese settlement (*ban jin*).

8   Villagers who preferred to have their roads lit had to purchase the lights from local authorities and pay for the cost of installation and the monthly electricity bill. The state government only provided main roads with street lamps.

9   In 1903 the Duff Development Company had called upon the state's British administrators to have road and rail tracks laid from Kuala Lebir in the south to the port at Tumpat. However, the road and rail line that was to favor the Duff

Company's transportation of raw material was not approved (Mohd. Kamaruzaman 1990: 59).

10   On my way to Kota Bharu one morning, Pak Cik Soh, a Malay cab driver, pointed out the torn sacks of rice strewn along the road in front of Wat Nai. Speaking matter-of-factly of a common incident in the village, he noted, "this way the smugglers would only lose about RM200 [US$52.63]. If they were caught [with the rice] they could be fined up to RM5,000 [US$1,315.79]."

11   For a lighthearted account of smuggling in Kelantan, see Douglas Raybeck's 1996 book, *Mad Dogs, Englishmen, and the Errant Anthropologist.*

12   Early British reports on Kelantan mention cattle theft as the most widespread form of crime in the state. In 1915, there were 320 cases of animal theft in Kelantan, with 122 convictions (Straits Settlements Reports 1915: 10). Fourteen years later, the British had still not put an end to the "old national pastime of cattle lifting" (Kelantan Administrative Report 1929: 16). Cattle were stolen even after they had been placed in locked pens for the night. So prevalent was the practice of cattle raiding in the pre–World War II period in Kelantan that the colonial administration issued licenses for each cow purchased, thereby maintaining an inventory of cattle in the state. These licenses, called *ji tra* in Thai, were prepared by the *tok gawo*, the state-appointed district representative. Today, cows are largely stolen from Thailand and smuggled across the Golok River into Malaysia, where they are sold locally or to traders in Terengganu and other states.

13   Carabao's music is a genre of popular Thai sound known as *phleng phoea chiwit* (songs for life). It combines Euro-American rock elements with a unique Thai feel created through the use of indigenous instruments and vocal styles. Many of the songs center around rural concerns such as social marginalization, poverty, corruption, exploitation, urban labor, and so forth, which many of its long-haired Malaysian Thai male fans claim to identify with. Carabao's lyrics often critique global consumerism and "Western" modernity. So popular is Carabao among young men in these Tumpat villages that I was once approached by Jaran, a seventeen-year-old student from Din Sung, to tattoo the band's logo on his arm. Unsure of my tattooing skills, I politely declined his request.

14   Herzfeld (1987: 195) observed a similar practice of nostalgically associating the past with malicious spirits (*eksotika*) among Pefkiot villagers in Cyprus. Unlike Ban Bor On, where modernity has placed the spirits in a state of dormancy to be resurrected by ritual practice and the retelling of stories, Pefkiots transformed the *eksotika* into metaphors for contemporary human evildoers who were marginal members of the community. By treating the *eksotika* as people, Herzfeld argued, the Pefkiots were in fact doing theoretical anthropology. Like the academic anthropologists of old, they too had embarked on a process "to 'exoticize' flawed beings while insisting on their common humanity" (197).

15   Kelantanese Thais choose ordination dates after consultation with monks or

magical practitioners who are well versed in the cycle of auspicious and inauspicious days and times. No ordinations are conducted on Fridays. Until about twenty years ago, all ordinations in Kelantan had to be conducted by the chief monk of the state (*chao khana rat*), who resided in Bang Rim Nam in the district of Pasir Mas. The chief monk did not want ordinations to be held on Fridays because that was the day he met visitors to his temple or was engaged to visit householders and other temples across Kelantan. Today, a number of senior Kelantanese monks have received ecclesiastical appointments from Thailand's Buddhist Council (*mahatherasamakhom*) that enable them to conduct ordinations as primary preceptors (*upatcha*) without the direct participation of the *chao khana rat*. In practice, however, the *chao khana rat* is usually invited to oversee all ordinations in the state. The Friday ruling was indirectly connected with the dynamics of inter-cultural interaction in a predominantly Muslim society. During breakfast at Phi Rat's one morning, Tok Nai Suk told me "we live among Malays. If it was permissible to be ordained on Fridays, many Thais would do so and the Malays would know of it. They may say to each other, 'Look at the Thais, they become monks on Fridays too.'" In other words, the ruling can be seen as a deliberate attempt by the Thais to distance themselves culturally from the Muslim population by preventing the overlap of cultural symbols.

CHAPTER 2 / Gaps

1   For an analysis of the Kelantanese Thai *nura* (manora) theater, see Wavell 1965, Golomb 1978, Kershaw 1982, Omar 1989, Pin 1992, Sheppard 1973, and Johnson 1996, 1999.

2   The number (as are the population demographics) included temples on both banks. Kelantan today hosts twenty temples (*wat*) and four monks' residences (*samnak song*). The district of Tak Bai in southern Narathiwat is served by twenty temples (Wanipha 1992: 72). Of these, the oldest is Wat Sunantharam (Wat Bang Toei), which is no longer in use. Tak Bai also has the highest concentration of Thai Buddhists in the southernmost provinces of Narathiwat, Yala, and Pattani. In 1997, some 20,000 out of Narathiwat's 57,515 inhabitants were Thai Buddhists resident in Tak Bai (Sukansil 2000: 21).

3   Despite the Siamese government's argument for the antiquity of Wat Choltarasinghe, the temple was likely built in 1860, forty-nine years before the establishment of Tak Bai as a Siamese municipality (*Wat Choltarasinghe*, undated). As with most Thai temples in Kelantan, it is uncertain when the temple was founded. Construction dates for temples are often mere guesses from local memories or the dates inscribed on some monastic buildings.

4   Gerhard Jaiser (2009: 81) observed how the Wat Chehe murals, a feature rarely found in Kelantanese Thai temples, reflected local Siamese preoccupations with

cultural boundary maintenance in the face of British colonization. The murals were a visual testimony to an ethnic Thai and Buddhist presence in the Malay area of the deep south and an undeniable part of the Siamese imagined community.

5   This so-called Siamese cultural-political sphere in Narathiwat included present-day Kampung Tanjong, Kampung Che Hel (Chehe), Kampung Belawan (Ban Phrai Wan), Kampung Tabal (Ban Tak Bai), and Kampung Sungai Golok. It also incorporated areas watered by the Golok, Menara, Layar, Kayu Kelat, Padi, and Elong rivers (Mohamad 1974: 55n).

6   For further discussions on the development of ethnic typologies in Malaysian discourse, see Hirschman 1986, 1987 and Shamsul 1996, 2001.

7   The Malaysian Parliament has allowed for political representatives at the senatorial level for some of the country's "underprivileged" ethnic minorities, including the Thai (Abdul Rahman 2001: 80). Some politically aware Kelantanese Thais I knew were upset that the one ethnic Thai senator was nominated from the west coast states of Kedah and Perlis and had close associations with the ruling federal party. Malaysia's first Thai senator was sworn into office in 1996 for a renewable three-year term. To date, there have been three Thai senators in Malaysia, none of whom were Kelantanese.

8   The black velvety *songkok* and white *kopiah* are traditional cloth headgears worn by Malay Muslim men. Traditionally only men who have gone on the hajj pilgrimage wear the *kopiah* in Kelantan, although this is changing in Malaysia today. Thais, being Buddhist, never wear the *kopiah*. Some Thais may put on a *songkok* as part of Malaysia's national costume during important governmental or school functions.

9   In the Kelantanese Thai dialect of southern Thai, Malays are referred to as *khaek*. Unlike in standard Thai, where the term encompasses a broader pan-ethnic group of Malays, Indonesians, Middle Easterners, and South Asians, *khaek* here is restricted in its reference only to Malays. The term is also used to refer to Islam, as in *sasana khaek* or "the Islamic religion." Standard Thai definitions of *khaek* hint at the term's association with "foreignness" (and not just Islam), but I found no such wider meaning in Kelantanese Thai definitions of the word.

10   Malaysia's *bumiputera* policy was initiated as part of the New Economic Policy (NEP) *Bumiputeraism*, an integral component in both national and popular definitions of ethno-cultural personhood in Malaysia and structured largely upon a material basis. The *bumiputera* policy has attracted the attention of many Malaysianists. See, for instance, Faland et al. 1990, Hing 1984, Hua 1983, Jomo 1986, Lim 1985, Harper 1996, and Shamsul 1986, 1996b.

11   For a fuller discussion of the policies and history of the Malay Reserve Lands in Kelantan identity, see Kershaw 1984, Nik Haslinda 2007, and Azizah 2006.

12   For a discussion of the role of the Malaysian-Thai ferry service in facilitating

cross-border movements and its political ramifications for both nation-states, see Praphon Ruengnarong 1986.

13 Although documents of citizenship in legal border crossings were officially necessary as early as 1950 and came under the Federation of Malaya Agreement, Section 124 (1) (e), it was likely that most Kelantanese Thais did not pay much attention to them. Kershaw (1984: 57) noted that at the Pasir Puteh District Office only two or three such documents were issued to Thai villagers from Ban Semerak between 1951 and early 1952.

14 A chapter of at least five monks is needed to conduct ordination ceremonies and to receive the annual offering of *kathin* robes at the end of the rainy-season retreat (*duen phansa*).

15 The concept of a national Buddhist examination was the brainchild of Prince-Patriarch Wachirayan (1859–1921), abbot of Bangkok's Wat Boworniwet and the half brother of King Chulalongkorn. On the life of the monk and his role in reforming Thai Buddhism, see Craig Reynolds's 1972 and 1979 works, as well as Niramol 1986. For a discussion of the history of the examinations, see Suchaowana Phloichum's short book, *Prawat Naktham* (2002).

16 See Tambiah (1970: 127–28) for a further discussion of the *nak tham* examinations in Thailand.

17 Almost everyone passes the *nak tham* examinations. Although each candidate sits at his own table and the exams are proctored, copying and cheating are easy and rampant. "If you really can't answer a question, just ask the proctor and he will give you the answer," said my monk friend Khun Phom smiling.

18 No one has been able to ascertain when Patani monks first arrived in Ban Bor On. Patani men were also believed by older Ban Bor On residents to have built the last remaining wood pavilion in Wat Nai. It is plausible that the influx of Patani migrants to Kelantan happened during the years of Bangkok's attacks on the Malay kingdom during the early part of the twentieth century.

19 Kelantanese Thais are not the only viewers of Thailand's television programs. Some Kelantanese Chinese from the Tumpat district also enjoy watching Thai television. Many speak some Kelantanese Thai and have picked up standard Thai by watching Thai programs (Yeo 2007: 48).

20 On the use of central Thai as Thailand's national/standard language, see Diller 2002.

CHAPTER 3 / Forms

Parts of this chapter have been reproduced in an article published in the *Journal of the Royal Anthropological Institute* 17 (2011): 116–34.

1 Much has been written about Tok Kenali in Kelantanese historiography. For a good introduction to the biography of the thinker, see Ismail Bakar 1997 and

Abdullah Al-Qari 1974.

2   Marc Askew (2006: 177) has noted that Chinese Malaysian and Singaporean pil-
      grims travel to the Buddhist and Chinese shrines in what he calls lower southern
      Thailand not only to worship but also to shop, seek out sexual services, and tour
      the region.

3   Not much ethnographic research has been conducted on the relationship between
      Kelantan's urban Chinese population and the predominantly rural Thai. The best
      works to date on the subject remain Golomb's study of interethnic adaptation
      (1978) and Mohamed's analysis of social organization in a Kelantanese Buddhist
      temple (1993a). Similarly very little has been written on the interaction Thais had
      with Hakka and Hainanese-speaking Kelantanese Chinese in Gua Musang and
      Tumpat.

4   For a discussion of Chinese participation in Kelantanese Thai ritual life, see
      Winzeler 1985 and Mohamed 1993a, 1993b.

5   The origins of Tua Pek Kong are uncertain. Scholars of Chinese religion have
      variously accredited him with being the Earth god, the god of prosperity, a Sini-
      cized Malay tutelary spirit, and a deified Chinese pioneer. On Tua Pek Kong wor-
      ship among Southeast Asian Chinese, see Middlebrook 1939, Cheo and Speeden
      1988, Sakai 1981, Kok 1993, and Debernadi 2004. Lung Dam, an elderly magical
      practitioner (*tok mo*) from the Thai village of Bang Rim Nam who had recently
      passed away, once told me that Tua Pek Kong was the Chinese equivalent of the
      Thai *chao the*—invisible spirits that guarded the peripheries of a place. To him,
      Tua Pek Kong and the *chao the* were one and the same. Other villagers I spoke
      to disagreed and were quick to point out that Thais never worshipped Tua Pek
      Kong, as the god was not part of the Thai pantheon, which was based on Bud-
      dhism and Brahmanism.

6   On Chinese political sponsorship of Kelantan's Thai temples and villages, see
      Mohamed 1995, Leng 1990, and Mohd. Naim 1986–1987.

7   Similar to Wat Klang's social situation, Wat Din Sung has become a hub for what
      Mohamed (1995: 6) has termed "weekend pilgrims": Chinese who come to the
      temple only on weekends and holidays for the ritual services offered. Significant
      numbers of Chinese tourists from all over Malaysia visit the temple, which has
      many buildings built in the Chinese style.

8   Mohamed (1993b: 135–36) noted how the pamphlets (*sakala*) announcing
      upcoming temple celebrations in the mixed community of Chinese and Thai
      households he did ethnographic research in were printed in Thai and Malay
      rather than Chinese, hence providing an "authentic Thai atmosphere" for the
      event. This ensured that Thai ritual and organizational expertise at these celebra-
      tions was not compromised. Thais who couldn't read Thai were more likely to be
      able to read Romanized Malay than Chinese. Chinese parents rarely sent their
      children to Thai language classes in the temples and therefore most cannot read

or write Thai.

9   Kelantan's high crime rates in the first decades of the twentieth century have been noted by Ibrahim (1974: 72n), who examined small court cases for the Pasir Puteh district. According to the administrative reports (January 1914 to December 1915), Pasir Puteh's court recorded 28 cases of theft, 54 cases of cattle theft, 29 cases of assault, 9 housebreaking instances, and 20 cases of public wearing of *kris* (Malay daggers). Graham (1905: 18) had earlier noted the frequency of cattle theft in Kelantan. Interestingly, despite villagers' complaints of crime, few Thais were arrested in Kelantan during the years of British administration. This could possibly have been due to the relative inaccessibility of Thai villages and the ease with which villagers could sneak across the Tak Bai. In 1910, for instance, of the 345 prisoners incarcerated in the Kota Bharu Gaol, only 3 were Siamese (Thai). Perhaps the earliest indication of Thai involvement in violent crime in British Kelantan occurs in the *Straits Settlement Report* for 1910, in which it is mentioned that "a Siamese named Chou [Chao] Dam strangled a man named Ikan who was on intimate terms with his wife: he was convicted of culpable homicide not amounting to murder and sentenced to 15 years rigorous imprisonment" (1910: 11).

10 Temple lands are formally referred to in Kelantanese Malay documents kept by the state's Land Department as *tanah kerajan Kelantan kerana perguna'an bagi bekas ketik* (Kelantan state land for temple use).

11 See http://www.youtube.com/watch?v=sRu1Pjnuujs.

12 The book shows a photograph supposedly of the Phra Non Reclining Buddha. It is, however, not the Phra Non statue but a smaller one set in a temple in Penang.

CHAPTER 4 / Circuits

1   Covering some three hectares in a wooded grove, Istana Bukit Tanah was probably built during the final years of the reign of Sultan Muhammad IV (r. 1911–1920). The mansion sits on top of a man-made mound (Malay: *bukit tanah*) that was constructed to raise the height and thus the magnificence of the building above the surrounding flat terrain.

2   Kelantanese temple calendars often come with one of three standard images. Most popular with villagers are calendars featuring photographs of the Thai king and his family. Other pictures include those of revered monks and famous Buddha statues in Thailand as well as actors from Thai television soap dramas, which many Kelantanese Thais watch each night on Thai channels 5, 7, 9, or 11.

3   In his 1902 annual report on the state of Buddhism and education to the Ministry of Education (*krasuang thammakan*) in areas under the jurisdiction of Nakhon Sri Thammarat, the local director of education, Phra Sirithammamuni, observed that there were 39 temples housing 213 monks in Siamese Kelantan (1902: 10).

In a subsequent report two years later, he counted 43 temples. But by 1906, the number had dwindled to 40.

4   Wat Ban Kao is believed by Thai villagers to be Kelantan's oldest Buddhist temple that is still in use. Older temples such as those at Sungai Pinang and Kok Keli in Tumpat, Lubok Jong in Pasir Mas, Kampung Chepo in Kota Bharu, and Berhala Tambung in Besut, Terengganu, may have predated Wat Ban Kao's but nothing remains by way of visible remnants — only the fantastical memory of these sacred places in the minds of some villagers. Wat Ban Kao's large ordination hall (*bot*) was supposedly built in 1918. The material form of the building, with its high base and thick walls, resembles that of Wat Nai, and residents from both communities have suggested that the same artisans could have been responsible for designing and building the two halls. Than Khru Kio was also believed by some Thais I spoke with to have been instrumental in constructing Wat Khok Phrao's yellow-walled ordination hall.

5   These temples were Wat Kok Sawad, Wat Bang Noi (Wat Tharakorn), Wat Khok Mafueng, and Wat Sai Khao.

6   Wanipha does not provide us with further details of the conferment process. She does mention, however, that Pho Than Phut's monastic promotion resulted from his disciple, Phra Khru Srithong Narakhetsangkhakit, traveling to Bangkok to request his master's preceptor status. Phra Khru Srithong was the abbot of Wat Chehe from 1908 to 1912. He was originally from the Panare district in Patani.

7   Ecclesiastical titles of rank are further subdivided into four main grades, each with its own symbols of office. These are the grades of Tham, Thep, Rat, and Saman, with the grade of Tham being the highest.

8   According to Wanipha (1992), prior to Pho Than Phut, monastic administration in the Siamese *mueang* of Kelantan was in the hands of one Phra (Than) Khru In Suwanajarit (Than Thong), who was the first monk in the *mueang* to be granted the title of Phra Khru. The title may have been granted locally, as was the tradition in Kelantan prior to Siam's Sangha Act of 1902 and Bangkok's increasingly active monastic control over its faraway provinces with the implementation of King Chulalongkorn's national reforms.

9   In his annual report of 1907, Phra Sirithammamuni, director of monastic education in Nakhon Sri Thammarat, noted that he had appointed Than Khru Kio to be Phra Khru Phud's successor based on the former's many years in the monkhood and likeable personality. At the time, Siamese Kelantan was divided into four subdistricts (*tambon*), each headed by a monk of the rank of *phra khru*. On the Malayan (later British) side of the Tak Bai, Phra Khru Chai of Borsamed and Phra Khru Chai of Khao Din oversaw the administration of nineteen temples.

10   The story of Thit Sa is interesting. He had once been a monk of the rank of Maha, the scholarly title reserved for monks who were well-versed in Pali studies. During his years as a monk, he had hired Malay workmen to build Wat Ban Kao's abbot's

quarters (*mae tek*). In order to ensure that the Malays were given proper Muslim meals, the abbot had a Malay woman cook for them. However, the abbot soon fell in love with the cook and eventually married her. A wealthy Malay man from Bandar Tumpat, the Datuk Bijiwangsa, was glad that Sa had embraced Islam and rewarded him with a piece of land at Cik Tahir, an estuarine location close to the Tumpat rivermouth. After Thit Sa's wife and child died he donated the land to his younger brother. Prior to Thit Sa, Wat Ban Kao was under the abbotship of a certain Pho Than Lin Dam (the Black-Tongued Abbot).

11   These included areas such as Cik Tahir (Bang), Pa Trang, Kok Jao, and Becoh Resok. Than Khru Kio partitioned some of these royally offered landholdings to other temples in the Tumpat area. Wat Khok Phrao was placed in charge of the Pa Trang plot and Wat Din Sung, the Becoh Resok plot. The temple acted in the capacity of an absentee landlord and was presented with a small token each year by the land's Malay cultivators. To this day, Wat Din Sung receives about RM30 (US$ 9) annually from a Malay villager for use of the Cik Tahir holding.

12   Monks of the rank of Athikarn were often the chosen secretary or assistant to superior ecclesiastical office holders such as the Phra Khru (Tambiah 1976: 237).

13   Similarly worded certificates are still being printed and presented to monks today as part of their formal symbols of monastic promotion. All such certificates carry the seal of the Religious Affairs Department, the office of the Sangkharat, and that of the king.

14   These were the administrative divisions of the north, south, and central regions of Siam. The fourth administrative division was reserved for the Thammayud Order of monks established by King Mongkut.

15   Prior to 1902, ecclesiastical hierarchies remained largely in the hands of local rulers and chief monks, although the tutelary head of Buddhism was still the royally appointed Sangkharat (Somboon 1982).

16   Yoneo Ishii (1975) noted that the earliest documented case of a millenarian revolt in Siam's history probably occurred in 1699, when a Lao man by the name of Bun Kwang planned an attack on the capital of Ayuthaya after amassing troops and elephants. Such revolts often occurred when the state intervened in local politics.

17   Sultan Muhammad II was instrumental in developing the Kelantanese capital into the state's administrative and commercial heart. Kelantanese historian Abdullah bin Mohammed Nakula (1981) associates the founding of the city in 1777 with Long Yunus, Sultan Muhammad II's father. Graham (1908) documents the moving of the capital from the old site of Pulau Saba to Kota Bharu much later. He credits Phja Pak Daeng with the shift in the two Malay political centers. Kessler (1978) lists the founding of Kota Bharu as during the reign of Sultan Muhammad I (r. 1800–1838).

18   For a comprehensive account of the civil war see Cyril Skinner's monograph *The*

Civil War in Kelantan in 1839 and Abdullah b. Mohammed Nakula's *Keturunan Raja-Raja Kelantan dan Peristiwa-Peristiwa Bersejarah* (1981). The prominent nineteenth-century Singapore Malay author and thinker Abdullah b. Abdul Kader Munshi visited Kelantan during the "warring kinsmen" period and writes about it in his travelogue (Abdullah Munshi 1960).

19   Sultan Muhammad I had tried unsuccessfully to escape the yoke of Buddhist Siam's overlordship on a number of occasions before deciding on winning Siamese favor with the presentation of the gold and silver trees. His hostility toward Siam can be seen as a delicate balancing act on the part of a state that needed Siam's powerful military intervention but rejected being subservient to the Buddhist polity. Sultan Muhammad I eventually gave in to Siamese demands for vassalage and thus was protected by Siam's powerful forces from impending southern invasions (Talib 1995: 14).

20   The endowment of parcels of land to the *sangha* was a traditional practice of Buddhist kingship that clearly displayed the ruler's patronage of the religion, albeit without direct intervention in the affairs of the monastic order. See Wales 1965 and Tambiah 1970 on the contemporary practice of kingly duties in Thailand.

21   A similar but less elaborate purification ceremony was conducted at Wat Din Sung in 2003 after a coconut tree within the temple grounds was hit by lightning. Such an unnatural disaster is considered ritually dangerous and polluting and therefore the temple needed to be purified.

22   The sultan's invitation to the Thai monks and likely the Thai Buddhist lay magical specialists (*tok mo*), who were an inseparable part of any *cha roen* ritual, can be seen as part of a larger generalized Malay belief in the efficacy and potency of Thai magical prowess and the mutual respect that pervaded both communities (Winstedt 1951; Golomb 1978, 1985, 1986; Yusoff 1996).

23   The Kelantanese Malay term for temple (*ketik*) is used here instead of the standard Malay *kuil* or *biara*, thus emphasizing the unique Kelantanese-only association between Thai Buddhist monastics and their Malay rulers.

24   Images of monks at Datuk Nik Aziz's receptions have been posted on blogs and social networking sites, detailing the chief minister's friendly associations with his Thai supporters. See, e.g., the following Malay language blogs: http://sanggahtoksago.blogspot.com/2010/07/anuar-musa-nasharuddin-sami-antara-yang.html, http://kerabubersuara.blogspot.com/2010/07/anuar-musa-nasha-ruddin-sami-antara-yang.html, http://mrk-al-banjari.blogspot.com/2010/07/menghadiri-kenduri-kesyukuran-di-rumah.html (accessed 30 November 2010).

25   Thailand's *sangha* council produces a variety of fans in different shapes and colors to represent the various offices and ranks of its members. When a monk is promoted within this complex hierarchy, he has to exchange his earlier fan for a new one that corresponds to his appointed position.

26   Like Thai understandings of rule, Islamic notions of kingship in the Malay world

were heavily influenced by earlier Hindu *sastras* as well as pre-Hindu Buddhist ideals of rulership. For a study of the syncretic nature of Malay kingship in Muslim Southeast Asia, see Winstedt 1947, Wilkinson 1959, Wolters 1970, Milner 1981, 1983, and Woodward 1989.

27 On 26 February 2001, Afghanistan's Taliban issued an edict for the destruction of statues in all areas that came under its jurisdiction. The edict (announced on the Taliban's Radio Sharia) a day later read: "On the basis of consultations with the religious leaders of the Islamic Emirate of Afghanistan (IEA), religious judgments of the Ulema and rulings of the Supreme Court of the IEA, all statues and non-Islamic shrines located in different parts of the IEA must be destroyed [broken]. These statues have been and remain shrines of infidels and these infidels continue to worship and respect these icons [statues]. Allah (God) Almighty is the only real shrine and all false shrines [symbols] be destroyed. Therefore, the supreme leader of the IEA has ordered all the representatives of the Ministry of Promotion of Virtue and Suppression of Vice and the Ministries of Information and Culture to smash [destroy] all the statues [shrines)]. As ordered by the Ulema and the Supreme Court of the IEA all the statues must be annihilated [destroyed] so that no one can worship or respect them in the future" (Warikoo 2002: 163).

28 Pho Kae Bo was killed by a Malay man; the reasons behind the murder remain unclear. The murderer placed heavy palm fronds over the *nai ban*'s body so as to make it appear that the headman had died after being hit by the falling leaves.

29 This was a man who went by the Malay Muslim name of Salleh. Salleh lived before World War II. Unfortunately, not much is known about him other than his unusual name.

30 The privileged position of the sultan as the guardian of Malay customs and religion was spelled out by the British in Malaya's colonial constitution. Citizen allegiance to their sultan was strengthened in the national principle of *Rukunnegara* and disseminated through all levels of society via education, the mass media, etc. The code of *Rukunnegara* that every Malaysian was expected to uphold comprised belief in God, loyalty to the king and the state, supremacy of the constitution, sovereignty of law, and good behavior and morality (Noer 1983: 199).

CHAPTER 5 / Dreams

1 For a full discussion of the *thammathut* program in Thailand, see Tambiah 1976.

2 Pattana Kitiarsa (2010) noted the long history of Thai monks participating in missionary-type activities in the Theravadin world since the thirteenth century. Modern Thai Buddhist transnational missionization began with the establishment of a Thai temple in Bodh Gaya, India, in 1957. By the mid-1960s, the Thai government had initiated the building of Europe's first Thai Buddhist temple in

Wimbledon, England (116).

3   The Thai citizen monks entered Malaysia using entry visas issued for a duration between fifteen days and six months instead of international passports. The visas were granted by the Malaysian embassy in Bangkok. Today, monks from Thailand who choose to stay in Kelantan beyond the granted one-month period often switch between Thai passports and border passes when re-entering Malaysia. Border passes are official forms that allow a resident of one of Thailand's southern border provinces to enter a Malaysian border state without a passport. Monks from Thailand who do not reside in the border regions are issued such passes only if they can prove affiliation with a temple in one of these provinces.

4   See, for instance, Swearer 1991, McCargo 1999, and Mackenzie 2007.

5   Kershaw (1969: 208) noted that one of the first large-scale projects the consulate embarked upon was a "secret survey of the Thai population, land and livestock" holdings in Kelantan. The exact reason behind the survey is unclear, although Kershaw suggested that it could have been done to assess the possibility of Kelantanese Thai immigration into the *nikhom* schemes.

6   Some Kelantanese Thais are so obsessed with watching Thai television that they have cable boxes and small satellite dishes installed in their homes if they live beyond the reach of Thailand's broadcast signals. These illegal devices are easily set up and allow Kelantanese to watch their favorite Thai television programs in locales far beyond Thailand's sphere of transmission.

Conclusion

1   The study of narratives and spatial production has been the concern of many anthropologists, folklorists, and students of cultural studies since the 1980s. See, for instance, Bruner 1984, Dundes 1989, Johnstone 1990, Featherstone 1993, Frake 1996, Feld and Basso 1996, and Neumann 1999.

BIBLIOGRAPHY

Abdullah Al-Qari. 1988. *Kelantan Serambi Makkah dalam Zaman Tuk Kenali*. Kota Bharu: Pustaka ASA.

Abdullah Al-Qari b. Haji Salleh. 1974. "To' Kenali: His Life and Influence." In *Kelantan: Religion, Society and Politics in a Malay State*, edited by William Roff, 8–101. Kuala Lumpur: Oxford University Press.

Abdullah b. Abdul Kader Munshi. 1960. *Kisah Pelayaran Abdullah ka-Kelantan dan ka-Judah*. Edited by Kassim Ahmad. Kuala Lumpur: Oxford University Press.

Abdullah b. Mohammed Nakula. 1981. *Keturunan Raja-Raja Kelantan dan Peristiwa-Peristiwa Bersejarah*. Kelantan State Museum Monograph Series. Kuala Lumpur.

Abdul Rahman Embong. 2001. "The Culture and Practice of Pluralism in Postcolonial Malaysia." In *The Politics of Multiculturalism: Pluralism and Citizenship in Malaysia, Singapore, and Indonesia*, edited by Robert Hefner, 59–86. Honolulu: University of Hawai'i Press.

Abu-Lughod, Lila. 1988. *Veiled Sentiments: Honor and Poetry in a Bedouin Society*. Berkeley: University of California Press.

———. 1991. "Writing against Culture." In *Recapturing Anthropology*, edited by Richard G. Fox, 137–62. Sante Fe, NM: School of American Research Press.

———. 2005. *Dramas of Nationhood: The Politics of Television in Egypt*. Chicago: University of Chicago Press.

Adiele, Faith. 1987. "Freedom without Status: Buddhist Mae Chi ('Nuns') in Contemporary Thailand." Honors thesis, Harvard University.

Ahmad, Dusuki. 2002. "Sandiwara Nabi Suka Kelantan." *Mingguan Malaysia*, 27 January: 10.

Anderson, Benedict. 1983. *Imagined Communities: Reflections on the Origins and Spread of Nationalism*. New York: Verso.

Annandale, Nelson. 1900. "The Siamese Malay States." *Scottish Geographical Magazine* 59: 505–23 (microfilm).

Anzaldúa, Gloria. 1987. *Borderlands/La Frontera: The New Mestiza*. San Francisco: Aunt Lute Books.

Appadurai, Arjun. 1996. *Modernity at Large: Cultural Dimensions of Globalization*. Minneapolis: University of Minnesota Press.

Asaad Syukri. 1971. *Detik-detik Sejarah Kelantan*. Kota Bharu: Pustaka Aman.

Asad, Talal. 2004. "Where Are the Margins of the State?" In *Anthropology in the Margins of the State*, edited by Veena Das and Deborah Poole, 279–89. Sante Fe, NM: School of American Research Press.

Askew, Marc. 2006. "Sex and the Sacred: Sojourners and Visitors in the Making of the Southern Thai Borderland." In *Centering the Margin: Agency and Narrative in Southeast Asian Borderlands*, edited by Alexander Horstmann and Reed Wadley, 177–206. New York: Berghahn.

Auge, Marc. 1995. *Non-places: An Introduction to the Anthropology of Supermodernity*. Translated by John Howe. London: Verso.

Azizah binti Samat. 2006. "Sistem Pentadbiran Tanah Inggeris di Kelantan: Peringkat Pengukuhan 1915-1940." *Warisan Kelantan* 7: 16-31.

Aziz Al-Azmeh. 1997. *Muslim Kingship: Power and the Sacred in Muslim, Christian, and Pagan Polities*. New York: I. B. Tauris.

Bala, Poline. 2002. *Changing Borders and Identities in the Kelabit Highlands: Anthropological Reflections on Growing Up in a Kelabit Village near the International Border*. Kuching: Universiti Malaysia Sarawak.

Balfour, Patrick. 1935. *Grand Tour: Diary of an Eastward Journey*. New York: Harcourt, Brace.

Barme, Scott. 1993. *Luang Wichit Wathakan and the Creation of a Thai Identity*. Institute of Southeast Asian Studies, Singapore.

Barth, Fredrik. 1969. "Introduction." In *Ethnic Groups and Boundaries: The Social Organization of Culture Difference*, edited by Barth, 9-38. Oslo: Universitetsforlaget.

Berdahl, Daphne. 1999. *Where the World Ended: Re-unification and Identity in the German Borderland*. Berkeley: University of California Press.

———. 2001. "'Go, Trabi, Go!' Reflections on a Car and Its Symbolization over Time." *Anthropology and Humanism* 25, no. 2: 131-41.

Bird, Elizabeth. 2002. "It Makes Sense to Us: Cultural Identity in Local Legends of Place." *Journal of Contemporary Ethnography* 31, no. 5: 519-47.

———. 2010. "The Anthropology of News and Journalism: Why Now?" In *The Anthropology of News and Journalism: Global Perspectives*, edited by Bird, 1-21. Bloomington: Indiana University Press.

Blackburn, Anne. 2010. *Locations of Buddhism: Colonialism and Modernity in Sri Lanka*. Chicago: University of Chicago Press.

Bourdieu, Pierre. 1990. *The Logic of Practice*. Cambridge: Polity Press.

Brenner, Neil. 1998. "Global Cities, 'Glocal' States: Global City Formation and State Territorial Restructuring in Contemporary Europe." *Review of International Political Economy* 5, no. 1: 1-37.

Brubaker, Rogers. 1996. *Nationalism Reframed: Nationhood and the National Question in the New Europe*. Cambridge, UK: Cambridge University Press.

Bruner, Edward. 1984. *Text, Play and Story: The Construction and Reconstruction of Self and Society*. Washington, D. C.: American Anthropological Association.

Bunnag, Tej. 1962. "Khabot Phum Mi Bun Pak Isan R.S 121." *Sangkhom parithat* 5, no. 1: 78-86.

Carsten, Janet. 1998. "Borders, Boundaries, Tradition, State on the Malaysian Periphery." In *Border Identities: Nation and State at International Frontiers*, edited by Thomas Wilson and Hastings Donnan, 215-37. Cambridge: Cambridge University Press.

Carstens, Sharon. 2001. "Border Crossings: Hakka Chinese Lessons in Diasporic Identity." In *Chinese Populations in Contemporary Southeast Asian Societies: Identities, Interdependence and International Influence*, edited by Jocelyn Armstrong, Warwick Armstrong, and Kent Mulliner, 188-210. Surrey, UK: Curzon.

———. 2005. *Histories, Cultures, Identities, Studies in Malaysian Chinese Worlds*. Singapore: National University of Singapore Press.

Chantas Thongchuai. 1993. *Phasa lae Wattanatham Pak Tai*. Bangkok: Odeon.

Chatthip Nartsupha. 1984. "The Ideology of Holy Men Revolts in North East Thailand." In *History and Peasant Consciousness in South East Asia*, edited by Andrew Turton and Shigeharu Tanabe, 11-134. Osaka: National Museum of Ethnology.

Cheo, Kim Ban, and Muriel Speeden. 1988. *Baba Folk Beliefs and Superstitions*. Singapore: Landmark Books.

Clifford, Hugh. 1897. "A Journey through the Malay States of Trengganu and Kelantan." *Geographical Journal* 9, no. 1: 1-37.

———. 1938. *Report and Expedition: Trengganu and Kelantan*. Kuala Lumpur.

Clifford, James. 1988. *The Predicament of Culture: Twentieth-Century Ethnography, Literature, and Art*. Cambridge, MA: Harvard University Press.

———. 1997. *Routes: Travel and Translation in the Late Twentieth Century*. Cambridge, MA: Harvard University Press.

Clifford, James, and George Marcus. 1986. *Writing Culture: The Poetics and Politics of Ethnography*. Berkeley: University of California Press.

Cohen, Amnon. 1982. "On the Realities of the Millet System: Jerusalem in the Sixteenth Century." In *Christians and Jews in the Ottoman Empire: The Functioning of a Plural Society*, vol. 2, edited by Benjamin Braude and Bernard Lewis. New York: Holmes and Meier.

Cohn, Bernard. 1996. *Colonialism and Its Forms of Knowledge: The British Rule in India*. Princeton, NJ: Princeton University Press.

Coleman, Simon, and John Eade. 2004. "Introduction: Reframing Pilgrimage." In *Reframing Pilgrimage: Cultures in Motion*, edited by Simon Coleman and John Eade, 1-26. New York: Routledge.

Crapanzano, Vincent. 1977. "On the Writing of Ethnography." *Dialectical Anthropology* 2, no. 1: 69-73.

———. 1980. *Tuhami: Portrait of a Moroccan*. Chicago: Chicago University Press, 1980.

Cremation Volume. Undated. Printed on the occasion of the royal cremation of Phra Wijaranayanmuni (Chan Kesaro), Wat Uttamaram, Pasir Mas.

Cremation Volume. 1997. Printed on the occasion of the royal cremation of Phra Khru Vithet Thammaphitak (Daeng Thammasaro), Wat Phikulthongwararam, Tumpat.

Cremation Volume. 2005. Printed on the occasion of the royal cremation of Phra Wija-ranayanmuni, Wat Uttamaram, Pasir Mas.

Cremation Volume. 2008. Printed on the occasion of the royal cremation of Phra Khru Bowornyarnnahprasit (Than Di), Wat Maisuwankhiri, Tumpat.

Cribb, Robert, and Li Narangoa. 2004. "Orphans of Empire: Divided Peoples, Dilemmas of Identity, and Old Imperial Borders in East and Southeast Asia." *Society for the Comparative Study of Society and History* 46, no. 1: 164–87.

Cuisinier, Jeanne. 1934. "The Sacred Books of India and the Malay and Siamese Theatres in Kelantan." *Indian Art and Letters* 13, no. 1: 43–50.

Das, Veena, and Deborah Poole. 2004. "State and Its Margins: Comparative Ethnogra-phies." In *Anthropology in the Margins of the State*, edited by Das and Poole, 3–35. Sante Fe, NM: School of American Research Press.

Davies, Charlotte. 1998. *Reflexive Ethnography: A Guide to Researching Selves and Others*. New York: Routledge.

Davis, Sara. 2003. "Premodern Flows in Postmodern China: Globalisation and the Sip-songpanna Tais." *Modern China* 29 (2): 176–203.

DeBernadi, Jean. 2004. *Rites of Belonging: Memory, Modernity and Identity in a Malaysian Chinese Community*. Stanford, CA: Stanford University Press.

de Certeau, Michel. 1984. *The Practice of Everyday Life*. Berkeley: University of California Press.

De Coulanges, Fustel. 1864 (1980). *The Ancient City: A Study on the Religion, Laws, and Institutions of Greece and Rome*. Baltimore, MD: Johns Hopkins University Press.

de Pina-Cabral, Joao. 1987. "Paved Roads and Enchanted Mooresses: The Perception of the Past among the Peasant Population of the Alto Minho." *Man* 22, no. 4: 715–36.

Diller, Anthony. 2002 "What Makes Central Thai a National Language." In *National Identity and Its Defenders: Thailand, 1939–1989*, edited by Craig Reynolds, 71–108. Bangkok: Silkworm.

Dodge, Nicholas N. 1980. "Population Estimates for the Malay Peninsula in the Nine-teenth Century, with Special Reference to the East Coast States." *Population Studies* 34, no. 3: 437–75.

Dollah, Hanapi. 1987. "Komuniti Cina di Kampung Mata Ayer, Kelantan: Satu Kajian Asimilasi Social Budaya dalam Masyarakat Berbilang Kaum." In *Kajian Budaya dan Masyarakat di Malaysia*, edited by Mohd. Taib Osman and Wan Kadir Yusoff, 296–328. Kuala Lumpur: Dewan Bahasa dan Pustaka.

————. 1999. *Borders: Frontiers of Identity, Nation and State*. New York: Berg.

Dorairajoo, Saroja. 2002. "No Fish in the Sea: Thai Malay Tactics of Negotiation in Time of Scarcity." Ph.D diss., Harvard University.

Dundes, Alan. 1989. *Folklore Matters*. Knoxville: University of Tennessee Press.

Durkheim, Emile, and Marcel Mauss. 1903 (1963). *Primitive Classification*. Chicago: Uni-versity of Chicago Press.

Dwyer, Kevin. 1982. *Moroccan Dialogues: Anthropology in Question*. Prospect Heights, IL: Waveland Press.

Ebin, Victoria. 1996. "Making Room versus Creating Space: The Construction of Spatial Categories by Itinerant Mouride Traders." In *Making Muslim Space in North America and Europe*, edited by Barbara Metcalf, 92–131. Berkeley: University of California Press.

Eh Mooi a/l Eh Chit. 1997. "Latarbelakang Masyarakat Siam di Kelantan." *Warisan Kelantan* 16: 66–82.

Evans-Pritchard, Edward E. 1940. *The Nuer: A Description of the Modes of Livelihood and Political Institutions of a Nilotic People*. Oxford: Clarendon Press.

Faaland, Just, Jack Parkinson, and Rais Saniman. 1990. *Growth and Ethnic Inequality: Malaysia's New Economic Policy*. Kuala Lumpur: Dewan Bahasa dan Pustaka.

Falk, Monica Lindberg. 2007. *Making Fields of Merit: Buddhist Female Ascetics and Gendered Orders in Thailand*. Seattle: University of Washington Press; Copenhagen: NIAS Press.

Farrer, Roland John. 1916. *State of Kelantan (Unfederated Malay States) Report for 1915*. Singapore.

———. 1933. "A Buddhistic Purification Ceremony." *Journal of the Malayan Branch of the Royal Asiatic Society* 11, no. 2: 261–63.

Featherstone, Mike. 1993. "Global and Local Cultures." In *Mapping the Futures: Local Cultures, Global Change*, edited by John Bird, Barry Curtiss, Tim Putnam, George Robertson, and Lisa Tickner, 86–101. New York: Routledge.

———. 2004. "Automobilities." *Theory, Culture and Society* 21, nos. 4–5: 1–24.

Feld, Steven, and Keith Basso. 1996. "Introduction." In *Senses of Place*, edited by Feld and Basso, 3–13. Santa Fe: University of New Mexico Press.

Firth, Raymond. 1943 (1996). *Housekeeping among Malay Peasants*. New York: Humanities Press.

Frake, Charles. 1996. "Places, Past Times and Sheltered Identity in Rural East Anglia." In *Senses of Place*, edited by Steven Feld and Keith Basso, 229–58. Santa Fe: University of New Mexico Press.

Geertz, Clifford. 1973. *The Interpretation of Cultures*. New York: Basic Books.

———. 1983. *Local Knowledge: Further Essays in Interpretive Anthropology*. New York: Basic Books.

Gesick, Lorraine, ed. 1983. *Centers, Symbols, and Hierarchies. Essays on the Classical States of Southeast Asia*. Monograph series / Yale University Southeast Asia Studies, 26. New Haven, CT: Yale University Southeast Asia Studies.

———. 1995. *In the Land of Lady White Blood: Southern Thailand and the Meaning of History*. Ithaca, NY: Cornell Southeast Asia Program.

Gimlette, John. 1920. "A Curious Kelantan Charm." *Journal of the Straits Branch of the Royal Asiatic Society* 82: 116–18.

Goh, Beng-Lan. 2002. *Modern Dreams: An Inquiry into Power, Cultural Production, and the Cityscape in Contemporary Urban Penang, Malaysia*. Ithaca: Southeast Asia Studies Program Publications.

Golomb, Louis. 1978. *Brokers of Morality: Thai Ethnic Adaptation in a Rural Malaysian*

Setting. Honolulu: University of Hawai'i Press.

———. 1985. *An Anthropology of Curing in Multiethnic Thailand*. Chicago: University of Illinois Press.

———. 1986. "Ethnic Minorities as Magical/Medical Specialists in Malaysia and Thailand." In *Cultural Identity in Northern Peninsular Malaysia*, edited by Sharon Carstens. Ohio: Ohio University Monographs in International Studies no. 63.

Gomes, Alberto. 1999. "Peoples and Cultures." In *The Shaping of Malaysia*, edited by Amarjit Kaur and Ian Metcalfe, 78–98. London: Macmillan Press.

Graham, William. A. 1905. *Report on the State of Kelantan for the Period 1st August, 1904, to 31st May, 1905*. Bangkok: Government Printer.

———. 1908. *Kelantan: A State of the Malay Peninsula*. London: J. Maclehose and Sons.

Green, Sarah. 2005. *Notes from the Balkans: Locating Marginality and Ambiguity on the Greek-Albanian Border*. Princeton, NJ: Princeton University Press.

Gupta, Akhil, and James Ferguson. 1992a. "Beyond 'Culture': Space, Identity, and the Politics of Difference." *Cultural Anthropology* 7, no. 1: 6–23.

———. 1992b. "After 'Peoples and Cultures.'" In *Culture, Power, Place: Explorations in Critical Anthropology*, edited by Akhil Gupta and James Ferguson. Durham, NC: Duke University Press.

Hagesteijn, Renee. 1989. *Circles of Kings: Political Dynamics in Early Continental Southeast Asia*. Providence, RI: Foris.

Hansen, Anne R. 2007. *How to Behave: Buddhism and Modernity in Colonial Cambodia, 1860–1930*. Bangkok: Silkworm.

Harper, Tim. 1996. "New Malays, New Malaysians: Nationalism, Society and History." In *Southeast Asian Affairs 1996*. Singapore: ISEAS.

Harvey, David. 1990. *The Condition of Postmodernity: An Enquiry into the Origins of Cultural Change*. Cambridge: Blackwell.

Hasimah Mat Kasim. 2007. "Kampung Bendang Kerian: Perubahan Teknologi Dalam Penanam Padi." *Warisan Kelantan* 22: 113–36.

Herzfeld, Michael. 1987. *Anthropology through the Looking-Glass: Critical Ethnography in the Margins of Europe*. Cambridge: Cambridge University Press.

———. 1991. *A Place in History: Social and Monumental Time in a Cretan Town*. Princeton, NJ: Princeton University Press.

———. 1992. *The Social Production of Indifference: Exploring the Symbolic Roots of Western Bureaucracy*. Oxford: Berg.

———. 1997. *Cultural Intimacy: Social Poetics in the Nation-State*. London: Routledge.

———. 2001. *Anthropology: Theoretical Practice in Culture and Society*. Oxford: Blackwell.

———. 2004. *The Body Impolitic: Artisans and Artifice in the Global Hierarchy of Value*. Chicago: University of Chicago Press.

Heyman, Josiah. 1994. "The Mexico-United States Border in Anthropology: A Critique and Reformulation." *Journal of Political Ecology* 1: 43–65.

Hing, Ai Yun. 1984. "Capitalist Development, Class and Race." In *Ethnicity, Class and*

Development in Malaysia, edited by Syed Hussin Ali. Kuala Lumpur: Persatuan Sains Sosial Malaysia.

Hirschman, Charles. 1986. "The Making of Race in Colonial Malaya: Political Economy and Racial Category." *Sociological Forum*, Spring, 330-61.

———. 1987. "The Meaning and Measurement of Ethnicity in Malaysia: An Analysis of Census Classification." *Journal of Asian Studies* 46, no. 3: 555-82.

Ho, Engseng. 2006. *The Graves of Tarim: Genealogy and Mobility across the Indian Ocean.* Berkeley: University of California Press.

Ho, Hui Ling. 2007. "Kegiatan Komunis di Negeri Kelantan pada Zaman Darurat, 1948-1960: Satu Tinjauan." In *Kelantan: Dahulu dan Sekarang*, edited by Abdullah Zakaria Ghazali and Zahir Ahmad, 186-203. Kuala Lumpur: United Selangor Press.

Hobsbawm, Eric. 1983. "Introduction: Inventing Traditions." In *The Invention of Tradition*, edited by Hobsbawm and Terence Ranger, 1-14. Cambridge: Cambridge University Press.

Horstmann, Alexander. 2002a. "Dual Ethnic Minorities and the Local Reworking of Citizenship at the Thailand-Malaysian Border." CIBR Working Papers in Border Studies. Belfast.

———. 2002b. *Class, Culture and Space: The Construction and Shaping of Communal Space in South Thailand.* Tokyo: ILCAA.

Horstmann, Alexander, and Reed Wadley. 2006. "Introduction: Centering the Margin in Southeast Asia." In *Centering the Margin: Agency and Narrative in Southeast Asian Borderlands*, edited by Horstmann and Wadley, 1-27. New York: Berghahn Books.

Hoskins, Janet. 1998. *Biographical Objects: How Things Tell the Stories of People's Lives.* New York: Routledge.

Hua, Wu Yin. 1983. *Class and Communalism in Malaysia: Politics in a Dependent Capitalist State.* London: Zed.

Hughes-Freeland, Felicia. 2007. "Charisma and Celebrity in Indonesian Politics." *Anthropological Theory* 7, no. 2: 177-200.

Ibrahim Nik Mahmood. 1974. "The To' Janggut Rebellion of 1915." In *Kelantan: Religion, Society, Politics in a Malay State*, edited by William R. Roff, 62-86. Kuala Lumpur: Oxford University Press.

Ingold, Tim. 2007. *Lines: A Brief History.* London: Routledge.

Irvine, Judith, and Susan Gal. 2000. "Language Ideology and Linguistic Differentiation." In *Regimes of Language: Ideologies, Polities, and Identities*, edited by Paul V. Kroskrity, 35-83. Sante Fe, NM: School of American Research Press.

Ishii, Yoneo. 1975. "A Note on Buddhistic Millenarian Movements in Northeastern Siam." *Journal of Southeast Asian Studies* 6, no. 2: 121-26.

———. 1986. *Sangha, State, and Society: Thai Buddhism in History.* Translated by P. Hawkes. Honolulu: University of Hawai'i Press.

Ismail Bakar. 1997. "Tok Kenali sebagai Ulama dan Tokoh Islam." *Warisan Kelantan* 16: 50-66.

Jaiser, Gerhard. 2009. *Thai Mural Painting Volume 1: Iconography, Analysis and Guide.*

Bangkok: White Lotus.

Johnson, Irving. 1996. "Sacred Steps: The Nuuraa as a Magical Practitioner in the Kelantanese Thai Culture Region." Honors thesis, National University of Singapore.

———. 1999. "Seductive Mediators: The Nuuraa Performer's Ritual Persona as a Love Magician in Kelantanese Thai Society." *Journal of Southeast Asian Studies* 30, no. 2: 286-309.

Johnstone, Barbara. 1990. *Stories, Community, and Place: Narratives from Middle America.* Bloomington: Indiana University Press.

Jory, Patrick. 2002. "Thai and Western Scholarship in the Age of Colonialism: King Chulalongkorn Redefines the Jatakas." *Journal of Asian Studies* 61, no. 3: 891-918.

Jomo, Kwame S. 1986. *A Question of Class: Capital, the State, and Uneven Development.* Singapore: Oxford University Press.

Kapur-Fic, Alexandra. 1998. *Thailand: Buddhism, Society, and Women.* New Delhi: Abhinav.

Kejiam a/p Perak Kiau. 2007. "Kampung Siam Semerak." *Warisan Kelantan* 22: 74-87.

Kelantan Administrative Report for the Year 1928, no. 1429. R. J. B. Clayton. Singapore.

Kelantan Administrative Report for the Year 1929, no. 1429. R. J. B. Clayton. Singapore.

Kershaw, Roger. 1969. "The Thais of Kelantan: A Socio-Political Study of an Ethnic Outpost." Ph.D. diss., University of London.

———. 1973. "The Chinese in Kelantan, West Malaysia, as Mediators to Political Integration of the Kelantan Thais." *Review of Southeast Asian Studies* 3, nos. 3-4: 1-10.

———. 1977. "The 'East Coast' in Malayan Politics: Episodes of Resistance and Integration in Kelantan and Terengganu." *Modern Asian Studies* 11, no. 4: 515-41.

———. 1981. "Towards a Theory of Peranakan Chinese Identity in an Outpost of Thai Buddhism." *Journal of the Siam Society* 69: 74-107.

———. 1982. "A Little Drama of Ethnicity: Some Sociological Aspects of the Kelantan Manora." *Southeast Asian Journal of Social Science* 10: 69-95.

———. 1984. "Native But Not Bumiputera: Crisis and Complexity in the Political Status of the Kelantan Thais after Independence." *Contributions to Southeast Asian Ethnography* 3: 46-77.

———. 2001. *Monarchy in South-East Asia: The Faces of Tradition in Transition.* New York: Routledge.

Kessler, Clive. 1978. *Islam and Politics in a Malay State, Kelantan, 1838-1969.* Ithaca, NY: Cornell University Press.

Keyes, Charles F. 1971. "Buddhism and National Integration in Thailand." *Journal of Asian Studies* 30, no. 3: 551-68.

———. 1989. *Thailand: Buddhist Kingdom as Modern Nation-State.* Bangkok: Duang Kamol.

———. 1995. "Who Are the Tai? Reflections on the Invention of Identities." In *Ethnic Identity: Creation, Conflict, and Accommodation*, edited by Lola Romanucci-Ross and George A. De Vos, 136-61. London: Altamira Press.

Kobkua Suwannathat-Pian. 1988. *Thai-Malay Relations: Traditional Intra-regional Rela-*

tions from the Seventeenth to the Early Twentieth Centuries. New York: Oxford University Press.

————. 2002. "Special Thai-Malaysian Relations." *Journal of the Malaysian Branch of the Royal Asiatic Society* 75, no. 282: 1-22.

Kua, Kia Soong. 2005. *The Malaysian Civil Rights Movement.* Petaling Jaya, Malaysia: SIRD.

Kuwayama, Takami. 2003. "Natives as Dialogic Partners: Some Thoughts on Native Anthropology." *Anthropology Today* 19, no. 1: 8-11.

Laidlaw, Frank F. 1953. "Travels in Kelantan, Trengganu and Upper Perak: A Personal Narrative." *Journal of the Malayan Branch of the Royal Asiatic Society* 26, no. 4: 150-64.

Lamont, Michèle, and Virág Molnár. 2002. "The Study of Boundaries in the Social Sciences." *Annual Review of Sociology* 28: 167-95.

Leach, Edmund. 1954. *Political Systems of Highland Burma: A Study of Kachin Social Structure.* London: London School of Economics and Political Science.

Lee, Raymond, and Susan Ackerman, eds. 1997. *Sacred Tensions: Modernity and Religious Transformation in Malaysia.* Columbia: University of South Carolina Press.

Leibing, Annette, and Athena McLean. 2007. "'Learn to Value Your Shadow!' An Introduction to the Margins of Fieldwork." In *The Shadow Side of Fieldwork: Exploring the Blurred Borders between Ethnography and Life,* edited by McLean and Leibing, 1-9. Malden, MA: Blackwell.

Leng, Siang Yong. 1990. "Peranan Biku Siam di Wat Machi Maram, Kampung Jong Bakar, Tumpat, Kelantan." Honors thesis, Department of Anthropology and Sociology, Universiti Kebangsaan Malaysia.

Lim, Lian Chian. 1990-91. "Amalan Keagamaan dan Amalan Tradisi Masyarakat Thai di Kampong Terbok, Tumpat Kelantan." Honors thesis, University of Malaya.

Lim, Mah Hui. 1985. "Contradictions in the Development of Malay Capital: State, Accumulation and Legitimation." *Journal of Contemporary Asia* 15, no. 1: 37-63.

Lim, Pui H. 2009. *Through the Eyes of the King: The Travels of King Chulalongkorn to Malaya.* Singapore: ISEAS.

Loo, Heng Ann. 2003. "Peranan Masyarakat Cina Kelantan dalam Menghidupkan Wat Siam: Satu Kes di Wat Photikyan Phut Thak Tham di Kampung Balai, Bachok, Kelantan." Academic exercise, University Malaya.

Loos, Tamara. 2006. *Subject Siam: Family, Law, and Colonial Modernity in Thailand.* Ithaca, NY: Cornell University Press.

Mackenzie, Rory. 2007. *New Buddhist Movements in Thailand: Towards an Understanding of Wat Phra Dhammakaya and Santi Asoke.* New York: Routledge.

Marks, Thomas. 1997. *The British Acquisition of Siamese Malaya (1896-1909).* Bangkok: White Lotus.

Marriot, Hayes. 1916. "A Fragment of the History of Trengganu and Kelantan." *Journal of the Straits Branch of the Royal Asiatic Society* 72: 12-23.

Masquelier, Adeline. 2002. "Road Mythographies: Space, Mobility, and the Historical Imagination in Postcolonial Niger." *American Ethnologist* 29, no. 4: 829-56.

Matory, James L. 2005. *Black Atlantic Religion*. Princeton, NJ: Princeton University Press.

McCargo, Duncan. 1999. "The Politics of Buddhism in Southeast Asia." In *Religion, Globalization and the Political Culture in the Third World*, edited by Jeffrey Haynes, 213-39. Basingstoke, UK: Macmillan.

McDaniel, Justin. 2008. *Gathering Leaves and Lifting Words: Histories of Buddhist Monastic Education in Laos and Thailand*. Seattle: University of Washington Press.

Middlebrook, Stanley M. 1939. "Ceremonial Opening of a New Chinese Temple at Kandang, Malacca in December, 1938." *Journal of the Malayan Branch of the Royal Asiatic Society* 17, no. 1: 98-106.

Milner, Anthony C. 1981. "Islam and Malay Kingship." *Journal of the Royal Asiatic Society of Great Britain and Ireland*, no. 1: 46-70.

———. 1983. "Islam and the Muslim State." In *Islam in South-East Asia*, edited by M. Barry Hooker, 23-49. Leiden: E. J. Brill.

Mohamad Kamil Othman. 1980-1981. "Asimilasi dan Transformasi Komuniti Siam di Besut, Trengganu: Satu Kes di Kampung Keluang, Besut, Trengganu." Honors thesis, Department of Anthropology and Sociology, Universiti Kebangsaan Malaysia.

Mohamed b. Nik Mohd. Salleh. 1974. "Kelantan in Transition: 1891-1910." In *Kelantan: Religion, Society and Politics in a Malay State*, edited by William Roff, 22-61. Kuala Lumpur: Oxford University Press.

Mohamed Yusoff Ismail. 1980. *The Siamese of Aril: A Study of an Ethnic Minority Village*. Monograph no. 3, Faculty of Social Sciences and the Humanities. Bangi: Universiti Kebangasaan Malaysia.

———. 1982. "Tradition and Change in Aril, a Siamese Village in Kelantan." *Mankind* 13, no. 3: 252-63.

———. 1989. "Kata-kata Pinjaman Thai dalam Dialek Kelantan." *Warisan Kelantan* 8: 42-50.

———. 1990a. "Buddhism among the Siamese of Kelantan: Minority Religion in a Muslim State." *Jurnal Antropologi dan Sosiologi* 18: 55-69.

———. 1990b. "Membuat Pahala Sebagai Ritus Kebiaraan di Kalangan Masyarakat Buddha di Kelantan." *Jurnal Fakulti Sastera dan Sains Sosial Universiti Malaya* (SARJANA), no. 6: 51-69.

———. 1993a. *Buddhism and Ethnicity: Social Organization of a Buddhist Temple in Kelantan*. Singapore: ISEAS.

———. 1993b. "Two Faces of Buddhism: Chinese Participation in the Siamese Temples in Kelantan." In *Chinese Beliefs and Practices in Southeast Asia: Studies on the Chinese Religion in Malaysia, Singapore, and Indonesia*, edited by Cheu Hock Tong. Petaling Jaya: Pelanduk Publications.

———. 1995. "Survival Strategies of Siamese Buddhist Temples in the Malay Muslim State of Kelantan." *Ilmu Masyarakat* 25: 1-20.

———. 1996. "Pengaruh Siam dan Buddha Terhadap Sistem Kepercayaan Tradisional Orang Melayu Kelantan." *Akademika* 49: 23-37.

———. 2000. "Pengekalan Identiti Masyarakat Minoriti Thai di Kelantan." In *Masyara-*

kat, Budaya dan Perubahan, edited by Rahimah Abdul Aziz and Mohamed Yusoff Ismail, 113-24. Bangi: Universiti Kebangsaan Malaysia.

————. 2010. "Buddhism in a Muslim State: Theravada Practices and Religious Life in Kelantan." *Muslim World* 100, nos. 2 and 3: 321-36.

Mohammad Hashim Kamali. 1997. *Freedom of Expression in Islam.* Cambridge: Islamic Texts Society.

Mohd. Kamaruzaman A. Rahman. 1990. "Perkembangan Ekonomi Kelantan (1900-1920): Peranan Penasihat Inggeris." *Warisan Kelantan* 9: 44-62.

Mohd. Naim @ Mohd. Zuki bin Ismail. 1986-1987. "Integrasi dan Asimilasi Komuniti Siam dengan Masyarakat Sekitar di Kelantan Utara: Satu Kajian Kes di Kg. Jong Bakar, Tumpat, Kelantan." Honors thesis, Department of Anthropology and Sociology, Universiti Kebangsaan Malaysia.

Mohd. Sofi Aziz. 1984. "Masyarakat Siam di Kampung Seligi." *Jurnal Persatuan Muzium Malaysia* 3: 31-43.

Montesano, Michael, and Patrick Jory. 2008. "Introduction." In *Thai South and Malay North: Ethnic Interactions on a Plural Peninsula*, edited by Montesano and Jory, 1-27. Singapore: National University of Singapore Press.

Morris, Rosalind. 2009. "Photography and the Power of Images in the History of Power: Notes from Thailand." In *Photographies East: The Camera and Its Histories in East and Southeast Asia*, edited by Rosalind C. Morris, 121-61. Durham, NC: Duke University Press.

Mottahedeh, Roy. 2001. *Loyalty and Leadership in an Early Islamic Society.* New York: I. B. Tauris.

Mulder, Niels. 1969. *Monks, Merit, and Motivation.* DeKalb: Northern Illinois University.

N. Mohamed. 2007. "Komuniti Siam Kampung Terbok, Tumpat." *Warisan Kelantan* 19: 89-103.

Narayan, Kirin. 1993. "How Native Is a 'Native' Anthropologist?" *American Anthropologist* 95, no. 3: 671-86.

Nash, Manning. 1974. *Peasant Citizens: Politics, Religion, and Modernization in Kelantan, Malaysia.* Athens: Ohio University Center for International Studies.

Neumann, Mark. 1999. *On the Rim: Looking for the Grand Canyon.* Minneapolis: University of Minnesota Press.

Nik Haslinda Binti Nik Hussain. 2007. "Undang-undang Tanah di Kelantan, 1881-1941: Kesannya Terhadap Sistem Hak Milik Tanah Orang Melayu." In *Kelantan: Dahulu dan Sekarang*, edited by Abdullah Zakaria Ghazali and Zahir Ahmad, 165-86. Kuala Lumpur: United Selangor Press.

Nik Hassan Shuhaimi. 1987. "Sejarah Kelantan Sebelum Long Yunus—Satu Gambaran Umum." In *Kelantan Zaman Awal: Kajian Arkeologi dan Sejarah di Malaysia*, edited by Nik Hassan Shuhaimi, 1-14. Kota Bharu: Kelantan State Museum.

Niramol Kangsadara. 1986. "Prince Wachirayan's Reforms in the Buddhist Order (1898-1921)." In *Anuson Walter Vella* (In memory of Professor Vella), edited by Ronald D. Renard, 249-64. Chiang Mai: Walter F. Vella Fund.

Nishii, Ryoko. 2000. "Emergence and Transformation of Peripheral Ethnicity: Sam Sam on the Thai-Malaysian Border." In *Civility and Savagery: Social Identity in Tai States*, edited by Andrew Turton, 180-200. Surrey, UK: Curzon.

Noer, Deliar. 1983. "Contemporary Political Dimensions of Islam." In *Islam in South-East Asia*, edited by M. Barry Hooker, 183-215. Leiden: E. J. Brill.

Nordholt, Henk Schulte. 1997. "The State on the Skin: Clothes, Shoes and Neatness in (Colonial) Indonesia." *Asian Studies Review* 21(1): 19-39.

Omar Farouk Bajunid. 1989a. *Pengantar Kesenian Kelantan*. Kuala Lumpur: Hakcipta Asrama Za'ba.

————. 1989b. *Warisan Kesenian Kelantan*. Kuala Lumpur: Hakcipta Asrama Za'ba, 1989.

Ong, Aihwa. 1996. "Cultural Citizenship as Subject Making: Immigrants Negotiate Racial and Cultural Boundaries in the United States." *Current Anthropology* 37, no. 5: 37-762.

————. 1999. *Flexible Citizenship: The Cultural Logics of Transnationality*. Durham, NC: Duke University Press.

Oommen, Tharaileth K. 1995. "Contested Boundaries and Emerging Pluralism." *International Sociology* 10, no. 3: 251-68.

Othman bin Mohd Yatim. 1987. "Kelantan Dalam Sejarah Perhubungan dengan Tamadun Luar—Perhubungan Perdagangan." In *Kelantan Zaman Awal: Kajian Arkeologi dan Sejarah di Malaysia*, edited by Nik Hassan Shuhaimi, 61-72. Kota Bharu: Kelantan State Museum.

Pallegoix, Jean-Baptiste. 1854. *Description du Royaume Thai ou Siam: Comprenant la topographie, histoire naturelle, moeurs et coutumes, legislation, commerce, industrie, langue, littérature, religion, annales des Thai et précis historique de la mission-avec cartes et gravures*. Paris: Au profit de la mission de Siam.

Pattana Kitiarsa. 2010. "Missionary Intent and Monastic Networks: Thai Buddhism as a Transnational Religion." *Sojourn* 25, no. 1: 109-32.

Peri, Oded. 2001. *Christianity under Islam in Jerusalem: The Question of the Holy Sites in Early Ottoman Times*. Boston: Brill.

Phra Phutthathaksinmingmongkhol: Luang Pho Khao Kong Songkhla: K. U. Press (author unknown, undated).

Phra Sirithammamuni. 1902. *Rai Ngan Truat Cad Kan Kana Khammakan Phra Sasana Lae Kan Suksa Nai Monthon Nakhon Sri Thammarat*. Bangkok: National Archives of Thailand.

Pin a/l Endin Klap. 1992. "Sejarah Menora." In *Proceedings of the International Seminar on Southeast Asian Performing Arts 1992*. Penang: Universiti Sains Malaysia.

Population Distribution and Basic Demographic Characteristics 2000. Department of Statistics, Kuala Lumpur.

Postill, John. 2006. *Media and Nation Building: How the Iban Became Malaysian*. Oxford: Berghahn Books.

Praphon Ruengnarong. 1982. *Thaksin Sarakhadi*. Bangkok: OS Printing House.

————. 1986. *Pak Tai Chai Daen*. Bangkok: Mitrsayam.

Rabinow, Paul. 1977. *Reflections on Fieldwork*. Los Angeles: University of California Press.

Rabinowitz, Dan. 1994. "To Sell or Not to Sell? Theory versus Practice, Public versus Private, and the Failure of Liberalism: The Case of Israel and Its Palestinian Citizens." *American Ethnologist* 21, no. 4: 827-44.

Rachagan, Sothi, and Richard F. Dorall. 1976. "Rivers as International Boundaries: The Case of Sungei Golok, Malaysia-Thailand." *Journal of Tropical Geography* 42: 47-58.

Rahmat bin Saripan. 1987. "Pemerintahan di Kelantan dan Hubungan dengan Patani dan Terengganu Dalam Abad Ke-18." In *Kelantan Zaman Awal: Kajian Arkeologi dan Sejarah di Malaysia*, edited by Nik Hassan Shuhaimi, 48-60. Kota Bharu: Kelantan State Museum.

Ravi, Narasimhan. 2005. "Looking beyond Flawed Journalism: How National Interests, Patriotism, and Cultural Values Shaped the Coverage of the Iraq War." *Harvard International Journal of Press/Politics* 10, no. 1: 45-62.

Raybeck, Douglas. 1996. *Mad Dogs, Englishmen, and the Errant Anthropologist: Fieldwork in Malaysia*. Long Grove, IL: Waveland.

Rentse, Anker. 1934. "History of Kelantan." *Journal of the Malayan Branch of the Royal Asiatic Society* 12, no. 2: 44-62.

———. 1936. "Salsilah Raja-Raja Kelantan." *Journal of the Malayan Branch of the Royal Asiatic Society* 14, no. 3: 306.

———. 1947. "A Historical Note on the North-eastern Malay States." *Journal of the Malayan Branch of the Royal Asiatic Society* 20, no. 1: 23-40.

Reynolds, Craig. 1972. "The Buddhist Monkhood in Nineteenth-Century Thailand." Ph.D. diss., Cornell University.

———. 1979. *Autobiography, the Life of Prince-Patriarch Vajiranana of Siam, 1860-1921 / Prince Vajiranana-varorasa*. Athens: Ohio University Press.

Robert, Leslie R. 1971. "The Duff Syndicate in Kelantan, 1900-1902." *Journal of the Malaysian Branch of the Royal Asiatic Society* 45, no. 1: 81-110.

Roberts, John M., and Teela Sanders. 2005. "Before, During and After: Realism, Reflexivity and Ethnography." *Sociological Review* 53, no. 2: 294-313.

Roff, William. 1974. "Preface." In *Kelantan: Religion, Society and Politics in a Malay State*, edited by Roff, v-x. Kuala Lumpur: Oxford University Press.

Rogayah Estar Mohamad. 1999. "Ajaran dan Kepercayaan Agama Buddha: Satu Kajian Khusus Terhadap Masyarakat Siam di Kelantan." Thesis, University of Malaya.

Rosaldo, Renato. 1989. *Culture and Truth: The Remaking of Social Analysis*. Boston: Beacon.

———. 2003. "Introduction: The Borders of Belonging." In *Cultural Citizenship in Island Southeast Asia: Nation and Belonging in the Hinterlands*, edited by Rosaldo, 1-16. Los Angeles: University of California Press.

Roseman, Sharon. 1996. "'How We Built the Road': The Politics of Memory in Rural Galicia." *American Ethnologist* 23, no. 4: 836-60.

Rudie, Ingrid. 1989. "Development Ideologies, Family Systems, and the Changing Roles of Malay Village Women." In *Southeast Asia between Autocracy and Democracy*, edited by Mikael Gravers, Peter Wad, Viggo Brun, and Arne Kalland, 96-121. Aarhus,

Denmark: Aarhus University Press.

———. 1994. *Visible Women in East Coast Malay Society: On the Reproduction of Gender in Ceremonial, School and Market*. Oslo: Scandinavian University Press.

Rumley, Dennis. 1991. "Society, State and Peripherality: The Case of the Thai-Malaysian Border Landscape." In *The Geography of Border Landscapes*, edited by Rumley and Julian Minghi, 121-52. London: Routledge.

Sahlins, Peter. 1989. *Boundaries: The Making of France and Spain in the Pyrenees*. Berkeley: University of California Press.

Sakai, Tadao. 1981. "Some Aspects of Chinese Religious Practices and Customs in Singapore and Malaysia." *Journal of Southeast Asian Studies* 12, no. 11: 133-41.

Sharifuddin Ab. Rahman. n.d. *Penempatan Orang Thai, Kaitannya dengan Sejarah Pertubuhan Negeri Kelantan*. Kota Bharu: Kelantan State Library.

Shamsul Amri Baharuddin. 1986. *From British to Bumiputera Rule: Local Politics and Rural Development in Peninsular Malaysia*. Singapore: ISEAS.

———. 1996a. "Debating about Identity in Malaysia: A Discourse Analysis." *Journal of Southeast Asian Studies* 34, no. 3: 8-31.

———. 1996b. "The Construction and Transformation of a Social Identity: Malayness and Bumiputeraness Re-examined." *Journal of African and Asian Studies* 52: 15-33.

———. 1999. "Identity Contestation in Malaysia: A Comparative Commentary on 'Malayness' and 'Chineseness.'" *Akademika* 55 (July): 17-37.

Shaw, William. 1976. *Aspects of Malaysian Magic*. Kuala Lumpur: Yau Seng Press.

Sheppard, Mubin. 1973. "Manora in Kelantan." *Journal of the Malaysian Branch of the Royal Asiatic Society* 46: 161-70.

Skeat, Walter W. 1953. "The Cambridge University Expedition to the North Eastern Malay States and to Upper Perak, 1899-1900." *Journal of the Malaysian Branch of the Royal Asiatic Society* 26, no. 4: 148-65.

Skinner, Allan M. 1878. "Geography of the Malay Peninsula." *Journal of the Straits Branch of the Royal Asiatic Society*, no. 1: 57-62.

Skinner, Cyril. 1965. *The Civil War in Kelantan in 1839*. Kuala Lumpur: Malaysian Branch of the Royal Asiatic Society.

Somboon Suksamran. 1982. *Buddhism and Politics in Thailand*. Singapore: ISEAS.

Stark, Jan. 2004. "Constructing an Islamic Model in Two Malaysian States: PAS Rule in Kelantan and Teregganu." *SOJOURN* 19, no. 1: 51-75.

Steedly, Mary. 1993. *Hanging without a Rope: Narrative Experience in Colonial and Postcolonial Karoland*. Princeton, NJ: Princeton University Press.

Stewart, Kathleen. 2007. *Ordinary Affects*. Durham, NC: Duke University Press.

Straits Settlements Reports for 1910 on the States of Kedah and Perlis, Kelantan and Trengganu. Kuala Lumpur.

Straits Settlements Reports for 1915 on the States of Kedah and Perlis, Kelantan and Trengganu. Kuala Lumpur.

Suchaowana Phloichum. 2002. *Prawat Naktham*. Bangkok: Mahamongkut University Press.

Swearer, Donald K. 1991. "Fundamentalistic Movements in Theravada Buddhism." In *Fundementalisms Observed*, edited by Martin Marty and R. Scott Appleby, 628-90. Chicago: University of Chicago Press.

Tagliacozzo, Eric. 2001. "Border Permeability and the State in Southeast Asia." *Contemporary Southeast Asia* 23, no. 2: 254-74.

———. 2005. *Secret Trades, Porous Borders: Smuggling and States along a Southeast Asian Frontier, 1865-1915*. New Haven, CT: Yale University Press.

Tagliacozzo, Eric, and Andrew Willford. 2009. "History and Anthropology: Strange Bedfellows." In *Clio/Anthropos: Exploring the Boundaries between History and Anthropology*, edited by Willford and Tagliacozzo, 1-27. Stanford, CA: Stanford University Press.

Takamura, Kazue. 2004. "Not 'Divided Spaces' but a 'Living Space': Chinese Women on the Thai Malaysian Border." *Journal of Asian and African Studies* 68: 173-93.

Talib, Shahril. 1981. "Nineteenth Century Kelantan: A Malay Tributary State." *Journal Antropologi dan Sosiologi* 9: 43-59.

———. 1983. "Voices from the Kelantan Desa, 1900-1940." *Modern Asian Studies* 17, no. 2: 177-95.

———. 1987. "Industry in Kelantan: Notes on Research Directions." In *Kelantan Zaman Awal: Kajian Arkeologi dan Sejarah di Malaysia*, edited by Nik Hassan Shuhaimi, 154-60. Kota Bharu: Kelantan State Museum.

———. 1995. *History of Kelantan, 1890-1940*. Kuala Lumpur: MBRAS.

Tambiah, Stanley. 1970. *Buddhism and the Spirit Cults in North-east Thailand*. Cambridge: Cambridge University Press.

———. 1976. *World Conqueror and World Renouncer: A Study of Buddhism and Polity in Thailand against a Historical Background*. Cambridge: Cambridge University Press.

———. 1977. "The Galactic Polity: The Structure of Traditional Kingdoms in Southeast Asia." *Annals of the New York Academy of Sciences* 293: 69-97.

Tanabe, Shigeharu. 1984. "Ideological Practice in Peasant Rebellions: Siam at the Turn of the Twentieth Century." In *History and Peasant Consciousness in Southeast Asia*, edited by Andrew Turton and Tanabe, 75-110. Osaka: National Museum of Ethnology (Senri Ethnological Studies 13).

———. 2008. "Introduction: Imagined and Imagining Communities." In *Imagining Communities in Thailand: Ethnographic Approaches*, edited by Tanabe, 1-21. Chiang Mai: Mekong.

Taylor, Philip. 2007. *Cham Muslims of the Mekong Delta: Place and Mobility in the Cosmopolitan Periphery*. Singapore: NUS Press.

Teo, Kok Seong. 2003. *Peranakan Chinese of Kelantan: A Study of the Culture, Language & Communication of an Assimilated Group in Malaysia*. ASEAN Academic Press:

———. 2008. "Chinese-Malay-Thai Interactions and the Making of Kelantan Peranakan Chinese Ethnicity." In *Thai South and Malay North: Ethnic Interactions on a Plural Peninsula*, edited by Michael Montesano and Patrick Jory, 214-230. Singapore: National University of Singapore Press

Thak Chaloemtiarana. 2007. *Thailand: The Politics of Despotic Paternalism*. Ithaca, NY: Cornell Southeast Asia Program.

Thongchai Winichakul. 1994. *Siam Mapped: A History of the Geo-body of a Nation*. Chiang Mai: Silkworm.

Thrift, Nigel. 2004. "Driving in the City." *Theory, Culture and Society* 21, nos. 4 and 5: 41-59.

Tiyavanich, Kamala. 1997. *Forest Recollections: Wandering Monks in Twentieth-Century Thailand*. Honolulu: University of Hawai'i Press.

Truitt, Allison. 2008. "On the Back of a Motorbike: Middle-Class Mobility in Ho Chi Minh City, Vietnam." *American Ethnologist* 35, no. 1: 3-20.

Tsing, Anna. 1993. *In the Realm of the Diamond Queen: Marginality in an Out-of-the-Way Place*. Princeton, NJ: Princeton University Press.

———. 2003. "The News in the Provinces." In *Cultural Citizenship in Island Southeast Asia: Nation and Belonging in the Hinterlands*, edited by Renato Rosaldo, 192-223. Los Angeles: University of California Press.

Turton, Andrew. 1991. "Invulnerability and Local Knowledge." In *Thai Constructions of Knowledge*, edited by Manas Chitakasem and Turton, 155-82. London: School of Oriental and African Studies, University of London.

Urry, John. 2004. "The System of Automobility." *Theory, Culture and Society* 21, nos. 4 and 5: 25-39.

Vella, Walter. 1957. *Siam under Rama III, 1824-1851*. Monograph of the Association of Asian Studies, New York.

———. 1978. *Chaiyo! King Vajiravudh and the Development of Thai Nationalism*. Honolulu: University Press of Hawai'i.

Verdery, Katherine. 1994. "Ethnicity, Nationalism, and State-Making. Ethnic Group Boundaries: Past and Future." In *The Anthropology of Ethnicity: Beyond "Ethnic Groups and Boundaries,"* edited by Hans Vermeulen and Cora Govers, 33-58. Amsterdam: Het Spinhuis.

Wales, Horace Q. 1965. *Ancient Siamese Government and Administration*. New York: Paragon Book Reprint Corp.

Wanipha Na Songkhla. 1992. *Wat Choltarasinghe*. Bangkok: Fine Arts Department.

Warikoo, Kulbhushan, ed. 2002. *Bamiyan: Challenge to World Heritage*. New Delhi: Third Eye.

Wat Choltharasinghe. n.d. Educational Office of the Amphoe of Tak Bai, Narathiwat.

Wattana Sugunnasil. 2000. "A Study of the Culture of Daily-Rated Workers in Amphoe Tak Bai, Narathiwat Province." Paper presented at the Annual Conference on Culture and Development in Southern Thailand, 21-23 January.

———. 2005. "Consuming Modernity in a Border Community." In *Dynamic Diversity in Southern Thailand*, edited by Sugunnasil, 63-97. Chiang Mai: Silkworm.

Wavell, Stewart. 1958. *The Lost World of the East: An Adventurous Quest in the Malayan Hinterland*. London: Souvenir Press.

———. 1965. *The Naga King's Daughter*. London: George Allen and Unwin.

Wee, Khoon Hock. 1987. "Kelantan and the Chinese Kelantanese." In *Kelantan Zaman Awal: Kajian Arkeologi dan Sejarah di Malaysia*, edited by Nik Hassan Shuhaimi, 216-28. Kota Bharu: Kelantan State Museum.

Wilkinson, Richard J. 1959. *A Malay-English Dictionary (Romanised)*. London: Macmillan.

Wilson, Constance. 1997. "The Holy Man in the History of Thailand and Laos." *Journal of Southeast Asian Studies* 22, no. 2: 345-64.

Winstedt, Richard O. 1935. "A History of Malaya." *Journal of the Malayan Branch of the Royal Asiatic Society* 13, no. 1: 1-270.

———. 1947. *The Malays: A Cultural History*. Singapore: Kelly and Walsh.

———. 1951. *The Malay Magician: Being Shaman, Saiva and Sufi*. Kuala Lumpur: Oxford University Press.

Winzeler, Robert. 1985. *Ethnic Relations in Kelantan: A Study of the Chinese and Thai as Ethnic Minorities in a Malay State*. Singapore: Oxford University Press.

Wolters, Oliver W. 1970. *The Fall of Srivijaya in Malay History*. Ithaca, NY: Cornell University Press.

———. 1982. *History, Culture, and Religion in Southeast Asian Perspectives*. Singapore: Institute of Southeast Asian Studies.

Woodward, Mark. 1989. *Islam in Java: Normative Piety and Mysticism in the Sultanate of Jogyakarta*. Tucson: University of Arizona Press.

Wyatt, David. 1969. *The Politics of Reform in Thailand: Education in the Reign of King Chulalongkorn*. New Haven, CT: Yale University Press.

———. 1974. "Nineteenth Century Kelantan: A Thai View." In *Kelantan: Religion, Society and Politics in a Malay State*, edited by William Roff, 1-21. Kuala Lumpur: Oxford University Press.

Yeo, Hun Chew. 2007. "Komuniti Cina Wakaf Bharu." *Warisan Kelantan* 22: 42-74.

Zainuddin bin abdul Rahman. 2007. "Hubungan Komuniti Melayu dan Siam di Kampung Aril." *Warisan Kelantan* 18: 55-74.

Internet Resources

http://www.highbeam.com/doc/1P1-138837558.html

http://sanggahtoksago.blogspot.com/2010/07/anuar-musa-nasharuddin-sami-antara-yang.html

http://kerabubersuara.blogspot.com/2010/07/anuar-musa-nasharuddin-sami-antara-yang.html

http://mrk-al-banjari.blogspot.com/2010/07/menghadiri-kenduri-kesyukuran-di-rumah.html

INDEX

British colonialism (cont.)
  policy of, 57–58, 61, 109;
  sultan position under, 195n30; village
  administration under, 142
Brubaker, Roger, 21–22
Buddhadasa Bhikkhu, 153
Buddhism: Chinese belief systems and,
  93; Dhammakaya society and, 152–53;
  education in, 150; festivities and celebrations, 42–43, 46–49, 73–74, 115,
  161–62, 174–75; national examinations on, 75, 189nn15–17; and nationalism, 91, 148; standards of behavior
  in, 98–99, 100, 106–7; Thailand and,
  128, 134; *thammathut* movement
  and, 150; Theravada, 75, 86, 102, 129,
  184n2. *See also* monks
Buddhist temples, statues, and monuments, **88**, **95**; categories of, 90;
  Chinese-style, 91, 94–96, 98, 102–4;
  as cross-cultural encounter, 101–2;
  destruction of, 112–13; donating
  money to, 98, 105; festivals at, 73–74,
  115–16, 161–62; financing and costs of,
  98, 103; and Kelantanese Thai agentive role, 97; as lucrative industry,
  108; number in Kelantan, 58–59, 128,
  187n2, 191–92n3; obtaining materials
  for, 107–8; purification ceremonies
  at, 130–31, 194n21; and temple lands,
  111–12, 130, 140, 191n10, 194n20; terrorist threats against, 139–40, 195n27;
  and Thainess, 86–87, 91, 102, 117;
  tourists and, 7, 87, 89–90, 190n2; at
  Wat Bang Rim Nam, 99; at Wat Ban
  Kao, 108; at Wat Ban Phai, 90, 95–96;
  at Wat Bot Ngam, 86, 108; at Wat Din
  Sung, 86, 107; at Wat Khao Kong, 91;
  at Wat Khok Phrao, 96; at Wat Klang,
  89, 103–4, 114, 140; at Wat Krai, 96;
  at Wat Nai, 87–89, 90–91, 108; at Wat
  Nak, 89, 91, 104; at Wat Nok, 96–97;

at Wat Phra Non, 89–90, 101, 107, 114
bumiputera policy, 6, 110, 111; about, 67,
  181–82n3, 188n10; Kelantanese Thai
  view of, 68
Bush, George W., 168

C

calendars, temple, 121, 167, 191n2
Carabao rock band, 43, 186n13
Carstens, Sharon, 23, 92
cattle theft, 38, 186n12
census figures, 5, 6, 32, 92, 182n4
Chai, Pho Than, 76
Chan, Than Chao Khun, 131
Chan Kesaro, Phra Maha, 75, 131, 132
Chang, Khru, 68–69
Chi, Kae, 24–27, 49, 61, 67
Chinese community and influence,
  39–40, **95**, **99**, 110; belief systems of,
  93; under British colonialism, 109;
  and Buddhist monuments, 91, 94–96,
  98, 102–4; Kelantanese Thai interac-
  tion with, 91–92; Kelantanese Thai
  tensions with, 102–6, 107, 190n8; Kel-
  antan population of, 92; urban and
  rural, 92–93, 190n3
Chong Cheng, 38
Chu, Lung, 76
Chulalongkorn, King, 59, 128, 182n10; and
  Buddhist centralization, 148, 150, 170;
  and Kelantan, 9, 124, 127
Chum, Pho, 37
citizenship, 17, 170; dual, 6, 165; Kelantanese Thai and, 83–84, 116; obtaining
  Malaysian, 17; obtaining Thai, 156;
  surnames and, 64
Clementi, Sir Cecil, 11
Clifford, Sir Hugh, 4–5, 16, 19–20
Cohn, Bernard, 61
Coleman, Simon, 25, 46
colonialism. *See* British colonialism
communes, *Nikhom*, 154–58, 160–62

Ibrahim Nik Mahmood, 191n9

identity, 12, 55–56, 62; borders and, xi–xii, 37; of Kelantanese Thai, 7, 12, 21, 79–80; and Thainess, xvi–xvii, 63–65, 68–69

Imagined Communities (Anderson), xiii

indigenism, 67, 68, 110

Ingold, Tim, 146, 178

In Suwanajarit, Phra (Than) Khru, 192n8

Irvine, Judith, 7

Ishii, Yoneo, 134

Islam, 171, 188n9; conversions to, 117; sultan as protector of, 138, 143; teachings and doctrines, 99, 138–39, 169

Islamic extremism and terrorism, 164, 168, 171

Islamism: and Islamization efforts, 4, 140, 142, 178; PAS and, 3–5, 112–13, 140, 142, 143

Ismail, Sultan, 31, 185n6

Ismail Petra Yahya Petra, Sultan, 119, 121–22, 134–35, 139

Istana Bukit Tanah, 119, 191n1

J

Jaiser, Gerhard, 187–88n4

Jim, Chao, 89, 90, 103, 105

Joi, Tok, 158, *159*

Jory, Patrick, 176, xiv

Journal of the Malayan Branch of the Royal Asiatic Society, 18–19

K

Kaya Budi, Datuk, 31, 185n6

Kedah, 10, 62, 75, 129

Kelantan: administrative districts in, 32, 181n2; British colonialism and, 9, 32–33; Chinese community in, 92; civil war in, 130, 193–94n18; clientelism in, 129, 142, 143; contemporary literature on, 20–21; crime in, 106, 191n9; ethnic and religious diversity in, 61, 102, 139; Islamic party in, 3–5, 112–13, 140, 142, 143; marginality of, 3, 19, 181n1; market traders in, 18, 25, 34; as Mecca's Verandah, 3, 4, 5, 117, 139, 177; monk influx to, 76, 77; number of temples in, 58–59, 128, 187n2, 191–92n3; political playing field in, 142, 143; population of, 5, 13, 92, 182n4; railroads in, 10–11, 183n12; rising cost of living in, 77; road building in, 10, 32–33; as Siam dependency, 10; and sovereignty, 60–61, 127; sultan role in, 134–37, 138, 139, 143, 195n30; Thai Consulate in, 137, 160, 161, 196n5; Thai migration to, 23; tourists and pilgrims to, 7, 34, 49, 87, 89–90, 94, 177, 190n2; tribute to Siamese court by, 8–9, 130, 194n19. *See also* Thai, Kelantanese

Kelantanese Thai Association, 116

Kelantan River, 20, 29

Kenali, Tok, 3, 5, 85

Kershaw, Roger, 26, 97, 129, 152, 196n5; on Thai kingly image, 144, 145

Kessler, Clive, 193n17

Keyes, Charles, 82, 148

Khron, Pho Than, 7

Khron, Than Chao Khun, 131, 133

Kio, Than Khru, 123–28, **125**, 130–31, 192n4, 192n9

Kobkua Suwannathat-Pian, 129

Kota Bharu, 4, 5, 16, 33, 92

Kuala Krai, 92

Kwan Im folk divinity, 91, 94, 95, 96, 102

L

Lai, Na Chao, 67

Lamont, Michèle, xi

Lan, Phi, 171

language, 12–13, 33, 62

Leach, Edmund, x

Leibing, Annette, ix

Lin, Lung, 158–60, **159**
Long Jenal, 130
Loo Heng Ann, 104

M

magical powers and spirits, 6, 44–45, 47, 186n14
Maha Chakri Sirindhorn, Princess, 80, 135
Maha Menteri, 20
Maha Mentri, Datuk (Saad bin Ngah), 5
Mahathir Mohamad, 113
Mak Yong dramas, 4, 31
Malaysia Boleh, 113–14
Malaysia Book of Records, 114
Malaysia/Malaya: academic studies on, 18–19; administrative divisions in, 31–32; *bumiputera* policy of, 6, 67, 110, 111, 181–82n3, 188n10; colonial history of, 18; communal riots in, 109; communism in, 111; creation and independence of, 11, 59; ethnic policies of, 6, 8, 17, 61–63, 67, 68–69, 188n7; Kelantanese Thai political identification with, 7, 17, 23, 47, 48, 146–47; National Culture Policy in, 109–11, 113; nationalism in, 109; patriotism in, 47, 48, 113–14, 115
Malaysian Chinese Association (MCA), 94
Malaysian-Thai border, xvi, 72, 178; Anglo-Siamese Treaty's establishment of, 10; border passes for crossing, 145–46, 189n13, 196n3; demarcation of, 60, 164; ease in crossing, 146, 165; smuggling across, 14, 38
Malay-Thai relations: as amicable, 61, 66–67, 107, 111, 118, 128, 141, 171; communal riots, 109; discord in, 61, 112–13, 141, 164–65; and terrorist attacks, 162–63, 164–65

maps, 41, 174–75
marginality, xvi, 22, 108; and agency, 7; of Kelantan, 3, 19, 181n1; of Kelantanese Thai, 37, 54, 83–84, 126; Thainess and, 57
Masquelier, Adeline, 43
Mat, Cikgu, 142–43
Mauss, Marcel, x
McLean, Athena, ix
millenarian revolts, 128, 193n16
Mit, Than Chao Khun, 131, 136
mobility: culture of, xii–xiii, 10; inter-village, 26; and modernity, 32, 36; monks and, 74–75, 76, 77–78, 93–94; and stasis, 27, 49, 82, 145; and travel, 25, 77
modernity, 32, 36, 44, 64, 186n14
Mohamed bin Nik Mohd. Salleh, 10
Mohamed Yusoff Ismail, 26, 97, 98, 103, 134, 190n8
Mohammad Hashim Kamali, 138
Mohd. Kamaruzaman A. Rahman, 33
Molnár, Virág, xi
monks, 35, 76, 189n18, 195–96n2; Bangkok control over, 64, 75–76, 123–27, 129–31, 138–39, 144; at Buddhist festivals, 73–74, 116; construction projects by, 100–101; Graham account of, 122; hierarchies and titles of, 116, 123, 127, 192n7, 193n15, 194n25; schools for, 150–51; sultanate relationship with, 134–35; temple staffing by, 75, 189n14; Thai citizen-monks, 77, 196n3; and *thammathut* movement, 149–52; travel by, 74–75, 76, 77–78, 93–94. *See also* Buddhism
Montesano, Michael, xiv, 176
Mottahedeh, Roy, 138
Muhammad I, Sultan, 130, 194n19
Muhammad II, Sultan (Phja Pak Daeng), 130, 193n17

Thai, Kelantanese (cont.)
   majority, 61, 66–67, 107, 111,
      112–13, 118, 128, 141, 164–65, 171; and
      resettlement schemes, 156–58; social
      invisibility of, 6, 56, 63, 66, 83, 107,
      116, 175; sultan's relationship with,
      129–30, 142–44; Thailand and, 49–50,
      52, 55, 79–82, 86, 108, 128–29, 137, 161;
      and Thai monarchy, 121–22, 123, 126,
      132–33, 144–45; Thainess of, 23, 35, 49,
      83–84, 151–52, 170–71, 176; villages of,
      13, 42, 74, 183n13. *See also* Malay-Thai
      relations
Thailand: and Buddhism, 128, 134; Communist Party in, 154; consulate in
   Kelantan, 137, 160, 161, 196n5; and
   Kelantanese Thai, 49–50, 52, 55,
   79–82, 86, 108, 128–29, **136**, 137, 144–
   45, 161; Malaysian settlers in, 155–56;
   monarchy of, 82, 120, 121, 122, 132–33;
   monastic control from, 64, 75–76,
   123–27, 129–31, 138–39, 144; nationalism in, 148, 157; negative stereotypes
   of, 72–73; obtaining citizenship in,
   156; red-shirt protests in, 169; southern insurgency in, 163–64; terrorism
   in, xvi, 73, 139–40, 162, 164–65; and
   Thai diaspora, 22, 82, 108; and *thammathut* movement, 149, 154–56; tourism in, 49, 77–79; village authorities
   in, 141–42. *See also* Siam
Thainess, xiv–xvii; ambiguity in, 49, 69,
   129, 171, 178; and boundaries, 7; Buddhist monuments and, 86–87, 91,
   102, 117; and creative agency, 105; as
   cultural space, 41, 83, 137, 179; and
   ethnicity, 46, 62–63, 65–66, 168,
   171; and geographic locatedness, 50,
   174–75; and identity, xvi–xvii, 63–65,
   68–69; Kelantanese Thai and, 23, 35,
   49, 83–84, 151–52, 170–71, 176; and
   marginality, 57; ordination parades

celebrating, 42–43, 46–49; shaped
   by diaspora, 81–82, 83; social and
   cultural definitions of, xi, 56, 66; Thai
   word for, xv, 56, 176; visual markers
   for, 53, 55, 56
Thak Chaloemtiarana, 155
thammathut program, 149–52, 154
Thanom Kittikachorn, 150
Thit Sa, 126, 192–93n10
Thong, Phi, 52–53, 54, 133–34
Thongchai Winichakul, xiv, 56, 82
Tok Janggut rebellion (1915), 33
tourism, 49, 94, 177; to Buddhist statues
   and monuments, 7, 87, 89–90, 190n2
Tsing, Anna, 167, 170
Tuan Long Senik, 59, 182n7
Tua Pek Kong folk divinity, 95–96, 97,
   103, 107, 190n5
Tumpat, 5, 31–32, 85, 185n7
Tumpat Tak Bai dialect, 12–13, 81, 183n13
Tun Abdul Razak, 109
Tunku Abdul Rahman, 48

U
Ulu, 3, 10; mining in, 5, 19, 32–33, 184n18

V
Vajiravudh, King, 148–49
vegetable cultivation, 14, 15–16
Vella, Walter, 148
Voices from the Kelantan Desa, 1900–1940
   (Talib), 20

W
Wachirayan, Prince, 189n15
Wadley, Reed, xiii
Wakaf Che Yeh, 16
Wanipha Na Songkhla, 123–24, 192n6
Wat, Chao, 169, 170
Wat Bang Rim Nam, 99, 133
Wat Ban Kao, 108, 130, 192n4
Wat Ban Phai, 90, 95–96